Letter Lessons
— AND —
First Words

HEIDI ANNE MESMER

Letter Lessons

— AND —

First Words

Phonics Foundations That Work

PreK–2

HEINEMANN
Portsmouth, NH

Heinemann
361 Hanover Street
Portsmouth, NH 03801–3912
www.heinemann.com

Offices and agents throughout the world

The author and publisher wish to thank those who have generously given permission to reprint borrowed material:

Evidence-Based Characteristics of Good Phonics Instruction from *Reading Research at Work: Foundations of Effective Practice* edited by Katherine A. Dougherty Stahl and Michael C. McKenna. Copyright © 2006 by The Guilford Press. Reprinted with permission from the publisher.

Excerpts from Just the Facts . . . Information Provided by The International Dyslexia Association, Dyslexia Basics, www.DyslexiaIDA.org. Copyright © 2017. Reprinted with permission from The International Dyslexia Association, Inc.

Alphabet Lines reprinted with permission from North Star Teacher Resources, Grand Rapids, MI, www.nstresources.com.

Cataloging-in-Publication Data is on file at the Library of Congress.
Name: Mesmer, Heidi Anne E., author.
Title: Letter lessons and first words : phonics foundations that work / Heidi Anne Mesmer.
Description: First edition. | Portsmouth, NH : Heinemann, [2019]. | Series: The research-informed classroom. | Includes bibliographical references and index.
Identifiers: LCCN 2019012436 | ISBN 9780325105444
Subjects: LCSH: Reading—Phonetic method—Study and teaching (Primary). | English language—Study and teaching (Primary). | Vocabulary—Study and teaching (Primary).
Classification: LCC LB1573.3 .M467 2019 | DDC 372.46/5—dc23

LC record available at https://lccn.loc.gov/2019012436

Acquisitions Editor: Margaret LaRaia
Production Editor: Patty Adams
Cover and Interior Designs: Vita Lane
Cover Photograph: © Fat Camera/E+/Getty Images/HIP
Typesetter: Shawn Girsberger
Manufacturing: Steve Bernier

Printed in the United States of America on acid-free paper
23 22 21 20 19 RWP 1 2 3 4 5

Contents

How to Access Online Resources

To access the online resources for *Letter Lessons and First Words*:

1. Go to http://hein.pub/letterlessons-login
2. Log in with your username and password. If you do not already have an account with Heinemann, you will need to create an account.
3. On the Welcome page choose, **"Click here to register an Online Resource."**
4. Register your product by entering the code: **FIRSTWORDS** (be sure to read and check the acknowledgment box under the keycode).
5. Once you have registered your product, it will appear alphabetically in your account list of My Online Resources.

Note: When returning to Heinemann.com to access your previously registered products simply log into your Heinemann account and click on **"View my registered Online Resources."**

Resources

VIDEO ▶

For the downloadable video clips, go to http://hein.pub/letterlessons-login.

DOWNLOADABLE PDFS

Daily Whole-Group, Teacher-Managed Activities for Teaching the Alphabetic Principle and Print Concepts (Pre-K)

Activities by Lesson Part

REVIEW-IT (LETTERS AND WORDS)

HEAR-IT

TARGET LETTER ACTIVITY (LETTER LESSONS)

DECODE-IT (FIRST WORDS AND BEYOND FIRST WORDS)

SPELL-IT

READ-IT

Foreword

Nell K. Duke

WE HAVE GOT TO GET PHONICS INSTRUCTION RIGHT. THE stakes are so high—not only because the ability to read words is important to success in school and life, but also because there is so much else to teach. We just cannot afford to spend the better part of the school day on phonics instruction. We need to be highly efficient and effective in teaching phonics so that we have as much time as possible to develop comprehension, composition, science knowledge, social studies knowledge, and so much else that is important to young children's development. Put another way, whatever your passion, you have a vested interest in providing the most efficient as well as effective phonics instruction possible.

With stakes as high as they are for phonics instruction, I thought very deeply about who to ask to write this book. It had to be someone who knows the research well—not just reviews of research but many, many hundreds of individual studies on letter–sound knowledge development and instruction. It had to be someone who knows practice well—who has a long history of teaching children to read and teaching teachers to teach children to read. It had to be someone who can communicate all this knowledge in an accurate and engaging way. And it had to be someone with innovative ways of connecting research, theory, and practice. Who could meet a bar this high? Dr. Heidi Anne Mesmer.

Heidi Anne did not disappoint. In the introduction, Heidi Anne provides the "big picture" of effective phonics instruction, including some fundamental understandings young children need in order for phonics instruction to be most productive. In Chapter

1, she builds key knowledge about English orthography and children's development of letter–sound knowledge. As she explains, it is crucial for us to have this knowledge in mind when examining children's early efforts at word reading and spelling and providing instruction accordingly. In Chapter 2, she moves on to assessment, providing an actual assessment that yields detailed information about letter–sound relationships each child currently knows and needs to learn next. You can use this tool along with observations to differentiate phonics instruction and accelerate teaching and learning as needed to get every child to grade-level expectations in this area. Chapter 3 tackles how to plan lessons that reflect research on phonics instruction. The lessons include a powerful mix of explicit instruction; hands-on, minds-on activities; and opportunities to read texts that reinforce letter–sound relationships taught. Chapters 4, 5, and 6 provide a much-appreciated level of detail, with three specific units that bring young children from alphabet learning through reading single-syllable words with complex letter–sound relationships. As the book concludes, you'll have a wealth of knowledge and tools available to support your quest to get phonics instruction right.

Introduction
Reimagining Phonics Instruction

F I SAID, "CLOSE YOUR EYES AND IMAGINE A PHONICS LESSON IN first grade," what would your picture be? Children sitting in rows with worksheets? A teacher holding a card with a word written on it? Would everyone have a number 2 pencil?

Would there be smiling? Jokes? Laughter? Puzzles? Riddles? Anticipation? I sure hope so, but this second list might not be what you associate with phonics instruction.

For a proficient adult reader, phonics can feel like a cumbersome distraction to the "real" work of reading and writing. But what this actually shows is that we've lost our awareness of what it is to be new to the printed word. As proficient readers, we read most words by sight and decoding is rarely a part of our reading and writing experience. Because phonics feels unnecessary to us, some teachers decide not to teach it or to give it only cursory attention. Others view it as necessary but don't make the connection between phonics principles and real reading and writing. The latter kind of phonics instruction involves lifeless routines; odd, dreary activities; excessive repetition; or whole-group, scripted lessons that soar over the heads of some children and bore others. Instead of rejecting phonics outright, we might want to consider that it's not phonics but how we teach it that is the problem. The teaching of phonics is a means to an end. Children need to decode in order to independently read and write. Phonics shouldn't feel like an interruption or detour away from these authentic experiences. Phonics should be the building of a curiosity—developed by a passionate, informed teacher—about how words work, an inquiry about how the sounds of our language are mapped onto visual symbols. It is discovering the purpose of letters, how letters can work alone or be combined to symbolize sounds, and later in the journey, how the spelling of words quite often intersects with their meaning. Phonics instruction simply gives children the information about how letter–sounds work so that they can build automatic word recognition that *frees their conscious attention* to concentrate on meaning.

I know many of us did not experience this kind of phonics instruction, so my intention in writing this book is to give you a vision of what that looks like and the tools to make it happen in your own classroom. Instead of quiet, passive students, imagine children spread out in groups on a brightly colored carpet spelling words with dry erase markers and boards. Imagine a first grader telling his teacher, "Look! *Some*, *done*, *none*, and *above* are the pattern!" Picture a small group of students with a teacher building words with magnetic letters. See a first grader sounding out a word for the first time: "/d/ /i/ /g/, *dig*? Oh! *Dig*! That's it!" Envision a prekindergarten student using letter–sounds to recognize her friend's name: "*T, Taylor. T* for *Taylor.*" This is phonics! Engaged word solving! Using letter–sounds to read and spell! The "I can do it!" smile on a child's face when the grown-up world of words is unlocked. (And you won't have to imagine these scenes, as this book includes many video clips of real children doing this work.) When children are taught to decode words, they become fluent readers; they understand that they can use strategies when they encounter new words, which means they get stuck less often and we decrease the risk of them becoming disengaged readers.

Years of research show us that while some children intuit phonics on their own, the majority of children require phonics instruction in order to learn to read. In the past, phonics instruction was viewed as competing with or even threatening reading for meaning. Today, we better understand the role of phonics instruction as one of the building blocks for meaningful comprehension and composition and that research allows us to create curricula specific to individual children's needs.

To Make Use of Phonics, Children Must Understand How the System of Writing Works

Because of its discrete nature, people sometimes think that teaching phonics is uncomplicated and easily applicable. You teach letters and sounds and then children learn how to decode and spell. But this is not true. Yes, you can get kids to learn the visual shapes of letters, just as you might teach them the characteristics and names of circles, squares, and other shapes. And you can teach them to pronounce the sounds, but this doesn't mean they will know how to use that information. There are two fundamental understandings children must develop as they are learning letter–sounds: the alphabetic principle and concept of word in print.

Graphemes Represent Speech Sounds: The Alphabetic Principle

When phonics instruction is *used*, children understand the big picture—how the system of writing works. In English one part of the big picture is the **alphabetic principle**, the system of symbols that puts speech into print. In an alphabetic system, visual symbols (graphemes made up of letters) represent speech sounds (phonemes) (/e/ /k/). So if we want to write the oral word *cat*, we use these alphabetic symbols (*c* = /k/, *a* = /a/, *t* = /t/) instead of drawing a picture of a cat. The basis for written communication is breaking down speech into sounds and then matching those sounds in letters. We combine and recombine letter symbols to form words.

The alphabetic system is abstract, but teaching phonics without simultaneously developing awareness of the system will fail. Mrs. McCall's question to a group of kindergartners illustrates what children will say and do when they don't understand the alphabetic principle, when they don't know how the system works.

"What sound do you hear at the beginning of *cat*?" Mrs. Mc Call asked her twenty prekindergartners as she raised her pen during the morning meeting.

"Meow!" volunteered Hannah.

"Um, um, um *cat*?" answer Felix.

"/s/?" explained Aleksey.

Each of these answers tell us something about what the child understands or misunderstands about print and letter–sounds. Hannah is thinking not about the structure of the word but about the meaning, so she provides her teacher with a sound that a furry four-legged creature makes. She doesn't understand the *question.* Hannah's response reminds us that when we teach children how to read and spell words, we are asking them to have awareness about how printed language works and, in doing so, to suspend their knowledge about the meaning of words. It's like asking children to look at a candy store and tell us that it's built of bricks, with a flat roof and two windows, but not discuss that it's a candy store—a tall order for a little kid. And it's a tall order for the human brain, period.

Felix understands the abstraction built into the question, that the teacher is asking about the structure of the word and the way that it sounds, not about what it means. But Felix does not have insight about the separate sounds /c/, /a/, and /t/. He focuses on what he hears as one sound, the entire word—*cat.*

Aleksey connects with the idea of the question—to pay attention to the way the word sounds. He actually gets closer to the idea of focusing on separate sounds within the word, but he produces a sound that is not in the word. Perhaps he knows that *cat* starts with the letter *c* and is thinking about the soft /s/ sound of that letter. (Note: The letter *Cc* can represent two sounds: the hard sound, /k/, as in *cat* and the soft sound, /s/, as in *cent*.)

None of the children completely understand the question or the layers of the system that organizes how we put speech into a printed, visual form. And this lack of understanding will hinder *any* attempts to teach them the smaller pieces of the system–phonics. What we know about learning and cognition is that the brain best stores and retrieves information when it is organized and categorized. The brain wants and needs a "big picture," and it wants and needs a strong filing system to store information around that big picture. When we present children with details and questions

> The brain wants and needs a "big picture," and it wants and needs a strong filing system to store information around that big picture.

ahead of their understanding of the system or big picture, our teaching will not be successful. They will try to make us happy by taking a stab at our questions. They may even memorize what they are supposed to say when we ask these questions (e.g., "I'm supposed to say /c/ when my teacher asks what sound is at the beginning of *cat*"). But they will not truly understand and will not be able to transfer their knowledge to novel situations (e.g., "What sound is at the beginning of *cut*?"). They will not retain or use knowledge that we are trying to teach them.

As an adult, you probably think, "Well, yeah. Okay. I can teach that. I'll just tell them, 'See this letter *g*, it stands for the sound /g/ as in *girl*. The word *girl* starts with the sound /g/ that we make with this letter *g*.'" But you can do that until you are blue in the face (and the children can "give" you the right answer), but then when you ask them the sound at the beginning of *go*, they may not know. Helping children construct the alphabetic principle is not that simple. In order to make these kinds of major changes in children's thinking, especially with something as abstract and arbitrary as written language, we have to show them and show them over and over and over again in many different ways.

Vygotsky explained it like this:

> *Direct teaching of concepts is impossible and fruitless. A teacher who tries to do this usually accomplishes nothing but empty verbalism, a parrot like repetition of words by the child, simulating a knowledge of the corresponding concepts but actually covering up a vacuum. (Vygotsky 1986, 149–50)*

With young children we develop the alphabetic principle by modeling the writing of words, by playing with language, by reading "big books" and pointing to words, and by using letter–sounds to figure out words. (See Chapter 3 for many specific strategies.) This conceptual development of the alphabetic principle must be pervasive and consistent along with the explicit teaching of specific letter–sounds. Without the alphabetic principle, phonics instruction is futile.

WATCH

VIDEO 0.1

Alphabetic Principle

In this short clip, I explain the alphabetic principle. It's a central concept, so watching the video might be helpful.

Concept of Word in Print

Imagine teaching children to read without ever explaining what a "word" is. Seems impossible, right? At a basic level, children must understand what a word is—a collection of letters that represent a meaningful unit. They must understand that words can be represented orally and visually, in speech and in writing. Children can only own this understanding by interacting with and observing others interacting with printed materials.

When children begin to try to "read" books or watch a teacher point to the words in a big book, they notice that the words stay the same each time, that there is a connection between print and voice, that words are made of groups of letters, and that white space separates words. As they interact with print, children acquire increasingly more detailed understandings of what a word is. Imagine looking at a plant cell under a microscope. At first, it is fuzzy and you can see that it is green and yellow. Then, as you turn the knob on the microscope, you can see that the shape is rectangular and very regular. You keep turning the knob and you can see that the borders are green and the interior has more structures inside. You see small floating green shapes (chlorophyll) and a large kind of brownish blob in the middle (nucleus). A child's concept of word comes into focus gradually, like the increasing magnification of the microscope. Below is an example of increasing understandings that children might have about how written words work.

Words are what a person "reads" when they interact with a book.
Words are not pictures, but a special code.
Words are made up of letters.
Words are collections of letters separated by white spaces.
The letters in words represents speech sounds.

You can see how the development of **concept of word in print** bleeds into the alphabetic principle. Children acquire concept of word in print by attempting to point to words as they say them in a line of print or by reading simple little books and finger pointing (Ehri and Sweet 1991; Henderson and Beers, 1980; Morris 1983; Morris et al. 2003). They eventually use alphabetic information to inform their concept of word. Although it sounds easy, it is not! Below is an example of a child reading and pointing to a memorized line of a nursery rhyme. Notice that at the end, the child points to the word *another* when he comes to the second syllable of *a-gain*. He doesn't yet understand that some words have two syllables.

Text:	*Come*	*again*	*another*	*day.*		
Child Reciting:	"Come	a-	gain	a-	nother	day."
Child Pointing:	✓	✓	✓	✓	?	(no print left)

If you are teaching in kindergarten or prekindergarten, try asking a child to point to the words in a chart or big book, a line of print that they have memorized. It can be very interesting and informative to see what they do.

WATCH

VIDEO 0.2

Concept of Word in Print

In this video clip, I explain the principle concept of word in print.

Phonics Is Teaching Children How to Organize Information for Use

Teaching phonics is about organizing information so that kids can store it in a systematized way. Once children begin to have some notion of the alphabetic principle and concept of word, they start to develop emerging cognitive structures. You might think of these cognitive structures as "file cabinets" and "file folders" into which they will store stuff about our written language. Concept of word provides a learner with a cognitive space, or "file cabinet," for storing "literacy symbols" or letters. The alphabetic principle and some visual discrimination drive a highly sophisticated and specific file folder system for each letter. What happens cognitively is that at first the filing system in the cabinet is not that sophisticated. Yes, letters are put into the cabinet, but they may not be well differentiated. So a child might, for example, have one file that stores both *Cc* and *Gg* together (erroneously) because the features have not been well differentiated. (This happens a lot with *Bb* and *Dd*.) Increasingly, the files become specific and correct so that each letter has its own file with the letter–sound, visual shape, written form, and other information (e.g., "That letter starts my name").

That system for learned letter–sounds means that children can quickly and easily access that information for *use*, such as in decoding words. When information is organized, it can be more easily retrieved or even expanded. For example, if we teach consonant digraphs together (e.g., *th, wh, sh, ch*), children might create a consonant digraphs folder. That "consonant digraph" category allows them to build from existing knowledge so that when they learn new information, say the digraph *ph*, they have a folder to put that information in (e.g., "Oh, that's like *th* and *ch*").

So teaching phonics requires a plan. Groups of letter–sounds are taught with a plan and an order, from easiest to hardest. This is called a scope and sequence, and by using it, teachers respond to the way that the brain organizes and stores information.

WATCH

VIDEO 0.3

Importance of Organizing Phonics Information

For a video explanation of why organizing information is very important for phonics instruction, watch this clip.

Phonics Learning Must Be Active

Good phonics instruction is about learning the architecture of words—what they are made of. It's about putting words together and taking them apart. Think about Legos and how children learn from assembling and disassembling. Words are the same way. To learn how they work, children must work with them, understand the parts, put them together, and take them apart. The best phonics instruction relies on active, manipulative, engaging activities in which students read and spell words.

Children learn it by *doing it*. They should have dry erase boards to practice spelling words and listening for sounds. They should have magnetic letters for building words. They should have (child-safe) scissors that allow them to cut the words apart and put them back together.

VIDEO 0.4

Active Phonics Instruction

Weak phonics instruction often happens when active application is missing. So here's a short clip to explain the importance of active phonics instruction.

WATCH

VIDEO 0.5

Phonics Strategies

Good phonics instruction engages the *mind* and encourages the process as much as the right answer. When readers *use* information to decode or spell a word, they will store that word more securely. Sometimes, this means that phonics instruction honors successive approximations and imperfect answers, answers that show thinking and hard work. Take Zaida, a girl in a kindergarten classroom. For several weeks during phonics instruction, Zaida had been struggling with letter order. She would write words like *no* as *on*. You might first think that she didn't know left-to-right directionality, but she did. Her letter order confusion occurred because she was trying to "memorize" words and did not really connect letter–sounds with spellings. She knew that print ran from left to right, but she was not thinking about letter–sounds.

Mrs. Taylor explained, "I would read back words to her. 'Look you wrote *on*. See the first sound is /o/ and then you wrote /n/.' I kept doing this and sometimes I would stretch out a word while I was spelling it: 'I am going to write the word *look*. *lllllook, llll*. How would I start it, Zaida?'" After two weeks, Zaida had a breakthrough. She was writing in her journal and wanted to spell *get*. "Say it, Zaida. What do you hear?" Mrs. Taylor asked. Gradually Zaida engaged in a process of saying the word slowly, listening for each sound, and then writing each letter as she heard the sound. This multistep process of saying, thinking, and writing went on for about two long minutes until she finally wrote *git*.

> Sometimes, this means that phonics instruction honors successive approximations and imperfect answers, answers that show thinking and hard work.

"I was so happy!" Mrs. Taylor recalled. "I praised her to the hilt. 'Wow! Look at that. You listened for the sounds and then you wrote them down. You didn't just copy. You heard the sounds. The word had three sounds and you got them in order!'" Mrs. Taylor knew that Zaida's work to spell *git* was so transformative and important that the correct answer, at that time, was not important. "Yeah, that short *e* is tough," she explained. "It's so close to the short *i* sound, as in *sit*. I knew that there would be plenty of time to deal with that. But I had just watched Zaida cross a major milestone, showing she knew how to *use her letter–sounds*, and I wanted to praise that." (Note: Often spellings that are logical but not exactly correct, like *git*, are called, "invented spelling." I prefer the term "temporary spelling," to convey that these spellings will change into conventional ones as children develop. This term is very useful for communicating with parents.)

WATCH

VIDEO 0.6

Explanation of Temporary Spelling

For a video explanation of temporary spelling and the importance of honoring successive approximations, watch this short clip.

VIDEO 0.7

Temporary Spelling

For a video example of a child using temporary spelling, watch this short clip about Hot Rod the turtle.

Isn't Just Following a Phonics Program Enough?

No doubt, if you are a teacher in the early grades, you have encountered programs. I define a phonics program as a "one-stop shop" for instruction with scripted lessons, worksheets, matching books, teacher's editions, posters, workbooks, and other shiny shrink-wrapped consumable items. Programs provide a day-by-day listing of what to do in each and every lesson for each and every minute. You may even use one of these programs now. You may be asking yourself, "Why not just keep relying on the ready-to-go program? It's right there. It's all set up. All I have to do is pick it up and go." There is nothing wrong with leaning on a program, especially as you learn content that may be new to you. You can't tell a whole classroom full of first graders, "Hey, I will figure it out in a year. So just hang on." Those kids have only one first-grade year and their literacy development is dependent upon getting phonics.

What does the research say about programs? The key to effectiveness is not a program but a systematic and explicit approach. In a 2005 analysis, my colleague and I (Mesmer and Griffith 2005) reviewed definitions of *systematic* and *explicit* going back to 1967, noting that "historically, *explicit, systematic* phonics instruction has converged upon three features . . . (a) a curriculum with a specified, sequential set of phonics elements (e.g., scope and sequence); (b) instruc-

> The key to effectiveness is not a program but a systematic and explicit approach.

tion that is direct, precise, and unambiguous; and (c) practice using phonics to read words" (69). Programs can deliver a systematic, explicit approach, *but* so can knowledgeable teachers not using a program. In fact, I went to the What Works Clearinghouse, and when I surveyed eight of the most well-known pre-K programs focusing on phonics, I found that only five had had "potentially positive" or "positive" impacts on print knowledge. I did the same with nine well-known programs for K–2 and found that only five had had "potentially positive" or "positive" impacts on alphabetics and only four had had "potentially positive" or "positive" impacts on reading achievement. In addition, both a recent meta-analysis of phonics instruction and a comparison study showed that both programs and nonprograms were effective (Suggate 2016; Tivnan and Hemphill 2005). Although a program can certainly make things easier for the teacher and, *if implemented with fidelity*, can result in learning, a program does not guarantee that. Why not invest in your own professional knowledge? We know that one of the most critical factors in any instructional situation is the *teacher* (Bond and Dykstra 1967).

Another challenge with teaching according to the script of a program is that programs are typically designed for whole-class instruction. These kinds of one-size-fits-all programs are not flexible or adaptive. Everyone gets the same thing, both students who are completely bored by too-simple content and students who are overwhelmed by content that is over their heads.

WATCH

VIDEO 0.8

Why a One-Size-Fits-All Approach Is Less Effective in Kindergarten

In this short clip, learn about why a one-size-fits-all approach can be less effective in kindergarten.

What This Book Offers: An Adaptable Approach to Phonics Instruction

The approach in this book is to empower teachers with need-to-know content about phonics instruction and to walk them through a process for teaching phonics that adds to their instructional prowess. In order to teach phonics, you must

- know the content (e.g., English letter–sounds),

- know how to find out what your kids need to learn, and

- know how to teach that content.

The information in this book is pared down to be accessible, concise, and efficient, because in many resources phonics instruction is unnecessarily overcomplicated. The book has six chapters that reflect a process of creating phonics instruction:

Chapter 1, "Know the Code," provides basic information about the English alphabet and how the twenty-six letter symbols are used to read and spell. It can be used as a resource to revisit.

Chapter 2, "Assessment That Shows You What to Teach," gives the scope and sequence for phonics instruction and a simple test to use. The scope and sequence is organized around three main units—Letter Lessons, First Words, and Beyond First Words. These units take about twenty-three to twenty-seven weeks to do and match to important milestones, learning letter–sounds, decoding simple words, and decoding words with multi-letter units.

Chapter 3, "Phonics Lessons for Real Literacy," provides a small-group lesson framework that can be used across the different units and also tweaked for whole-group instruction. This framework includes the types of activities that support students in applying their knowledge of letter–sounds to reading.

Chapters 4–6 are unit specific, providing specific guidelines for teaching children at each of the stages, with activities as well.

(Note: In this book, I provide mnemonics and labels for different types of letter–sound patterns [e.g., "We Are Family" for c-v-c (consonant-vowel-consonant) word families, "Sneaky Silent *e*" for the c-v-c-*e* pattern (consonant-vowel-consonant silent *e*), and "*R* the Robber" for *r*-controlled vowels]. These may or may not be useful, appropriate, or desired in all classrooms. Share these with children only as you see fit. What is most important is not what we call these patterns but that they are categorized in some memorable way for children to learn and understand.)

The book is a streamlined approach to phonics, a quick reference to move forward and lay groundwork that will empower informed and inspired teaching. The basics can be enhanced and creatively expanded by resourceful and reflective educators teaching young children. As always, children achieve more when they are working with teachers who know them and are thoughtful of their needs. I'm grateful for the opportunity to share this work that's been inspired and influenced by so many wonderful teachers and children. My hope is to plant a seed and to watch the seed grow into the type of innovative practice that changes the lives of children.

chapter 1

Know the Code

Teacher's Reference on How English Works

I N THIS CHAPTER, I'VE CREATED A CONCISE REFERENCE FOR YOUR teaching. The purpose is to provide you with basic information about how the English system of writing works so that when you teach, you have an understanding of the system. Keep in mind that this is an abbreviated treatment of the topic specific to *teaching*. Within the field of linguistics there continue to be debates about categories, divisions, and labels (Moats 1998). I organize categories of letter–sounds together and present figures for each group. These groups match the categories of letter–sounds taught in the three main units—Letter Lessons, First Words, and Beyond First Words. Throughout the chapter, I identify the unit in which a group of letter–sounds is taught. For example, as I describe the basic consonant sounds in English, I note that these are addressed in Letter Lessons. Read this chapter to check what you know and what's new to you, from details to definitions to understandings. In the next chapter, we will get into the meaty, rewarding work of using this knowledge to support children.

Speech Versus Writing: What's the Difference?

Although to literate adults, the connections between oral language and written language are obvious, some very important differences exist. These distinctions can actually make it challenging for a young child to acquire the written system. Use the brief written conversation between Robby and his mom in Figure 1.1 to think about the difference between oral and written language.

FIGURE 1.1

Oral Language	Written Language
Robby: Aymom. Goin'ta jimz.	**Robby:** Hey, Mom. Going to Jim's.
Mom: Waid uh minud.	**Mom:** Wait a minute.
Robby: Beback afree.	**Robby:** Be back at three.
Mom: Kay don be too lawn.	**Mom:** Okay. Don't be too long.

Funny, isn't it? But this is actually how we sound in our everyday speech. We blur things together, don't enunciate sounds, and often do not even speak in complete sentences. It's no wonder that children get confused when we begin teaching reading and start separating words or talk about "sounds in words." To them, words blend altogether and the "sounds in words" are larger units of meaning.

Speech does not operate like writing. First, speech and oral language have been around for far longer than writing. According to many, while humans have a biological predisposition to create and use oral language (Chomsky 1986), writing is an invention. The first record of a written language is generally believed to be the Sumerian language in the third century BC. Even today, there are still languages that do not have a written form.

Second, speech is less permanent than writing. The very purpose of writing is to record, or hold permanent, the spoken word. In writing, there is a cue where one word ends and the next begins: a white space. As we saw in the example of Robby's conversation with his mom, people do not pause between each word when they speak. Writing is discrete and there are clearly distinguishable parts and a hierarchy for organization. The building blocks of speech are sounds and the building blocks of writing are visual symbols: you hear speech (unless you are hearing impaired) and you see writing and then hear it again when it is read aloud, as shown in Figure 1.2.

FIGURE 1.2

Phonemes, Speech Sounds Building Blocks of Speech	**Graphemes,** Letters Building Blocks of Writing
It is important to understand that phonemes are *speech* sounds, not just *sounds*. Think about sounds in your world that are not *speech sounds*—a lawn mower, two hands clapping. A *phoneme* is the smallest unit of sound in speech that distinguishes one word from another.	A grapheme is a letter or group of letters that represents a phoneme. The *grapheme* for a speech sound can be made up of one letter, as in the /a/ sound in *hat,* or it can be made up of more than one letter, as in the /a/ sound in *wait.* The vowel sound in *wait* has a grapheme made up of the letters *ai.*

Figure 1.3 shows the parts of words and how those parts map onto print.

- A **word** is a single element of meaning that has a specific function (more about morphology below). Words can have one or more syllables.

- A **syllable** is a word or word part with at least one vowel, made with one push of breath. Syllables have vowels. Find the vowel groups in a word and you usually find the number of syllables in that word.

- A syllable can usually be broken down into an **onset** and a **rime**. The onset is the consonant sound(s) that comes before the vowel (e.g., *c*-an, ***th***-at, ***tr***-ip). Not all words have onsets (e.g., *at*, *in*). The rime is the part of the word with the vowel and all that comes after it (e.g., *c*-**at**). Teachers often use the term *word family* or *phonogram* for the more technical term *rime*. The words *rime* and *word family* will be used interchangeably throughout the book. The rime can further be broken into a *nucleus* (which is always a vowel sound) and the *coda*, which is the part in a syllable what follows the vowel or ends the word.

- Lastly, words in English are broken down into **phonemes**.

FIGURE 1.3 **Parts of a Word**

Word:
treatment

Syllable:
treat ment

Onset / Rime:
tr-eat   m-ent

Nucleus / coda:
(tr) ea-t   (m) e-nt

Phoneme / Grapheme:
t-r-ea-t-m-e-n-t

If this breakdown seems unnecessarily tedious, know that it is extremely useful in explaining how words work to a child. A teacher of prekindergarten, kindergarten, first grade, or second grade needs to show children how the parts work within this visual, written system. Teachers are making clear the relationships between the visual parts of writing and the spoken parts of English. When we teach children to read, we are teaching them how to *decode* or translate the *graphemes* into spoken words. We are also teaching them how to *encode* or *spell*: how to take spoken words and put them into a written form.

If we think about humans' invented writing systems and pay attention to the earliest attempts, we see that alphabetic approaches are complex, efficient, and parsimonious, but not natural or intuitive. They are also quite imperfect. The first attempts to "write down" speech were pictures or pictographs, symbols that directly represented the meaning of the spoken word (e.g., *table, man, girl*). We actually use pictographs today for signs and even in written texts. Of course, while pictographs are simple and straightforward because you only have one symbol for each word, they present several problems. First, it is difficult to represent words that are not concrete or imaginable, like abstract ideas (e.g., *love*), function words (e.g., *through, into*), or certain verbs (e.g., *wants*). Second, representing the words in a language in this way generates too many symbols for people to remember because oral languages have *at least* five thousand words that are essential and used heavily. For this reason, languages very quickly had to develop logographs or symbols representing words that could not be pictured.

Smallest Word Units: Phonemes and Graphemes

Inventors of writing quickly learned that it is more efficient to develop a system based on a visual code that maps the sounds in a language. One way to be more efficient is to create symbols for sounds in speech and then recombine symbols to represent different words. In some languages with consistent syllable structures, like Japanese, developers created visual symbols to match *syllables*, a sound-based approach called a syllabary. In other languages, like English, developers created symbols to represent individual phonemes or speech sounds. Theoretically, an alphabetic system has a visual code for each speech sound. Although sound-based systems like syllabaries and alphabets are harder to learn initially, once you learn twenty to forty symbols, you are set up to read words.

In the simplest, most *transparent* alphabets, there is a symbol or grapheme for each speech sound / phoneme. This means, that once you learn the graphemes and sounds, you can recognize any word. Each grapheme is simply one alphabet letter. There is a direct, straightforward relationship between speech and print. The number of symbols closely matches the number of sounds. Cross-linguistic studies indicate that reading accuracy in very transparent languages (e.g., Greek, Finnish, German, Italian, French, Spanish) is almost complete for both words and nonwords by mid–first grade (Ziegler and Goswami 2005).

Pictures Are Natural for Young Children Too

As young children are becoming literate, they are like our early ancestors in that they use pictures to represent their ideas. In fact, their early approaches to symbolic representation are important and show cognitive development. At the initial stages of writing, children use pictures exclusively to represent their ideas. Then they begin to differentiate pictures from "writing," and often we see letter-like scribbles around their pictures, representing an important insight. Teachers can show young children how our alphabetic writing system works by drawing pictures and labeling them with words, thereby showing children how words differ from pictures.

English is not a *transparent* alphabet and it takes longer to learn. It is a *deep orthography*. (*Orthography* is a fancy name for spelling.) In deep orthographies, there is not a one-to-one sound–symbol relationship. Usually there are more sounds than symbols, so the letter symbols must be combined or altered to capture all the sounds (e.g., *sea*, *chip*). English has about forty-four sounds and twenty-six letters, but this number of sounds is often up for debate (Bizzochi 2017). In English, a deep orthography, children are only about 40 percent accurate with words and pseudowords by mid–first grade (Ziegler and Goswami 2005).

(Note: This does not mean that the incidence of dyslexia or severe reading difficulty at the word level is lower in Italian or Finnish. For about 5 to 10 percent of the population, serious word-reading difficulties occur regardless of the transparency of language because children still must have insight about the phonemic structure of words.)

Teachers of beginning readers must have a basic fluency with the letter–sounds or *phoneme–grapheme* relationships. I've included several figures that list this information, first for consonants and then for vowels. These figures will serve as a reference as you teach phonics. The vocabulary and language for particular letter–sounds will be used throughout the book. This is the toolbox of early literacy instruction. The divisions here are made mostly because they help organize the teaching of letter–sounds.

Some Consonant Sounds Can Be Similar

Say the sound for each consonant pair. What do you notice?

/p-b/ /t-d/ /k-g/ /v-f/ /z-s/

Place your hand on your vocal chords as you say each pair. How are the sounds the same? How are the sounds different? Do you feel your voice box (vocal chords) vibrate or "buzz" on one sound in the pair and not another?

Each of these pairs is made in the same *place* in the mouth and in the same *manner* or *way*. The sounds /p/ and /b/ are both bilabial (both lips) stop sounds. A stop sound is produced when air is blocked and then released to make the sound. The only thing that makes /p/ and /b/ different is that /b/ is voiced (vocal chords buzz or make a noise) and /p/ is unvoiced (vocal chords are silent).

How Does This Affect Teaching?

Because these pairs of sounds are so very similar, it is best *not* to teach them adjacently. For example, don't teach *Kk* and *Gg* in the same week or *Tt* and *Dd* in adjacent weeks. It might be easy for children to confuse these sounds because they make the sounds the same way in their mouths. For instance, for both /t/ and /d/, children start with their tongue against their teeth (place) and then push a breath of air out (manner) to make each sound. The only difference between these two sounds is that for /g/ there is voicing (the vocal chords vibrate or buzz). Understanding these similarities is also helpful in interpreting children's spelling approximations. For example, it makes sense for a child to confuse the /k/ and /g/ sounds in spelling *go-kart* as *ko-grt*.

Single Consonants

Consonant sounds are made by closing off or partially constricting the flow of air through the vocal tract. When we make consonant sounds we tend to close our mouths, and when we make vowel sounds we open our mouths.

There are consonants graphemes (letters) that duplicate sounds already represented by other letters. These letters do not represent a unique sound. The letter *Cc* does not represent a unique sound, but represents the /s/ sound or the /k/ sound. The *Cc* will represent the /k/ or "hard sound" when followed by a *u*, *o*, or *a* and will represented the "soft sound" when followed by the *e*, *i*, or *y*. Another example of letters that do not represent unique phonemes are *Xx* and *Qq*. The letter *Xx* represents a consonant blend /ks/ or the sound /z/. The letter *Qq* is almost always accompanied by *u* and represents mostly the blend /kw/ but sometimes represents /k/. What's important to remember is that each letter does not have *its own sound*. So watch out when teaching *Cc*, *Xx*, or *Qq*.

The single consonant sounds are taught in the Letter Lessons unit in Chapter 4, which for most children should take place in kindergarten or prekindergarten. Both the name of the letter and common phoneme are taught. Letters like *Xx* and *Qq* are taught with the blended sound associated with the grapheme. Both the hard and soft *c* and *g* are taught as shown in Figure 1.4.

FIGURE 1.4

Single Consonant Sounds: Sounds made by partially or fully restricting sound as it moves through the vocal tract (Content taught in Letter Lessons unit.)					
	Phonemes/ Speech Sounds	Letters	Graphemes/ Common Spellings (Letter Lessons)	Graphemes/Some Less Common Spellings (Most not taught in Letter Lessons and First Words)	Notes
1	/b/[1]	Bb	*b*ag		
2	/k/	Cc Kk	*c*at *k*ite	ck ro*ck*	ch *ch*ord
3	/d/	Dd	*d*ad		
4	/f/	Ff	*f*un	ph *ph*one	gh rou*gh*
5	/g/	Gg	*g*ift	gu *gu*ess	gh *gh*ost

continues

1 The slash marks around a letter are used to denote the phoneme or sound represented by the letter. These marks are actually the tool of linguistics and speech pathologists, and they are often used to record sounds using the International Phonetic Alphabet, a system with unique symbols for each English phoneme. That system is not used here because it is complex and unknown to most educators.

Single Consonant Sounds: **Sounds made by partially or fully restricting sound** **as it moves through the vocal tract** **(Content taught in Letter Lessons unit.)**					
	Phonemes/ Speech Sounds	Letters	Graphemes/ Common Spellings (Letter Lessons)	Graphemes/Some Less Common Spellings (Most not taught in Letter Lessons and First Words)		Notes
6	/h/	Hh	*h*at			
7	/j/ /g/	Jj Gg	*j*oy *g*iraffe	*g*em ca*ge*		The letter *g* typically makes a /j/ sound after *e, i,* or *y* (e.g., *gem, gym, lodge*).
8	/l/	Ll	*l*eg			
9	/m/	Mm	*m*an			
10	/n/	Nn	*n*et	kn *kn*ot	gn *gn*ome	
11	/p/	Pp	*p*at			
12	/r/	Rr	*r*ob	wr *wr*ing		
13	/s/	Ss Cc	*s*un	c *c*ent ni*c*e		The letter *c* typically makes the /s/ when followed by *i, e,* or *y.*
14	/t/	Tt	*t*old			
15	/v/	Vv	*v*et			
16	/w/	Ww	*w*ork			
17	/y/	Yy	*y*ell			
18	/z/	Zz	*z*oo	rat*s* wa*s*	x e*x*am	

Note: Not every letter in the English alphabet represents a unique sound (*Cc, Xx, Qu*). Also see chapter notes.

The first eighteen sounds shown are generally represented by a single consonant grapheme or letter, and generally single consonants are fairly predictable. That is, if you read a word with a single consonant, especially at the beginning of the word, it will make a predictable sound.

Consonant Digraphs

The consonant digraph sounds in Figure 1.5 include seven unique phonemes that are represented by combinations of consonant letters. A consonant digraph is two consonant letters that produce a new or unique speech sound. The most common consonant digraphs are *sh*, *ch*, and *th*. When these letters are adjacent to each other, they usually represent unique sounds. The *th* digraph has a voiced sound as in *th*at, in which the voice box or vocal cord "buzzes." It also has an unvoiced sound as in *th*in, in which the voice box does not buzz. (See the box "Some Consonant Sounds Can Be Similar," p. 6.) The voiced and unvoiced versions do not represent meaningful differences in English. The digraph subunit in the First Words unit is called Two for One because two letters are representing one sound.

FIGURE 1.5

	Phonemes/ Speech Sounds	Graphemes/ Common Spellings	Notes
19	/sh/	sh **sh**ip	
20	/hw/	wh **wh**y?	The /hw/ sound is spelled with the *wh* and has a slight breath before the /w/ sound. This is a unique sound, but it is difficult to distinguish from /w/.
21	/ch/	ch **ch**ip	
22	/th/ (voiced)	th **th**ose o**th**er	The "voiced" *th* sound will produce a "buzz" or a sound in the throat, as in *this*, *that*, or ga*th*er.
23	/th/ (unvoiced)	th **th**ick	The "unvoiced" *th* sound will not produce a "buzz" or sound in the throat, as in *th*in or *thought*. The voiced and unvoiced *th* are different phonemes / speech sounds, but they both are spelled the same way. Note: Although there are two sounds for /th/, voiced and unvoiced, these are not typically differentiated in *instruction*. Both voiced and unvoiced /th/ are taught together. This distinction does not differentiate meanings in words.

continues

	Phonemes/ Speech Sounds	Graphemes/ Common Spellings	Notes
24	/ng/	ng bri**ng**	Generally this sound, which is made in the back of the mouth, occurs in -*ing* words.
25	/zh/	s mea**s**ure z a**z**ure	This sound is almost always in the middle of words.

Consonant Blend or Digraph? Keeping These Two Terms Straight

I have found that people confuse the terms *blend* and *digraph*. Most often, they use the term *blend* when they are really talking about a digraph like *sh*. Remember, a blend (or consonant cluster) is a combination of consonant letters *in which each sound can still be heard.* In the word *grin*, both the /g/ and /r/ sounds can be heard. A digraph is a combination in which two letters represent one sound. In consonant digraphs, a different sound results from the combination of letters. In the digraph *sh*, you do not hear /s/ or /h/ but hear a new sound. (Note: It is important to use the term *consonant* before *digraph* because there are also vowel digraphs.) The easiest way to keep these words straight is to remember that the word *blend* has two consonant blends in it and the word *digraph* has a digraph, *ph*. See Figure 1.5. (Note that this *ph* digraph is used to spell the /f/ sound, but it is nonetheless a digraph.)

Consonant Blends/Clusters

Consonant blends or clusters are groups of consonants pronounced quickly with each consonant retaining its own sound. Most consonant blends have two consonants, like *gr*, but some have three, like *scr*, and some combine a blend with a digraph, like *thr*. The most common consonant blends found at the beginning of words are those with *l*, *r*, or *s*. Teach these in groups. Once students can hear the sounds in words with these blends, they can spell them. Some blends at the end of words are more subtle and more difficult to hear. For example, whenever an /n/ or /m/ sound is also followed by a consonant, it is hard to hear (e.g., *lump*, *bend*). Other ending blends like *-st* (e.g., *best*) are a bit more clear. With the more challenging ending blends, additional time and patience will be needed. See Figure 1.6. (Note: The list of ending blends in Figure 1.6 is not comprehensive. All are not included here. Other less common blends can be taught after the Beyond First Words unit.)

FIGURE 1.6

Consonant Blends or Consonant Clusters: Two or more adjacent consonants pronounced together within a syllable in which each consonant retains its separate sound. (Content taught in First Words unit.)		
Beginning Sound Blends: Blends at the beginning of words.		
	Most Common	**Less Common**
r-blends consonant + *r*	tr-, gr-, br-, cr-, dr-, fr-, pr- **tr**ip, **gr**ab, **br**ing, **cr**ib, **dr**ip, **fr**og, **pr**od	
s-blends s + consonant	sp-, st-, sw-, sk- **sp**ot, **st**op, **sw**at, **sk**ip	sc-, sm-, sn- **sc**oot, **sm**ell, **sn**ap
l-blends consonant + *l*	bl-, cl-, pl-, gl-, fl-, sl- **bl**eed, **cl**ip, **pl**ant, **gl**ue, **fl**ip, **sl**ap	
Others		tw- **tw**ist
Three Consonants	str- **str**ing	spr-, scr-, spl- **spr**ig, **scr**ape, **spl**it
Digraph Blend digraph + consonant	thr-, shr- **thr**ill, **shr**ink	
Ending Sound Blends: Blends at the end of words.		
n = blends n + consonant	-nd, -nt, -nk be**nd**, spe**nt**, ri**nk**	It is very difficult to hear the /n/ or /m/ sound when followed by another consonant. These are challenging. Teach slowly with repetition.
m = blends m + consonant	-mp ju**mp**	
t = blends consonant + t	-st, -ft mu**st**, le**ft**	
l = blends l + consonant	-ld, -lk, -lp, -lf mo**ld**, mi**lk**, he**lp**, e**lf**	

Source: Most common beginning blends are from Groff (1971).

Vowel Sounds: Short, Long, Diphthongs, "Other," and *R*-Controlled

Vowel sounds are made by opening the vocal tract. They are said to be the "song" of language, and, indeed, without vowels we would all go around clenching our jaws and spitting on each other. Just try to say, "This is happy" without saying the vowel sounds. All words have vowel sounds and most have vowel graphemes (e.g., *fry* does not have a vowel letter but has the /i/ sound). The twenty vowel categories offered here are useful for teaching reading, but they may not be the exact categories that linguists or speech pathologists use. Often linguists and speech pathologists include more categories and subdivide groups more than we do in literacy education. Linguists are interested in accurately representing all features of the language, not teaching people how to read. Speech specialists are focused on helping students *articulate* sounds, so they give more attention to describing how the sound is made. Vowels are organized into five categories: short vowels, long vowels, diphthongs, "other vowels," and *r*-controlled vowel sounds.

The words *short* and *long* make it seem as though the distinction between these sounds is how long you say them, but actually this is a misconception (Odden 2011). A long vowel sound and a short vowel sound are completely different. Long vowel sounds are the names of the letters. For example, the long *a* is /ay/ as in *day*. Long vowels are commonly denoted with a straight line, called a macron, over the vowel (e.g., ā). The short vowel sounds are the not the names. It would be the /a/ as in *cat*, often denoted with a breve over the vowel (e.g., ă). One distinction between short and long vowel sounds is that long vowel sounds are "tense." If you say the sounds /ay/, /ee/, /ie/, /oa/, and /ue/, you can feel that your tongue and the muscles in your jaw are tight or tense. If you say /a/, /e/, /i/, /o/, and /u/, you can feel that you are more relaxed or loose. Short vowel sounds are very consistent in single-syllable words. Usually when you have a single vowel in a word that ends in a consonant, the vowel is "short." Often this pattern is called a c-v-c pattern, which stands for consonant-vowel-consonant. Short vowels usually occur in words that end in a consonant. These are called "closed" syllables because the vowel sound is "closed" off by a consonant, as in *mat* and *top*. In contrast, an "open" syllable ends with a vowel sound, as in *go* and *bee*. Often short vowels are taught in what are called *rimes*, *phonograms*, or *word families* because at the very early stages of reading first words, it is easier to add a consonant sound to this unit than to fully sound out an entire word (e.g., c*at*, b*at*, s*at*, m*at*). See Figure 1.7. Linguistically the term *phonogram* means a sound written down, but in education people use this term to mean *rime* or *word family*.

Long vowel *sounds* have the most variety of *spellings*. Learning long vowels takes a long time because since we have only five vowel graphemes, we have to double up or combine letters to represent the different long vowel sounds. So, in order to represent the long *a* sound, the two vowels *ai* are written adjacently. The difficulty with long vowels is that each long vowel sound also has several variations. So long *a* can also be spelled with an *ay*. The long vowel sounds also employ the "silent" *e*, which marks a long vowel sound. The Sneaky Silent *e*, as it is called in the subunit in Beyond First Words, is pretty consistent. Figure 1.7 lists the most common spellings for each of the long vowel sounds and the less common patterns. In the Beyond First Words unit in Chapter 6, the letter–sound patterns listed under "Most Common Graphemes/ Spellings" are taught. Also, within that chapter are statistics from several studies that report how consistent these patterns are, so that you can know when you are teaching a pattern how likely that pattern is to occur again.

The sounds listed under "Diphthongs" in Figure 1.7 are /oi/ as in *noise* and /ou/ as in *shout*. These are generally called diphthongs because the sound changes quality in the middle of the sound. If you put your hands around your jaw as you say the sound, you can feel your mouth change. When children are trying to spell these, you can observe their confusion. If they try to write the word *oil*, for example, they might include up to three different vowel letters because they hear so many different sounds (e.g., *aeol*). (Note: Linguists use different definitions for diphthongs.)

"Other Vowels" in Figure 1.7 are sounds that are not short, long, or *r*-controlled. The sound /aw/ as in *law* is one of these. There are two sounds that the grapheme *oo* represents: the sound that is in *book* and the long *u* sound as in *boot*.

R-controlled vowels are sounds that have a vowel sound along with an *r*. The *r* in these words can be called a "robber" because it steals the "vowelness" of a sound. In the Beyond First Words unit in Chapter 6, the *r*-controlled vowels are taught in a subunit called *R the Robber*. The first three *r*-controlled vowels are the least complicated: *or*, *ar*, and *er/ir/ur*. The /er/ sound is a little more difficult, as it has three different spellings: *ur*, *er*, and *ir* as in *hurt*, *her*, and *shirt*. The last two sounds combine an *r* with a vowel pattern (e.g., *ear*, *eer*).

FIGURE 1.7

Short Vowel Sounds: Sounds made with the vocal tract open in which the target sound is not the name of the letter. (Content taught in First Words unit.)				
	Phonemes/ Speech Sounds	Graphemes/ Common Spellings	Less Common Graphemes/Spellings or Silent Letters	Notes
1	/a/	c*a*b			Most single vowels without an *r* in single-syllable words are short, especially if they are in a closed syllable. (Gates and Yale 2011).

continues

2	/e/	g*e*t	ea h*ea*d	ai s*ai*d		
3	/i/	f*i*t				
4	/o/	h*o*t	a w*a*sh, sw*a*p			
5	/u/	n*u*t				

Schwa: An unstressed vowel sound made in the middle of the mouth in which the target sound is /u/; found most often in multisyllabic words. (Not addressed in this book due to this book's focus on single-syllable word learning.)

| 6 | /ə/ | *a*bout,
b*a*lloon
tak*e*n
penc*i*l
ph*o*tography
s*u*pply | There are countless spellings of the schwa sound, particularly in multisyllabic words. | | | |

Long Vowel Sounds: Sounds made with the vocal tract open in which the target sound is the name of the letter. (Content taught in Beyond First Words unit.)

	Phonemes/ Speech Sounds	Most Common Graphemes/Spellings			Less Common Graphemes/Spellings	
7	/a/	a-e b*ake*	ai w*ai*t	ay d*ay*	ei *ei*ght	
8	/e/	ee b*ee*t	ea m*ea*t		**y** bab**y**	e_e P*e*t*e* th*ese*
9	/i/	i-e l*i*k*e*	y fr**y**	igh n*igh*t	**ie** p*ie*	
10	/o/	o-e h*o*p*e*	oa b*oa*t	ow thr*ow*	o (with -*ld*) c*old*	

11	/u/	u-e fl**u**t**e** **u**se[1]	ew f**ew**[1] gr**ew**	oo g**oo**se	ue bl**ue**	ui s**ui**t

	1 The sound in words like *few* and *use* have the sound /y/ at the beginning, making the sound /yoo/. For teaching purposes, the pure /u/ sound (e.g., *hoot, grew*) and this sound are not differentiated.

Diphthongs (Content taught in Beyond First Words unit.)

	Phonemes/ Speech Sounds	Graphemes/ Common Spellings				
12	/oi/	oy t**oy**	oi n**oi**se			
13	/ow/	ow n**ow**	ou sh**ou**t			

Other Vowels

14	/aw/	aw cl**aw**	au c**au**ght			
15	/oo/	oo b**oo**k t**oo**k				

R-Controlled Vowels: A vowel + *r* with a sound that is influenced heavily by the /r/ sound. (Content taught in Beyond First Words unit.)

16	/ar/	ar c**ar**				
17	/or/	or f**or**	ore ch**ore**	our t**our**		
18	/ir, er, ur/	ir f**ir**	er p**er**ch	ur b**ur**n		
19	/air/	are c**are**	air f**air**			
20	/eer/	ear d**ear**	eer st**eer**			

Glass Half Empty or Half Full? The Consistency Question in English

Many teachers, when given information about English, kind of throw their hands up and say, "Well, kids, you just have to memorize it 'cause it doesn't make sense!" That's not really helpful and not true. Really, we should ask, "Is English more consistent than it is inconsistent? Or vice versa? Should I teach as if there is something predictable or not?" The first thing to remember is that English is primarily an alphabetic language, meaning that the foundation of putting the language into a written form is based on using letters to represent phonemes. So we must teach the alphabetic principle and letter–sounds. Here are some facts. In terms of consistency, Moats (1995) found that 50 percent of English words are completely regular or consistent and another 37 percent are irregular at only one sound layer (e.g., *do, said*). Further, single consonants are pretty consistent, with most representing only one sound. If there is complexity, it is at the vowel level and usually for vowels that are not short and/or found in multisyllabic words. But even some of these are pretty consistent. (See Chapter 3, "Phonics 'Rules'?" box, p. 43.) For example, the *ee* pattern as in *bee* was consistent 90 percent of the time. So don't throw your hands up! The best way to teach children phonics is to start with the letter–sounds that are most consistent (e.g., single consonants, short vowels, and consonant digraphs) and then add on. There is also another level of representation that influences how we put speech into writing: "morphology." Often word parts are added to beginnings or endings that influence the meaning and the spelling (Bowers and Kirby 2010).

Smallest Unit of Meaning: Morphemes

This book focuses on reading and spelling single-syllable words, which in the early grades mostly involves learning phoneme–grapheme relationships. However, English is actually morphophonemic; letter–sounds do not fully drive the system. This information is relevant for more advanced readers.

A morpheme is the smallest unit of *meaning* in a language. Often a word can have multiple word parts that convey meaning, or multiple morphemes. Take, for example, the word *runner*. There are two morphemes in this word, the first part, *run*, and the second part, *er* (a person who *runs*). The first morpheme, *run*, is a free morpheme, a verb conveying a way of moving, and the second morpheme, *er*, is a bound morpheme that changes the verb to a noun and the meaning to "one who runs."

The first morphemic layer, words, is called **free morphemes**. These are units of meaning that can stand independently by themselves—words. There are two types of free morphemes: content words and function words. Content words are nouns, verbs, adjectives, and adverbs, and these words add meaning to sentences, paragraphs, and

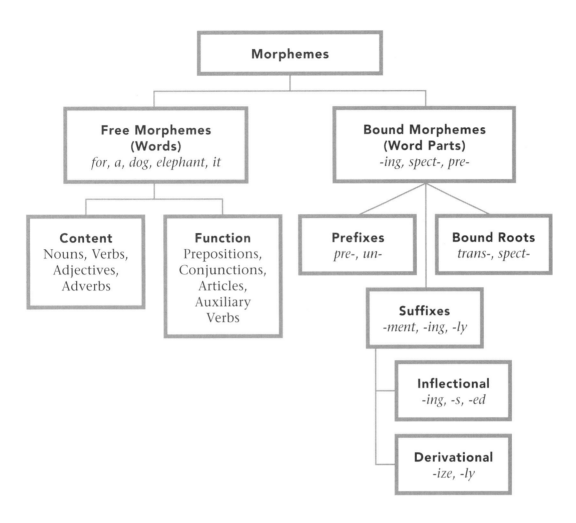

passages. Function words are like the glue that holds those content words together, and they consist of prepositions, conjunctions, articles, and auxiliary verbs.

The group of morphemes that really affects teaching students to read words is called **bound morphemes**, which are word parts added to free morphemes to communicate some level of meaning. The *runner* example above illustrates this combination. There are three types of bound morphemes, prefixes, suffixes, and bound roots. Prefixes are word parts like *pre-*, *re-*, and *un-* that affect the meaning of a word through their addition (e.g., *preheat*, *rerun*, *unrepentant*). Bound roots are typically Greek or Latin word parts that must be combined with other morphemes, yet carry the main meaning in a word (e.g., **spect**ator, in**spect**, **spect**acle). Suffixes can be two types, inflectional and derivational. Inflections are parts that change tense or number, like *-ing*, *-ed*, and *-s*. Derivational morphemes change the part of speech (e.g., *-ment*, *ly*). If you add *-ly* to the word *happy*, you make it into an adverb, *happily*.

In the United States, the discussions about phonics tend to focus almost exclusively on letter–sounds, but really our language is morphophonemic. After learning how to read and spell the patterns in single-syllable words (those addressed in this book) students should have systematic instruction in meaningful word parts or morphemes as well (Kirby et al. 2012). In English multi-morphemic words outnumber single-morpheme words by a factor of four to one (Moats 1995), and although morphemic instruction becomes substantive in the upper-elementary grades, there are certain morphemic layers that are taught earlier. For example, adding inflections like *-s*, *-ing*, and *-ed* and learning about compound words happens in the primary grades.

If your mind is swimming after this chapter and you feel a bit overwhelmed, remember that this is a basic reference to return to when you are teaching. What is most important is that you come away with "file folders" or cognitive categories for types of sounds (e.g., single consonants, digraphs, consonant blends, short vowels, long vowels) and that you have an understanding of how these work.

Access to this information may actually prove more useful than you think. Let's say a parent challenges you and asks, "Why do you teach the consonant sounds first? Why don't you teach phonics rules?" You have information at your fingertips. I know you already know some of it, maybe all of it, but now the information is in one place, and you and I have the same understanding of terms and concepts. Let's get to work using this information to make children powerful, joyfully literate people!

For a downloadable glossary of terms, go to http://hein.pub/letterlessons-login.

2

Assessment That Shows You What to Teach

THE PHONICS INSTRUCTION IN THIS BOOK SETS UP A FLEXIBLE system that actually frees you from *figuring out* the more tedious parts of teaching phonics (e.g., content and order, finding out what a child needs to learn) so that you can concentrate on the interesting, engaging, and fun parts. The idea is to quickly locate a student along a developmental continuum and access a scope and sequence so that you can *teach*. Why reinvent the wheel with assessment and scope and sequence when what you really want to do is be creative about word building, spelling, and immersive reading and writing? So take the scope and sequence and the assessment parts of this book, use the instructional units and lessons in Chapters 4–6, and feel free to expand, invent, and innovate when it comes to the teaching parts. Use the base recipe and then craft it with a new sauce, ingredient, or twist. Let this assessment help you do what you love—engage kids with spot-on teaching that invigorates them and you.

The *Letter Lessons and First Words* Placement Test in this chapter can be quickly administered and should take only about fifteen minutes per child. The focus in this chapter is on how to give the Placement Test. Section introduction preceding Chapters 4–6, Where to Start: Using the Letter Lessons and First Words Placement Test to Identify What to Teach, describes how to use the test data to select the correct unit and subunit for each student or group of students.

An Argument for Individualized Assessment and Instruction

Chapter 1 described phonics "vocabulary"—the labels for categories of letter–sound patterns—but this isn't enough to teach phonics because it tells you nothing about the sequence in which *children* learn patterns. It tells you nothing of how children *use* letter–sound information. If you internalized all the content in Chapter 1, you would be a great linguist but not necessarily an effective teacher. As a teacher you need to know how to organize content for kids—how to present it and pace it so that students will respond. You need answers to questions such as "Should I teach consonants or vowels first?" and "Should I start by teaching *r*-controlled vowels or words with short vowels?"

It's easy to get overwhelmed. We know that's why teachers and schools choose prepackaged programs. Although programs do have advantages and can address gaps in teachers' content knowledge, you do not need a *program* to teach phonics well.

> As a teacher you need to know how to organize content for kids—how to present it and pace it so that students will respond. You need answers to questions such as "Should I teach consonants or vowels first?" and "Should I start by teaching *r*-controlled vowels or words with short vowels?"

What you need is a scope and sequence and a way to find out where to start teaching each child. Debra, a teacher in the Southwest, explains, "I have kids in kindergarten who don't know their letters and other kids who are already reading simple chapter books. If I tried to start teaching them all the same thing, half of them would be rolling their eyes and the other half would be like deer in the headlights. Assessment is survival for them and for me!"

When I recently discussed using this test to guide phonics instruction, one brave teacher raised her hand and said, "Are you seriously asking me to give another test? I am spending almost 25 percent of my time testing." I could not argue with her. The struggle is real and there is indeed *too much testing*, but if instruction is going to match needs, some type of assessment is necessary. The Letter Lessons and First Words Placement Test takes no more than fifteen minutes per child and will ultimately *save* time by preventing you from teaching things that a child already knows or from forging ahead when foundational knowledge is not known.

Before we get into the details of learning how to give the assessment, let's do a quick overview of the research on developmental progression of letters, sounds, and words that informs our assessment.

The Foundation of the Assessment and Scope and Sequence: Research on Development

The assessment and the units (Chapters 4–6) in this book are organized around what we know about how children develop phonics knowledge, an order supported by research (Ehri 1991, 2005; Henderson and Beers 1980; Share 2004; Stahl, Duffy-Hester, and

Stahl 1998) and reflected in the Common Core State Standards for English Language Arts and in other state standards. This gives us a rough scope and sequence that allows us to create a plan for individual children. Phonics instruction has a defined content (scope) taught in a specified order (sequence), but this does not mean that everyone in a class starts at the same place, on the same unit. The key to developmentally responsive teaching is finding out what content students already know and what they do not. Some children in kindergarten, for example, will not need to be taught letter–sounds. They will be ready to blend words in the First Words unit. Other kindergartners will need letters and will start in Letter Lessons. I have never encountered a classroom where everyone, even at the beginning of the year, is at the same place instructionally.

What follows is a general progression of letter, sound, and word knowledge (for greater detail about the research supporting progressions, see each specific Chapters 4–6). Generally, children learn letter names and then acquire letter–sounds (e.g., *t* = /t/), the simplest phoneme grapheme associations. Once letter–sounds are mastered, children apply this knowledge to sound out single-syllable words with short vowels. These words begin and end with a single consonant. The words occur in a consonant-vowel-consonant pattern (c-v-c), and there is a one-to-one correspondence between letter and sound (grapheme and phoneme). For each letter, there is a sound. Along the way, they will also learn high-frequency words that contain more complex letter–sounds (e.g., *the*, *have*), graphemes using multiletter combinations. A high-frequency word is a word that appears often in English—words like *the*, *at*, and *some*. Next, they read words that have digraphs (e.g., *ch*) in short vowel words and also consonant blends (e.g., *tr, sl*). After learning words with one-to-one relationships, they move on to study single-syllable words with two-to-one grapheme/ phoneme relationships (e.g., *seat, part*). These are words that have long vowels and other spellings. See Figure 2.1.

FIGURE 2.1

1. Learn Letters	2. Read short vowel words: Single-syllable words with mostly one-to-one relationships		3. Read long vowel words: Single-syllable words with two-to-one relationships	
Letter names Letter–sounds Single consonants Short vowels Concept of word	Short vowels and single consonants (e.g., *hit, bat*)	Short vowels with consonant blends (e.g., *stop, must*) and digraphs (e.g., *thin, ship, chin*)	Words with long vowel patterns (e.g., *eat, take*)	Words with *r*-controlled and other vowel teams (e.g., *car, hoot*)

This developmental progression is the basis of the three units, *Letter Lessons*, *First Words*, and *Beyond First Words* shown in Figure 2.2. Each unit is divided into four to six subunits, which further break down the content. The assessment matches the units directly. The content of phonics instruction in this book covers the decoding of single-syllable words because evidence suggests that this is what children learn first (Ehri 1991, 2005; Ehri and McCormick 1998). Of course, this is not to suggest that children should not be taught and learn multisyllabic words in prekindergarten through second grade. It is only to say that phonics instruction in these early grades typically builds a foundation of how vowels and consonants work in single-syllable words. The Letter Lessons and First Words Placement Test is for the early stages of phonics knowledge development; see other resources for later assessment, for example, of knowledge of more complex syllable types, multisyllabic word decoding, and morphological knowledge (see Johnston, et al. 2005).

FIGURE 2.2

Units		Subunits	Examples	Weeks
Letter Lessons		Learning letter–sounds: Can the child automatically recognize all uppercase letter names, lowercase letter names, and letter–sounds?		
Prekindergarten	1	**Letter Cycle 1: What's in a Name?** Learning letters for your name For students with little entering knowledge		2–3
	2	**Letter Cycle 2: First Pass** Letter–sound instruction For students who know some letter–sounds Slower, more thorough		11
		Note: The first two cycles of Letter Lessons can be taught in pre-K. These two cycles can also be taught in kindergarten depending on assessment information.		
Kindergarten (first half)	1	**Letter Cycle 1: What's in a Name?** Learning letters for your name For students with little entering knowledge		2–3
	2	**Letter Cycle 2: First Pass** Letter–sound instruction For students who know some letter–sounds Slower, more thorough		11

Kindergarten (first half) *(continued)*	3	**Letter Cycle 3: Second Pass** Solidifying letter–sounds For students who know more letter–sounds		6
	4	**Letter Cycle 4: Word Building** Learning 25 high-frequency and decodable words For students who know most letter-sounds	to, it, is, the	7
First Words		Applying letter–sounds to read simple c-v-c words: Can the child read short vowel, single-syllable words?		26 weeks
Kindergarten (second half) First grade (first half)	1	**Consonant Review**		1–2 if needed
	2	**We Are Family** Short vowel word families	-at, -op, -ip	10
	3	**Two for One** Digraphs	sh-, ch-, th-	5
	4	**Beginning Blends** Consonant blends at the beginning of words	gr-, tr-, sl-, st-	5
	5	**Final Blends** Consonant blends at the end of words.	-st, -nt, -nk	4
Beyond First Words		Learning vowel patterns with two letters: Can the child read single-syllable words with multi-letter patterns?		24 weeks
First grade (second half) Second grade (first half)	1	**Sneaky Silent *e*** Silent *e* long vowel pattern and exceptions	a_e, i_e	5
	2	**Teamwork** Common vowel digraphs	ai, oa, oo	8
	3	***R* the Robber** *R*-controlled vowels	ar, ir, or, are, air	7
	4	**Diphthongs** Diphthong glides (*oi, aw*)	aw, oi, oy	3

Note: All "grade-level" specifications are approximate and will depend on assessed knowledge.

The Letter Lessons and First Words Placement Test: Diagnosing What Individual Children Need

What children need to learn is what they don't already know. The Letter Lessons and First Words Placement Test helps you find out what each child needs to learn and match them to the unit and subunit within that unit that they need next. You'll find the full test reproduced, in sections, at the end of this chapter. See Figures 2.3–2.9.

You can also download a copy and powerpoint slides for easy administration, by going to the online resources, see http://hein.pub/letterlessons-login.

How to Give the Letter Lessons and First Words Placement Test

The whole purpose of the Letter Lessons and First Words Placement Test is to find out what to teach. It is *not* administered to prove what children in a school have learned or to justify grades on report cards or to qualify students for special education. The test is divided into three sections that correspond to the three units in the book and the units match milestones in phonics learning. Using the guidelines on the Cover Sheet to determine which part of the tests to start with. Prekindergartners, kindergarteners, and first graders all start with Part A and second graders start with Part B. After giving each part, follow the directions on the Cover Sheet to determine whether or not the next part needs to be given.

Part A: Letter Lesson

Part A: Letter Lessons has three sections in which students name letters and produce the letter–sounds for the twenty-six alphabet letters. It is given in prekindergarten through first grade. Students take all sections. In Part A.1 students name uppercase letters, in Part A.2 they name lowercase letters, and in Part A.3 they provide letter–sounds. Letter-naming measures are easier, but letter–sound measures reflect what we really want children to know—the information that they use during reading. For this reason, Part A.3 is used when deciding which subunit to do within Letter Lessons. This does not mean that we do not *teach* letter names. We teach letter names and sounds together, but it is the letter–sounds that children need to go on to blend words together. Automatic recognition of letter-sounds supports decoding first words. The letters in Parts A.1–A.3 are not presented in alphabetic order so that students cannot use alphabetic order to help them.

> Letter-naming measures are easier, but letter–sound measures reflect what we really want children to know—the information that they use during reading.

The results on A.3 indicate whether to give the next part of the test, Part B: First Words.

- If the child receives a score of 21/26 *or higher* on Part A.3, then administer Part B: First Words.

- If the child receives a score of 20/26 *or lower* on Part A.3, stop; Letter Lessons is the right unit for this student. See the directions section intro between Chapters 3 and 4, Where to Start: Using the Letter Lessons and First Words Placement Test to Identify What to Teach.

Part B: First Words

In Part B: First Words, students read single-syllable words with short vowel sounds with the c-v-c word family pattern. This part of the test shows if a child can put together letter–sounds as words, a skill that is quite different from simply naming letter–sounds. Students in second grade start with Part B. Depending on Part A results most first graders will also take Part B. (Note. First graders who do not achieve a score of 21/26 on Part A, do not need Part B.) All parts of Part B are given. From easiest to hardest, the subunits in First Words are (1) We Are Family, (2) Two for One, (3) Beginning Blends, and (4) Final Blends. (See Figure 2.2.)

Part B has four sections that match the names of First Words subunits:

- **Part B.1: Short Vowels (We Are Family)** has simple words with the c-v-c word family pattern. There are ten items in this section, five real words, and five pseudowords. Pseudowords are made-up words that fit patterns in English. They are particularly useful for determining if readers can blend a novel word using their knowledge, the very purpose of phonics. That said, some people do not like using pseudowords. See the box about the advantages and disadvantages of pseudowords.

- **Part B.2: Digraphs (Two for One)** has short vowel, c-v-c words with digraphs like *ship*, *th*is, and *ch*at.

- **Part B.3: Beginning Blends** includes fifteen words with blends at the beginning and end of words. This section has r-blends (e.g., *cr*, *dr*, *fr*), l-blends (e.g., *gl*, *pl*), and s-blends (e.g., *sk*, *st*).

- **Part B.4: Final Blends** includes eight words with blends in the ending position, including -*mp* and -*nt* (e.g., *hump*, *lent*), -*st* (e.g., *nest*), and -*nk* and -*ng* (e.g., *bank*, *wing*).

When students read words on any parts of the Letter Lessons and First Words Placement Test, let them blend the word together *themselves*. To be correct, the word has to sound like a natural pronunciation of the word without coaching. Sometimes a reader can say all the sounds separately, like /b/ /i/ /t/, but not put them together in a natural pronunciation of the word. This provides important information about a child's development; for example, there may be a phonemic blending problem as discussed in Chapter 3.

After giving Part B: First Words, look at the scores. If any score in Part B has two or more wrong, then stop testing (sections B.1–B.4); First Words is the correct unit. To find the right subunit look for scores with two or more items wrong. If a student has two or more incorrect on a section (B.1–B.4), then the content has not been mastered and the corresponding subunit should be taught. If a student had a score of 3/5 on Digraphs, then the Two for One subunit would be taught. However, always start with the easiest subunit. So if a student had 10/15 on Beginning Blends B.3 and 2/4 on Final Blends B.4, start with the Final Blends subunit. Generally, if a student has one or fewer wrong (0–1 items wrong) on a section B.1–B.4, we consider that content mastered and the corresponding subunit is not taught. So if a student had 9/10 on Short Vowels B.1, that subunit would not be taught.

Part C: Beyond First Words

In Part C: Beyond First Words, students read single-syllable words with long vowel sounds or words with vowel teams and digraphs (e.g., *oo*). This part of the test shows if a child recognizes some of the more common vowel combinations. From easiest to hardest, the subunit tests in Beyond First Words are the following:

- **Part C.1: Silent *e* (Sneaky Silent *e*)** tests one of the most common vowel patterns and usually one of the first that readers learn due to its wide generalizability (Gates and Yale 2011; Johnston 2001).

- **Part C.2: Vowel Digraphs (Teamwork)** tests if a reader knows some of the more common vowels used to represent long sounds.

- **Part C.3: *R*-Controlled (*R* the Robber)** focuses on *r*-controlled sounds, with the first set of words testing the simple *ur, ir, er, or,* and *ar* sounds and the second set testing a vowel team + *r* (e.g., *air, ear*).

- **Part C.4: Diphthongs** addresses words with sounds like *oi* and *aw*.

Part C is given to students who have mastered all the First Words subunits, as indicated by scores on *all* First Words subtests, with only 0–1 incorrect. After giving Part C start on the lowest subunit in which a reader misses two or more words using the same guidelines as used for finding subunits in Part B.

Language to Support Assessment

- **To keep tension and worry down:**

  Teacher: Do your best. I just want to learn what you know so that I can teach the right things.

- **To praise effort (not correctness):**

  Teacher: You are working so hard!

- **To keep the student moving through the assessment and not focused on performance:**

  Teacher: Next one. [or] Keep going!

- **To respond to a student who has appealed for help:**

  Student: What's that?
  Teacher: I'm trying to learn what you know. Keep doing your best. You are working hard.

- **To *avoid* giving feedback on answers after each response:**

  Student: *H.*
  Teacher: Yes!
  Student: *V.*
  Teacher: Not quite.

As Kathy, a first-grade teacher, pointed out, often a teacher can gauge a child's confidence and efficiency with content during the one-on-one testing. Depending on the child, a teacher may choose to push a proficient student in a more challenging group or let the student lead in a lower group. Either choice has benefits. There are some children who will be off-task and irritated without continual challenge. There are other children who will shrink and become discouraged if they don't feel as successful as their peers. These are decisions that can be made only by teachers who know their students. Keep in mind that these assessments are designed to provide only ballpark estimates of where to start. Once teaching begins, observation, instructional judgment, and responsiveness will prevail.

More details about how to use the Letter Lessons and First Words Placement Test results to identify subunit can be found in "Where to Start: Using the Letter Lessons and First Words Placement Test to Identify What to Teach" (page 69).

FIGURE 2.3 Letter Lessons and First Words Placement Test Cover Sheet

Placement Test Cover Sheet

Student:_____ Grade:_____ Date:_____

Starting Unit:_____ Starting Subunit:_____

(Letter Lessons, First Words, Beyond First Words) (We are Family, Two for One, etc.)

Who takes it?	Part A: Letter Lessons (Pre-K–1)	Score
Prekindergarten Kindergarten First Grade	A1. Uppercase Letter Names	/26
	A2. Lowercase Letter Names	/28*
	A3. Letter–Sounds (Use this score for subunit placement)	/26

Decision Point

Score of 21/26 *or higher* on Part A.3: Letter–Sounds?
• Give test for Part B: First Words.

Score of 20/26 *or lower* on Part A.3: Letter–Sounds?
• STOP; IDENTIFY Letter Lessons subunit.
(See Letter Lessons Teacher Record, Figure 2.5,
and section introduction "Where to Start" after Chapter 3)

Who takes it?	Part B: First Words (Grades K–2)	Score
Kindergarten First Grade Second Grade	B1. Short Vowels (We Are Family)	/10
	B2. Digraphs (Two for One)	/5
	B3. Beginning Blends	/15
	B4. Final Blends	/8

Decision Point

Score of 0–1 *incorrect* on *any* section (B.1, B.2, B.3, B.4)?
• Give test for Part C: Beyond First Words.

Score of 2 or *more* incorrect on *any* section (B.1, B.2, B.3, B.4)?
• STOP; IDENTIFY First Words subunit.
(See First Words Teacher Record, Figure 2.7,
and section introduction "Where to Start" after Chapter 3)

Who takes it?	Part C: Beyond First Words (Grades 1–2)	Score
First Grade Second Grade	C1. Silent *e* (Sneaky Silent *e*)	/5
	C2. Vowel Digraphs (Teamwork)	/15
	C3. *R*-Controlled (*R* the Robber)	/10
	C4. Diphthongs	/5

* The Lowercase Letter Names test has 28 items because two forms of the lowercase letters *a* and *g* are used (*a, g, ɑ, ɡ*).

Note: This assessment is for the early stages of phonics development; see other resources for later assessment, for example, of knowledge of more complex syllable types, multisyllabic word decoding, and morphological knowledges.

FIGURE 2.4 PART A: Letter Lessons (Student Copy)

Part A: Letter Lessons (Student Copy)

A.1 Uppercase Letter Names

F	R	U	O	T	
J	G	Z	W	A	
P	V	D	I	M	
C	N	X	Q	E	
H	Y	S	K	B	L

Part A: Letter Lessons (Student Copy)

A.2 Lowercase Letter Names

i	x	u	p	c
q	k	m	z	r
a	y	t	f	g
j	d	v	o	w
n	s	l	h	b
e	a	g		

Part A: Letter Lessons (Student Copy)

A.3 Letter–Sounds

a	j	n	c	o
x	e	p	t	g
d	v	s	i	q
b	y	k	r	u
z	w	h	l	f
m				

FIGURE 2.5 PART A   Letter–Sounds (Teacher Record)

Part A: Letters Lessons (Teacher Record)

Student: _____ Date: _____

Who? Prekindergartners, kindergarteners, and first graders (beginning of the year).

Directions: Have the child **name** the letters as you point to them. "Please tell me the name of each letter." Record the child's responses in the chart below. Point to the first row and go across. Wait for five seconds; if the name is not given within that time, count the letter as incorrect and move to the next letter.

A.1 Uppercase Letter Names

F	R	U	O	T	
J	G	Z	W	A	
P	V	D	I	M	
C	N	X	Q	E	
H	Y	S	K	B	L
				Total:	___/26

If there is a score of 0, stop and do not give other Part A tests.

A.2 Lowercase Letter Names

i	x	u	p	c
q	k	m	z	r
a	y	t	f	g
j	d	v	o	w
n	s	l	h	b
e	a	g		
			Total:	___/28

A.3 Letter–Sounds

Directions: Have the child give the **letter–sounds** as you point to them. "Please tell me the letter–sounds." If the child only provides the letter name, say, "Tell me the sounds." For *c* and *g*, if the child provides the "soft sounds" (e.g., *cent*, *gem*) say, "Is there another sound that *c* can make?" The correct answer for this assessment is /k/ as in *cat* and /g/ as is *go*. For lowercase *l*, some children will say the sound for uppercase *I* since those letters tend to look the same. If so say, "That is a lowercase letter. Which lowercase letter is that? [Do not tell the letter name.] What sound does it make?" For the vowels, ask students to name the short sounds (e.g., *c̲a̲t*, *b̲e̲g*, *l̲i̲ck*, *h̲o̲t*, and *n̲u̲t*) because the long sounds are the same as the letter names. Do not use the labels *hard*, *soft*, *long*, and *short* with children. Wait for five seconds; if the sound is not given, count it as incorrect.

a	j	n	c	o
x	e	p	t	g
d	v	s	i	q
b	y	k	r	u
z	w	h	l	f
m			Total:	___/26

Diagnosing Part A Results

After giving all three parts, record the scores on the Placement Cover Sheet in Figure 2.3. The score on Part A.3 will determine if you give the next part of the test, B.1.

- **If the child receives a score of 21/26 *or higher* on Part A.3,** then administer Part B: First Words.

- **If the child receives a score of 20/26 *or lower* on Part A.3,** stop; Letter Lessons is the right unit for this student. See the section introduction before Chapter 4, "Where to Start; Using the Placement Test to Identify What to Teach," to identify the proper Letter Lessons subunit. (Note. The score *must* be on the letter–sounds part, A.3. Having a score of 23/28 for Part A.1 or A.2 on letter names *does not indicate* that a child is ready to blend words.) Research has indicated that with at least 21 letter–sounds students are usually ready to read words (Invernizzi et al. 2004).

- **Special instructions for students with scores of 21 or higher on Part A.3:** Students with a score of 21 or higher on A.3 could technically start in several subunits. They could start Letter Cycle 4: Word Building in *Letter Lessons* or Subunit 1: Letter Sound Review, in *First Words* or even Subunit 2: We Are Family in *First Words*. To decide which is best, consider the strength of the student's letter–sound knowledge and the amount of high-frequency words known. The Word Building subunit covers high-frequency words and most kindergartners would benefit from it. For first graders who already know many high-frequency words, starting with the *First Words* subunits is recommended.

FIGURE 2.6 PART B: First Words (Student Copy)

Part B: First Words (Student Copy)

B.1 Short Vowels

ham	rob	lid	tub	net

tup

san	zot	vig	wub	het

B.2 Consonant Digraphs

thin	chap	shut	wish	them

B.3 Beginning Blends
(*r*-blends)

brag	crop	drip	fret	grab

(*l*-blends)

bled	clip	flag	plop	glass

(*s*-blends)

skip	swim	snob	spill	stem

B.4 Final Blends and Digraphs

band	hump	wing	bank
nest	lent	link	lift

FIGURE 2.7 PART B: First Words (Teacher Record)

Part B: First Words (Teacher Record)

Student: _____   Date: _____

Who? First graders, after taking Letter Lessons test. Kindergartners who know 21+ letter–sounds on Part A.3. Second graders.

Directions: Have the child **read each word**. Say, "Please read these words." Wait for five seconds; if the word is not given within that time, count it as incorrect and move to the next.

B.1 Short Vowels (We Are Family)

ham	rob	lid	tub	net

Total: ____/5

Directions for pseudowords: Say, "These are made-up words. They are silly. They don't mean anything, but you can still read them. Look at this word [point to *tup*]. This word says *tup*. What is a tup? It's not anything because it's a made-up word. All these words will be like this."

tup

san	zot	vig	wub	het

Total: ____/5

B.2 Consonant Digraphs (Two for One)

thin	chap	shut	wish	them

Total: ____/5

B.3 Beginning Blends

(*r*-blends)

brag	crop	drip	fret	grab

(*l*-blends)

bled	clip	flag	plop	glass

(*s*-blends)

skip	swim	snob	spill	stem

Total: ____/15

B.4 Final Blends and Digraphs

band	hump	wing	bank
nest	lent	link	lift

Total: ____/8

Diagnosing Part B Results

Once a student takes Part B, record the scores for each of the parts on the Placement Cover Sheet in Figure 2.3.

- Generally, **if a student has *2 or more incorrect* on *any* subunit test** (e.g., Part B.1: Short Vowels (We Are Family) *or* Part B.2: Digraphs (Two for One, etc.), stop testing. The student will be in First Words. The section introduction before Chapter 4, "Where to Start: Using the Letter Lessons and First Words Placement Test to Identify What to Teach," will show how to find the right First Words subunit. Usually, you will simply start teaching the easiest subunit in which the student misses *2 or more* items.

  Having 2 or more incorrect on these subunits signals that the student needs more instruction. Always start with the easier subunit. For example, a student might have a score of 8/10 on Part B.1: Short Vowels (We Are Family) and 3/5 on Part B.2: Digraphs (Two for One), but you would start on the easier subunit, We Are Family, first.

- **If the student has only 0–1 incorrect on *all* other Part B sections** (e.g., Part B.1: Short Vowels (We are Family); Part B.2: Digraphs (Two for One) etc.), administer Part C: Beyond First Words.

When in doubt, I always suggest attempting the next test part. It's easier to stop a test if the child really struggles than to have to go back and get more data.

FIGURE 2.8 PART C: Beyond First Words (Student Copy)

Part C: Beyond First Words (Student Copy)

C.1 Silent *e*

case	ride	tube	rose	these

C.2 Vowel Digraphs and Other Vowels

sail	lay	weed	meal	bright
feast	main	goat	row	few
dry	glue	sigh	root	took

C.3 *R*-Controlled
(*r*-controlled *ur, ir, er, or, ar*)

harm	fort	fir	fern	burn

(vowel digraph + *r*-controlled)

dare	hair	fear	search	steer

C.4 Diphthongs

boil	joy	law	pout	now

FIGURE 2.9 PART C: Beyond First Words (Teacher Record)

Part C: Beyond First Words (Teacher Record)

Student: _____ Date: _____

Who? Second graders. First graders who mastered content in First Words.

Directions: Have the child **read each word**. Wait for five seconds; if the word is not given within that time, count it as incorrect and move to the next.

C.1 Silent *e* (Sneaky Silent *e*)

case	ride	tube	rose	these

Total: ____/5

C.2 Vowel Digraphs and Other Vowels (Teamwork)

sail	lay	weed	meal	bright
feast	main	goat	row	few
dry	glue	sigh	root	took

Total: ____/15

C.3 *R*-Controlled

(*r*-controlled *ur, ir, er, or, ar*)

harm	fort	fir	fern	burn

(vowel digraph + *r*-controlled)

dare	hair	fear	search	steer

Total: ____/10

C.4 Diphthongs

boil	joy	law	pout	now

Total: ____/5

Diagnosing Part C Results

Once a student takes Part C, record the scores for each of the parts on the Placement Cover Sheet in Figure 2.3.

- Generally, **if a student has *2 or more incorrect* on *any* subunit test** (i.e., Part C.1: Silent *e* (Sneaky Silent *e*); Part C.2: Vowel Digraphs (Teamwork); Part C.3: *R*-Controlled Vowels (*R* the Robber); or Part C.4: Diphthongs), the student will be in the Beyond First Words unit. The section introduction before Chapter 4, "Where to Start: Using the Letter Lessons and First Words Placement Test to Identify What to Teach," will show how to find the right Beyond First Words subunit. Having 2 or more incorrect on the subunits for learning vowel teams, the silent *e* pattern, *r*-controlled vowels, or diphthongs, signals that the student needs more instruction. Always start with the easier subunit. For example, a student might have score of 3/5 on Silent *e* (Sneaky Silent *e*) and 10/15 on Vowel Digraphs (Teamwork), but you would do the easier subunit Sneaky Silent *e* first.

- If the student **has only 0–1 incorrect on all other Part C subunit tests** (i.e., Part C.1: Silent *e* (Sneaky Silent *e*); Part C.2: Vowel Digraphs (Teamwork); Part C.3: *R*-controlled vowels (*R* the Robber); Part C.4: Diphthongs), the student is beyond the scope of Beyond First Words curriculum and will need phonics instruction that addresses reading multisyllabic words.

chapter 3

Phonics Lessons for Real Literacy

ALL TEACHERS OF YOUNG CHILDREN WANT CHILDREN TO love literacy, but many are not sure how (or whether!) phonics fits within their instruction. While some teachers fear that teaching phonics will overly mechanize the reading experience and strip the joy from reading, experienced teachers of beginning readers teach phonics within rich, multifaceted literacy instruction. It is *neither* book reading and writing instruction *nor* phonics instruction, but both. You cannot have one without the other. If you teach phonics without reading and writing, children cannot and will not use their knowledge. If you read and write without phonics instruction, children do not have the tools they need to unlock words or make sense of spellings. With effective instruction, phonics can be really exciting for children. They learn the "big kid" stuff about how to write their own messages, and they experience the stupendous accomplishment that comes from "sounding out" a word or building a word family (e.g., *cat*, *bat*, *hat*).

Research has established that phonics should be taught in the early grades and in certain ways (Ehri 2015; Snow, Burns, and Griffin 1998; Stahl, Duffy-Hester, and Stahl 1998). In 1998, a group of researchers published a literature review (Stahl, Duffy-Hester, and Stahl 1998) and provided a series of basic principles about phonics instruction that still hold true today:

Evidence-Based Characteristics of Good Phonics Instruction

Phonics instruction

- is **one part of reading instruction**
- should provide a thorough **grounding in letters**
- should **not teach rules**, should **not use worksheets**, should **not dominate instruction**, and does **not have to be boring**
- provides **sufficient practice in reading words** (in isolation and in text)
- should develop the **alphabetic principle**
- should develop **phonological awareness**
- leads to **automatic word recognition**

While this list is not comprehensive or conclusive, it continues to be supported by a host of research articles, literature syntheses, and books both in the United States and in other English-speaking countries (National Reading Panel and National Institute of Child Health and Human Development 2001; Rose 2006; Seidenburg 2017; Torgeson, Brooks, and Hall 2006; Willingham 2015).

Phonics "Rules"?

Simple, hard-and-fast rules don't work. If you want to find one rule for pronouncing English words that will be simply stated and apply all the time, you are out of luck (Gates and Yale 2011; Johnston 2001). As Johnston wrote, "Simplistic, broad generalizations do not capture the complexity of English orthography, yet when they are refined in more specific ways there is a danger that they will become clumsy and complex" (2001, 140). Often, if the generalization is made just a bit more specific, it is more applicable. For example, the silent *e* pattern is over 75 percent consistent in *a_e*, *o_e*, *i_e*, and *u_e*, but only 16 percent consistent in *e_e*.

Teach the most frequently occurring and consistent patterns (Fry 2004). Following is a list of generalizations that are fairly reliable in English:

Single consonants. In English, most single consonants have one sound or one of two sounds, which is why they are taught first (Calfee 1998; Gates and Yale 2011). If patterns are learned, then 95 percent of the time a given generalization can be applied to consonant sounds (Johnston 2001). Letters like *c* and *g* can be more challenging. They take both hard and soft sounds but still conform to certain patterns (e.g., when an *i* or *e* follows a *c*, it is usually the soft sound).

continues

Single vowels in single-syllable words usually have a short sound. The reason that we usually teach young children short vowel sounds is that short vowels usually have one sound (Gates and Yale 2011). Like consonants, most have a one-to-one letter–sound relationship (e.g., *hit* or *big* as opposed to *heat* or *sheet*). As discussed further in Chapter 6, all bets are off when there is that "robber" *r* involved (*-ar, -or*) or in certain word families like *-all.*

Usually the silent e *marks the long vowel pattern in single-syllable words.* Another pattern that is fairly consistent is the "sneaky" silent *e* at the end of single-syllable words (Gates and Yale 2011; Johnston 2001). The silent *e* usually makes the vowel sound long (e.g., *hope, rate, like*), but there is a larger collection of long *o* words that form their own collection of words that don't follow this pattern (e.g., *dove, some, come, done*). See Chapter 6 for a full list.

Usually vowel digraphs (e.g., -ea, -oa*) have a maximum of two sounds.* Long vowels are the most variable of all sounds in English. The problem is that English has about fifteen to twenty vowel sounds and only five vowel letters. Some vowel digraphs have one sound very consistently, but those that have more than one sound have only one *other* sound (e.g., *-ow, how, low*). (More on this in Chapter 6.) The "rule" that "when two vowels go walking, the first one does the talking" is often inaccurate. However, what is accurate is that when two vowels are together, they nearly always represent only one vowel sound (as opposed to two) (Bailey 1967).

What Should Children Do in a Lesson?

In an effective classroom, phonics instruction involves children and teachers participating in specific behaviors. Figure 3.1 summarizes these practices, as shown later in this chapter on p. 53.

Analyze and Read Individual Words

Learning to understand how words work is hard. A young child must focus on multiple visual symbols and then recall what each symbol refers to orally. Each part of the word must be understood in order. Effective phonics instruction isolates individual words so that children can study them. A purely embedded approach to phonics instruction is not effective. (Embedded means that phonics is taught *only* within the context of a book, during reading.) In 2000, an experienced first-grade teacher, Francine Johnston, did a very interesting study. She taught words in predictable big books using three different approaches: (1) reading the books repeatedly; (2) using sentence strips; and (3) analyzing the words in isolation, individually. The repeated readings involved reading the books about ten times. Students learned the least number of words in this way (Johnston 2000).

The idea of this study is not that context and big books are bad. In fact, reading books and charts to young children, pointing to words, and showing them print in a connected, contextualized way are essential practices, but teachers need to understand what shared reading accomplishes. These practices help children understand how letters are used to form words, how an alphabetic script encodes meaningful messages, and how we read connected texts (e.g., left to right, top to bottom). However, at the beginning stages, repeatedly reading words in a big book should not be the *only* approach to learning to read words because it does not specifically focus on the architecture of words and how they work. Learning words *only* through a contextualized approach will not lead to high levels of word learning for most children. Learners must carefully analyze individual words. They must think about why the words *can* and *cat* are different. Paying attention to these mechanics helps them store knowledge cognitively.

Analyzing the letter–sounds in words is a form of *metalinguistic awareness*, a way of thinking about language. It requires children to *suspend* focus on the word's meaning *temporarily*, in order to focus on features of the alphabetic system. To learn the system, students need to be freed from trying to balance both the meaning demands and the mechanical demands of words. Taking a word like *frog* out of a book and allocating space and time for cognitively organizing and analyzing letter–sounds does *not* mean that this word can't or won't—beforehand and afterward—be assigned its more primary

> Don't be drawn into a forced choice about word analysis. Ignore people who say that it is "wrong" to analyze words out of context or people who say that all children need is out-of-context phonics instruction. Research simply does not support either of those positions, especially for beginning readers.

purpose: conveying meaning. Don't be drawn into a forced choice about word analysis. Ignore people who say that it is "wrong" to analyze words out of context or people who say that all children need is out-of-context phonics instruction. Research simply does not support either of those positions, especially for beginning readers.

Orally Manipulate Words to Build Phonemic Awareness (If Needed)

From research we have learned that there is a skill that undergirds or supports phonics instruction called phonological awareness (Bus and Van Ijzendoorn 1999; Juel 1988; Landerl et al. 2018; Liberman et al. 1974; Lunderberg, Frost, and Peterson 1988). This is conscious attention to sound in spoken language. Children do not automatically understand that the word *dog* has three speech sounds or phonemes, /d/ /o/ /g/, or that the word *elephant* has three syllables or that the syllable *mat* has an onset /m/ and a rime /at/. A lot of children, particularly those who do not learn to read easily, actually struggle with insights about sound units in words (Shaywitz 2003). They will participate in instruction and learn what they are supposed to say in a very rote way. For example, they will know that when the teacher points to the letter *d*, they are supposed to say the sound /d/, but they don't understand that *dog*, *date*, and *dip* all have the same sound at the beginning. They need to learn how to think about the sounds in those words.

Phonological awareness has a very robust and strong research basis. As a teacher, you need a few essential understandings to support children in learning to read words. First, the term *phonological awareness* is an umbrella term that refers to the ability of children to manipulate and identify any size unit within the spoken word (e.g., a word, syllable, rime, or phoneme; see Chapter 1). The term *phonemic awareness* refers to the ability to consciously attend to and manipulate *individual* speech sounds or phonemes. A child with phonemic awareness could tell you that the words *bell* and *bag* have the same beginning sound or that the sound is /b/. A child with phonemic awareness could tell you that *bell* without the /b/ is /ell/. Generally, children's understanding of phonology moves from awareness of larger units (e.g., words or syllables) to insights about smaller units (e.g., phonemes) (Anthony et al. 2003).

Playing with syllables and rhyming are both very important but only when they are connected to phonemic awareness and phonemic blending. The awareness of initial sounds in words builds capacity to learn letter–sounds (Hulme et al. 2002) and is expected by sixty months on the *Head Start Early Learning Outcomes Framework* (United States Department of Health and Human Services 2016). Let's imagine someone teaching letters and telling a child, "A is for *apple*. Hear that? /aaaaaapple/. That's the sound that *a* makes." Without phonemic awareness, the child is not going to make sense of the mnemonic apple. He may memorize that he should say apple when the teacher points to *Aa*, or even realize that the word has the *Aa* at the beginning, but the sound at the beginning of *apple* and the target sound of the letter *Aa* will not be connected. When children can find new pictures that begin with the same sound or tell you the sound at the beginning of *sssssun*, then they understand the system for letter–sounds and they will retain letter–sound information. For this reason, in the Letter Lessons unit in Chapter 4, children work to listen for beginning sounds.

Phonemic blending (e.g., /s/ /u/ /n/ = *sun*) and segmentation (e.g., *sun* = /s/ /u/ /n/) help children learn to identify and transfer phonics knowledge. Segmentation especially supports or builds capacity to sound out or fully decode words (Nation and Hulme 1997; Muter et al. 1997). There are many wonderful practices that make this concrete for children like using Elkonin boxes or tapping words, and these instructional practices are used in the First Words unit in Chapter 5. Phonemic awareness is an important element of phonics instruction, and a recent literature review actually found that phonemic awareness instruction had particular staying power, long after it was given (Suggate 2016). Phonemic awareness instruction is oral but is delivered along with letter instruction. In my own work, I like to "front-load" phonics lessons with activities that are purely phonemic awareness so that students have a chance to work with the sound before attaching the visual symbol (Mesmer 2001; Mesmer and Griffith 2005). The letter–sound or decoding instruction follows right after the activity. (For activities, see the Letter Lessons unit in Chapter 4 and the First Words unit in Chapter 5.)

Meaningful Review and Practice for Transfer and Overlearning

Multiple exposures in multiple contexts are key. The purpose of phonics instruction is to develop automatic, error-free decoding during text reading. For decoding to become automatic, students need to practice and review associated letter–sounds. "I am really basic," explained David, a rather humble award-winning first-grade teacher in a large urban district. "When people ask me what my secret is, it's kind of embarrassing to tell them that I use a lot of repetition. That's not really sexy. It might make me sound like a boring teacher, but I'm not drilling the skills in decontextualized ways. I keep it fun and do it in different ways so that the kids don't get bored. Repetition is one of my secrets."

David has actually tapped into a phenomenon that neuroscience reinforces: over-learning. In order to become fully automatic with letter–sounds, students need to practice them a bit beyond the point of mastery. A recent article in *Scientific American*, "The Power of Overlearning," explains that practicing a skill beyond the point of mastery solidifies it (Turner 2017). As it turns out, when humans overpractice, even if they do not appear to add the skill immediately after that overpracticing, they tend to retain the skill for a longer period of time. At the same time, automatic knowledge must also transfer to multiple contexts, such as reading words in little books, sentences on charts, words in big books, word cards, and words in games. It's not okay, for example, to know the letter–sounds only when you see them on flash cards made by your teacher and not when you are reading books. For this reason, practice has to occur in multiple contexts (including reading and writing of extended texts, such as books, which is discussed in a later section, Daily Whole-Group, Teacher-Managed Activities).

Another important principle of instruction is distributed practice. Distributed practice involves shorter practice sessions that take place over longer periods of time, usually days, weeks, and months. This contrasts with longer practice sessions that take place over a shorter period of time, often called "cramming." With young children, shorter practice sessions keep attention at a high level and lead to automaticity or overlearning. This is one of the reasons that teaching a letter a week is not effective—children do not have distributed practice (see *No More Teaching a Letter a Week* by McKay and Teale [2015]). In this book, letters are taught in "cycles" to emphasize this idea of meaningful repetition and distributed practice (Jones and Reutzel 2012).

Who Is Holding the Book, Pen, or Letters?

Want to know who really owns an activity? Who is really running it? Who is really engaged? It's the person who is physically holding the materials used in the activity. This is especially true for young children. They are concrete and tactile and they want to physically hold, use, and manipulate items.

So if you want students to feel connected, engaged, or invested in something, *let them hold it*. This seems so obvious, but often you will see a teacher holding a small student-sized book and turning the pages as the student sits there with arms hanging down by his side.

Sometimes a teacher needs to demonstrate or show students how to do something. If this is the case, don't pass out materials. Ask students to watch. Ask them to repeat the directions and *then* give them the materials. In addition, clearly differentiate times for teacher demonstration and modeling from times of *student doing*. One example might occur during an interactive writing lesson when the teacher hands the pen to a student.

What Should Teachers Do in a Lesson?

Plan Systematic and Explicit Lessons

When planning useful phonics instruction, teachers should be *systematic* and *explicit* (Mesmer and Griffith 2005). *Systematic* means that phonics instruction should have a clear content of letter–sounds taught in a specific order—a scope and sequence— like the one offered in this book. It does not mean, however, that everyone must be learning the same sounds at the same time. *Explicit* means teacher language is clear and direct when explaining letter–sounds to children. For example, a teacher explaining *sh* might say, "When you see the two letters *s* and *h together*, they make one sound. So if you look at this word [*ship*], you see the *s* and *h* and you hear /sh/. The sound is /sh/. *S* and *h* next to each other make the sound /sh/."

Unfortunately, the words *systematic* and *explicit* have often been used to bludgeon teachers over the head with dry, lockstep programs, but that's not what researchers intended. *Planned, systematic* instruction can and should be lively, engaging, and effective. The scope and sequence and lesson framework in this book guide you as you are teaching. (Notice I used the word *guide*, not *dictate*!)

Use a Scope and Sequence

A scope and sequence is a characteristic of good phonics instruction. It details (1) the scope or content to be taught (e.g., letter–sounds and patterns) and (2) a sequence (i.e., order) in which the content is taught. The scope is the *what* and the sequence is the *when*. Having a scope and sequence is important because

- A sequence ensures that everything gets taught. Over the course of a year, it is easy for patterns to get forgotten or not receive the best attention.

- A scope and sequence helps make sure that content "sticks." The reader learns something today and knows it three months later because the sequence has facilitated long-term storage and retrieval.

Use Inductive Tension

With all the talk over the years about phonics instruction being clear and direct, I believe that a very powerful ingredient is being ignored or de-emphasized. Good instruction *is* organized, clear, and direct, but it also has what I call "inductive tension." Inductive thinking occurs when students are asked to look at a collection of facts, words, or details and figure out how things work or pull out a pattern. When students are asked to think inductively, they are not directly given the answer. For example, a teacher might put the words *bat*, *boy*, *big*, and *belt* on the table and ask students what makes them the same. Then students must do some work *on their own*, without the teacher telling them the answer. They must puzzle and figure things out. This is extremely powerful both for learning and teaching. When students are able to analyze and find a pattern, we know that they have really learned something; they truly "own" that information. We don't have to worry that they weren't listening or were daydreaming. There is a natural tension built into the activity.

When children use their own language to explain what they have figured out, they give us a window into their thinking. For example, imagine you show a group of children three words and then ask, "What do all these words have that's the same— *ship*, *shop*, and *shell*?" If a student says, "They all have *s*," you learn that the student does not recognize the digraph pattern, which is *sh*. If you had simply used a direct teaching approach and told them, "These two letters make the sound /sh/," you would have assumed that they heard and understood and retained what you said, when in actuality they did not.

Inductive approaches also keep students from getting bored. Take Nate, a bright but sometimes challenging student. With too much direct teaching he can get irritated, mostly because he knows many of the answers, but when there is a letter–sound puzzle to solve or a pattern to find or a word to analyze, things get more interesting for him. It's a challenge and he stays engaged. *Any* student will become disengaged and disempowered if they perceive teaching is a game of "guess what the teacher is thinking" rather than an invitation to figure something out on their own.

When using inductive approaches, it is always important for the teacher to bring closure to the exercise with direct and clear language by stating the pattern or solution.

So in the lesson about *sh*, the teacher might say something like this: "You figured out that the letters that represent the /sh/ sound are *s* and *h*. So when you see *sh* together, the letters will almost always make the sound /sh/."

In a group of students it is possible that some children did not see the pattern, and in any case your statement of the pattern is reinforcing. Inductive tension keeps content engaging and interesting for children, who feel accomplished when they figure things out. That said, it should not take too much time. A combination of direct teaching and inductive tension maximizes efficiency and effectiveness. It's like salt, a necessary seasoning in many dishes that is useful in limited quantities.

WATCH ▶

VIDEO 3.1

What Is Inductive Tension?

In this clip, I talk about what inductive tension is.

VIDEO 3.2

Inductive Tension

In this short clip, I use inductive tension to invite children to solve a problem, and then I explain the concept.

Provide Helpful Feedback

Talk during a phonics lesson should provide helpful feedback. What this means is that after a response, the teacher should provide information that expands on the reasons that an answer was correct or pinpoints the crucial correction needed to get a wrong answer "right." Typically, students are used to the response being evaluated for accuracy. But if a teacher explains why the answer is correct and how that answer was obtained, a correct answer can teach others. In this way, feedback uncovers the process or thinking that undergirds an answer. It also provides useful information to the other children in the lesson, not just the one whose answer is being evaluated. For a correct answer a teacher might say, "Yes, that's *pig*. You added /p/ to this word part, /ig/, and made *pig*. /p/ plus /ig/ is *pig*." This tells the student why the answer is correct and provides teaching for listening students. Contrast that with a simple "Yes, that's right." When an answer is not correct, clear and useful information can support the student in accurately completing the task: "You said *dig*. /d/ /ig/. *Dig*. The word is not *dig*. Look at the first sound, /p/ [pointing to the letter *p*]. Try it with /p/, /p/ /ig/." Note that in this example, the teacher repeated the incorrect answer (*dig*) and clearly stated that the answer was not correct ("The word is not *dig*"). Then the teacher pinpointed the error by visually directing the student to the letter and by saying the sound /p/. Note that the teacher did not say the name of the letter here because we don't say *peeig*, but pointed to the letter and said the sound because the *sound* /p/ is what the student needed to use.

WATCH

▶

VIDEO 3.3

Feedback

In this short clip, I talk about the value and how-to of giving feedback.

Avoid Verbal Clutter

In addition to using clear language and providing helpful feedback, teachers should be mindful of extra talk in their lessons. Verbal clutter is talk that fills the air during an instructional sequence that is (1) not meaningful (e.g., *okay*, *ummm*) or (2) not focused. Often verbal clutter is quickly delivered and nervous, leaving the young child little chance to process it. High-quality phonics instruction uses simple, purposeful talk that focuses the reader on just one thing at a time. The talk is delivered at a pace that can be processed by the learner, and the teacher punctuates the question or comment with a pause.

Without realizing it, a well-meaning teacher can fire five different questions and requests at a student: "Okay, what is that word? What does it say? Hmmm, what's at the beginning of the word? Look at the word. Um. Think about what other word this is like." The student is completely confused.

Avoiding Verbal Clutter

Follow these tips to avoid verbal clutter:

- **Add pauses to your teaching.** Everyone talks about wait time for students, but teachers need wait time too. Don't let yourself feel rushed or pressured to cover everything. Rushed teaching is bad teaching. So add more pauses before you talk. It will feel awkward at first, of course, but really all you're doing is giving yourself time to get centered on what's the best thing to say, rather than just talking. You can just say to yourself, "Pause," and just think for ten seconds.

- **Remember that less is more.** During instructional sequences, less talking and verbiage will usually be better, especially with young learners. The young learner is going to respond better to a simple question or prompt as opposed to a longer one. Try to avoid filling the instructional space with fillers (e.g., *like, okay, you guys, yeh?, right?*). These vary by region of the country, but they are equally distracting.

continues

- **Check the pacing of your voice.** Many people, when nervous, will talk more quickly and use a high pitch. This makes a direction or question even more difficult to follow. It can also add urgency and stress to the request, even if that is not the intention. For learners in pre-K through first grade, talk in a pace that is slightly slower than the pace you would use with adults.

- **Pause and give sufficient wait time after making a request.** One of the instructional mistakes that teachers make is not waiting long enough for students to respond and then asking another question quickly to remedy the situation. Sufficient wait time is usually around five seconds. It may feel uncomfortable to you, but children need it. Before rephrasing a question, simply ask it again and wait.

- **After giving a direction, look at the word or letter—the instructional target.** When young children hear someone talking to them, their obvious response is to look at the person and engage in conversation. This is central to oral language development. However, in a teaching interaction, the object of focus is not the other person but the activity—the word card, letters, or dry erase board. When a teacher visually focuses on the instructional activity, there is a clear message to the student to look as well. And that's what we want children to do as they read words: look at them.

- **Know how you want the learner to respond.** Often verbal clutter occurs because the teacher says the first thing that comes to mind and then realizes that something else is better for getting the desired response. Think about what the learner should do or say as the result of your prompt. This does not mean that you should be restrictive and limit children's inquiry; rather, you should be prepared for possible responses and should use language that is as precise as possible to help solicit responses.

- **Plan for verbal precision.** Good lesson preparation tends to decrease verbal clutter. Planning key parts of what you are going to say, even if only in your head, helps make your language more precise. You'll find that the more precise and focused your language is, the more precise and focused children's attention is. Talk is a major tool of teaching and we should treat it that way. Practice your lesson language in the car on the way to school, in the shower, or with your pet. Many teachers like to use a little sticky note or note card beside them as they are teaching to remember important language. Throughout the book, I'll be referring to such language as "catchphrases."

How to Plan a Phonics Lesson

FIGURE 3.1

Guidelines for an Effective Phonics Lesson	
Students Should	Teachers Should
Analyze and read individual words	Plan lessons that are organized, clear, and explicit
Orally manipulate words to build phonemic awareness	Use a scope and sequence
Review and practice for transfer and overlearning	Use inductive tension
Read, write, and *do*	Provide helpful feedback
	Avoid verbal clutter

Good phonics instruction is one part of literacy instruction. See Figure 3.1 above. Effective literacy instruction includes many elements, such as

- read-alouds
- shared readings of charts, big books, and other materials
- vocabulary instruction
- handwriting instruction
- writing
- interactive writing
- concept of word development, and
- small-group reading.

A study examined the types of activities in first-grade reading instruction (Connor et al. 2007), dividing activities based upon whether they focused on phonics/code or meaning and whether the child or the teacher managed the activity. A teacher-managed activity would be something that a teacher organized, guided, and taught, and a child-managed activity would be something the child did independently. The four categories of activities included teacher-managed code activities, teacher-managed meaning activities, child-managed code activities, and child-managed meaning activities. Essentially, this book concentrates on the code-focused side of instruction, either teacher managed or child managed. All types of activities are important. If you build a literacy program based only on meaning-focused activities and ignore code-focused work, children will not get the specific information that they need to read and write words. If you build a literacy program based only on code-focused activities, the entire point is missed since the code-focused activities serve the purpose of meaning getting. Of course, many of these activities blend throughout the school day. For example, a teacher who is reading a book aloud may make an observation about the spelling of a word. However, a fully embedded approach to phonics instruction—that is, letter–sound and decoding instruction that occurs *only* during contextual reading— is not effective because it depends on implicit learning and may not be specific or clear enough for the children who need it (Armbruster et al. 2003). In the early grades, dedicated time for phonics instruction is very important.

Daily Whole-Group, Teacher-Managed Activities

WATCH

VIDEO 3.4

Overview of Daily Whole-Group, Teacher-Managed Activities

In this short clip, I provide an overview of daily whole-group, teacher-managed phonics activities.

Phonics instruction develops the alphabetic principle, and teachers must model how to *use* letter–sounds and decode and spell words. In addition to the focused phonics lessons that follow the scope and sequence in this book, a collection of whole-group, teacher-managed code activities should also take place daily in classrooms.

Shared Reading with Print Referencing

In most kindergarten and prekindergarten classrooms, reading a big book or chart with the whole group is a daily occurrence. Joan does a daily shared reading of big books or charts in her kindergarten classroom. She explains, "We read poems or books like *Chicka, Chicka, Boom, Boom* every morning. I point to the words as we read and sometimes play games with the kids, like saying the wrong word to see if they are paying attention. When I first started teaching, I didn't really do that and I found that the kids would learn the letters but couldn't *do* anything with them."

A robust line of research provides information about how to do print referencing during a read-aloud that supports children's understandings of print (Justice, Pullen, and Pence 2008; Zucker, Ward, and Justice 2009). Usually the teacher will read and reread a book over the course of three to five days, using the book to reinforce letter–sounds, words, and decoding. The big books used for shared readings are usually rhymes, predictable stories, simple informational texts, or materials that use repetitive sentence stems (e.g., "I love my _____"). The idea is to support children in remembering the words of the book so that they can link that knowledge to emerging print knowledge. These books are not extended stories with lots of details. They usually measure about 1½ × 3 feet. The print is clearly situated in a consistent place on the page and is large enough so that a child sitting several feet away can easily read the words. Below is a suggested sequence for big book reading:

> Day 1: Read the book without pointing. Talk about the story, rhyme, or repetitive parts.
>
> Day 2: Read the book and point to the words. Ask children to read as *you* point.
>
> Day 3: Read the book and point. Read the book again and ask different children to come up and point.
>
> Day 4: Read the book and focus on *using* letters. Use a target letter–sound throughout the reading, and pause and get help. "Okay, here we are. Look at this beginning letter. What should I say?"

Teacher Prompts for Print Referencing

How Print Works

- If I wanted to read this book, where would I start?
- Where do I go next? [Indicate going from left to right.]
- When I am at the end of a line, where do I go? [Sweep back to the left.]

Using Letters

- Can you name a letter on this page? Is there a letter that's in your name?
- I see a letter that makes the sound /t/. Can you come find it?
- I want to read this word. How would I start that word? What is the sound?

Words

- Watch me point to each word as I say it. Can you come up and do it? [or] Say the words as I point.
- How many letters are in that word *the*?
- How many words are on this page?
- Look at the word _____. It is a long word. Listen to me say it. It even sounds long.

Interactive Writing

Interactive writing is another practice that supports the development of the alphabetic principle. Instead of copying words letter-by-letter from word walls or books, children learn how to apply letter–sounds to spell words in their own messages by watching their teacher model it.

As this photo shows, often the teacher will "share the pen" with students, who write in words. During interactive writing, a teacher works with a group to generate a novel message and then models the writing of it on chart paper, a Smart Board, or a dry erase board. There are many different ways to do interactive writing, but generally the teacher provides a "starter" of some sort, a reason to write (e.g., learning about pumpkins, saying thank you to a mom for sending cupcakes). Terrell, a prekindergarten teacher, describes his process: "First, we make a sentence. Sometimes we might be writing a note to someone, or recording something that we learned, or writing about how to do something. So let's say we started with 'Spring is.' The kids might say, 'Spring is bunny time.' Then we say the sentence together and then count the number of words. Second, we draw a blank for each word and then point to each blank as we are saying the sentence. Last, we work on writing each word. Right now we are working on consonants. So I will stop and ask them to tell me beginning sounds for words like *bunny* and *time*. I stretch the words and repeat them so they can hear the first sound. Then I just write the rest of the word. I try to hold them accountable for what I have taught them. So if I know that they know certain letters, I expect those to be correct. When we write a word that is on our high-frequency list, like *it*, *is*, or *the*, I insist that it get spelled correctly. Once we start doing word families, I get those spelled correctly. At different points in the year, I turn over different parts of the activity to them. At the beginning of the year I count words and draw blanks, but toward the end *they* can do that."

Learning about Pumpkins

Pumpkins have many colors. They can come in tan, yellow, blue, white and orange. Pumpkins have seeds. Pumpkins need water and sun to grow. A pumpkin has five parts. They have a shell

Language Play for Developing Phonological Awareness

Phonological awareness is the foundation of phonics instruction. If children cannot tell that words orally have the same beginning sound, then they will not make sense of a teacher's statement that the symbol *B* represents the /b/ sound. If children can't tell that a word like *hit* has three sounds, then decoding will be a challenge because they will not have the foundation. Thus, good phonics instruction includes brief, relevant language play with sounds or phonological awareness instruction. There are many levels of phonological awareness, but as I mentioned earlier, it appears that initial sound awareness and phoneme segmentation and blending are the most important for building capacity to learn and use letter–sounds. Following is a list of fun games focusing on these two skills that teachers can play with groups of children. (See also Chapters 4 and 5 for additional games and activities for small groups.)

Initial Sound Recognition Games

Which One? Place a group of items on the table that begin with one to three different sounds, and then say, "Show me one that starts like *ffffish*, /ffff/." This can also be done with tubs or bins. Children can "collect" items from around the room that start with a particular sound.

Tommy Tiger likes to eat _____. Use a puppet or a picture of an animal that begins with a specific sound (e.g., Tommy Tiger). Tell the children that Tommy only likes things that begin with *Tt*, things that make the sound /t/ at the beginning. Use a sentence frame and ask children to give their answers: "Tommy Tiger likes tuna." "Tommy Tiger likes turkey." *Make sure that the children say the sentence stem with the target sounds.* If the children don't say the target sounds themselves, they are missing half the activity. This game can be played waiting in line to go into art class or PE.

Picture Sorts Picture sorts are described in detail in Chapter 4 (p. 110). Children choose pictures that begin with a certain sound and put them together. Usually the sort has two to four different target sounds.

Share the Sound Toward the end of mastering beginning sounds, students are asked to say the sound at the beginning of a word. This is more difficult because they must "slice" off a sound and just say that sound. The teacher says, "Say the sound at the start of *big*."

Mother May I? Like in Tommy Tiger, children use the Mother May I? game format to name words that begin with a specific sound. The teacher stands at one end of the room or carpet and the children stand at the other end in a line. A target sound is named like /g/. Each child asks, "Mother may I take two steps with *girls*? Mother may I take three steps with *goat*?"

Beginning Sounds Bingo Each child has a bingo board with pictures that start with different sounds. The teacher calls out the *sounds only* (not the picture names) and the children can cover one item that begins with that sound. For example, the teacher says, "Find something that starts with /f/."

Once children have mastered many letter–sounds, phonemic segmentation and blending tasks can help them decode. In Chapter 5, strategies like Elkonin boxes, which are best done with small groups, are described (pp. 173–175). Here are some activities that you can do with large groups.

Blending Games

Secret Word This is a blending game. The teacher says a "secret word" in parts and the children have to say the correct word to their partner. For example, the teacher says, "/b/ /u/ /g/. What's the secret word?" Make sure that each child has a partner to whisper the secret word to. This keeps everyone engaged. Once children show some mastery, individual children can come up and do their own "secret word" for the group (see Chapter 5 for a description).

WATCH

VIDEO 3.5

Secret Word

In this short clip, teacher Kelly Linkenhoker plays Secret Word with her kindergartners.

Chugging Words This is described in the First Words unit in Chapter 5 as well, but it can be done with a large group. It works for items with two sound parts. The teacher uses two cubes for the two parts of the word and then "chugs" them closer and closer until they say the whole word. For example, the teacher says, "/a/ /t/, /a/ /t/, /a/ /t/, *at*." If students are working on word families, then they can chug the onset and the rime. For example, a student would chug blocks and say, "/b/ /ug/."

WATCH

VIDEO 3.6

Kelly Chugs Words in a Daily Whole-Group Activity

In this short clip, teacher Kelly Linkenhoker chugs words in a daily whole-group phonics activity.

Segmentation Games

Tapping Words This is a segmentation game. Many of the multisensory approaches show children how to use their fingers to tap the sounds in words. This is a simple, concrete way to break words up. For example, the teacher says, "Let's tap *pig*, /p/ /i/ /g/. Touch your fingers to your thumb for each sound." It is always easier to tap or segment two sounds, so start with words with two sounds first. In addition, certain sounds, called continuants, are easier when you first start segmenting. These are sounds like /s/, /m/, and /r/ that can be held or "continued" as you are saying them. They are different from stops like /b/ and /t/. For additional guidance about specific words to use with phonemic awareness activities, see Chapters 4 and 5.

Robot Talk This is also a segmentation game (or a blending game if you change it). Children learn how to say words in "robot" talk, which consists of segmented words. The teacher says, "Let's say this word *go* in robot talk with each sound, /g/ /o/. Can you say the word *at* in robot talk?" The game can also be turned around so the teacher says things in robot talk to the children, who then must blend the sounds together.

All of these whole-group phonological awareness activities are simple and efficient. There are literally hundreds of these on the web, and many teachers take these initial sound, segmenting, and blending activities and get really creative. These games are a great way to get up and move while still learning. In addition, they introduce simple routines that translate to other activities. For example, tapping words is a routine that children can use during journal writing.

Targeted Instruction for Needs-Based Small Groups

In most classrooms, especially kindergartens, students are at different places. Some children will actually be ready to read words and others will be ready to learn letter–sounds. For example, one child doesn't understand short vowels, whereas another doesn't understand consonant letter–sounds. The *reason* to create small groups is to differentiate instruction for a group of learners with similar needs. What that means is that the content that is taught in small groups *should not* be the same for each group. The focus of the instruction should be matched to the student's needs. Research shows that when teachers use small-group, differentiated instruction, there are better outcomes for students (Taylor et al. 2000).

Because the small group shrinks the scale of the instruction down considerably, it allows each child to have *multiple* opportunities to practice, as opposed to the occasional opportunities that occur in a whole-group lesson. In addition, the practice opportunities can be more equivalent, ensuring that even the quietest members of the group have the same number of chances to practice as the other members do. In a whole-group lesson, practice opportunities are unplanned and often depend on the confidence of the child, the teacher's field of vision, and the teacher's unidentified biases. (We all have biases that we often do not know about that cause us to call on certain children more than others.)

When working with children in a small group, teachers have ample opportunity to see exactly what each child is doing, to hear each child respond to questions, and to provide just-in-time feedback to each child. Think about it. During a whole-group lesson, the teacher can provide feedback, but it may not be relevant to the rest of the group. When children are doing independent work, the teacher is usually not there. The small group provides a golden opportunity to correct issues as they are happening. A seating arrangement in which the teacher is in very close proximity to each child is a great way to organize space so that feedback can be given promptly.

With needs-based grouping, it is important to be flexible in assigning children to groups. You should not end up with a set of static groups that are essentially the same from September to June. Groups should shift as students' needs change and focal standards shift, with the goal that every child meets grade-level expectations by the end of the year.

Five Questions to Answer *Before* Setting Up Small-Group Instruction

1. Why use small groups?

The reason to use small groups is so that young children can receive daily, focused instruction based on their needs. With small groups, children receive more teacher attention, feedback, practice, and targeted content. They don't have to relearn things they already know or "fake it" through content that is over their heads.

2. How many small groups can I reasonably handle?

Optimally, the number of groups should be completely driven by student needs. However, four, five, or six groups can be unwieldy. For new teachers or those just starting small-group instruction, three may be the most manageable number. With three groups, the organizational structure only requires three twenty- to thirty-minute rotations, and students do not have to work independently for too long.

3. What kinds of independent activities will my students do?

Nothing can derail small groups faster than inappropriate activities. If the activities are boring, messy, distracting, too hard, too short, or frustrating, then small-group instruction gets derailed. It might be helpful to think of these activities as you would homework because they must be done almost completely independently without adult help. The tasks also must be carried out at a brisk pace and require the "right" amount of time. Activities that are too short will result in off-task students. Tasks that are boring or too hard will also result in off-task students. Tasks should be useful, practice activities that have instructional purposes and are not simply busywork.

4. What will the routines and expectations be?

Small-group instruction requires a simple, understandable, easy-to-follow routine that guides students when they are not with the teacher. There are many of these routines in which students move through different centers, stations, or activities. Students also must know what to do if their pencil breaks or they don't know how to complete an activity, or if they run out of things to do.

5. How will we get there?

Usually, before fully implementing small groups, teachers spend a period of time training their students. They talk about activities and rules in centers, stations, or activities. They explain what students should do when they encounter a problem. They show students the places in the room where they should do activities. They also provide times for the class to "practice" working independently for shorter periods of time before doing so for an entire half hour. Ramping up to a full hour and a half of small-group instruction requires baby steps.

Reading specialists, experienced teachers, and university faculty often underestimate the importance of solid classroom management in maintaining small-group instruction. Small-group instruction should not begin until the routines and structures are in place that allow a teacher to work in a focused way with small groups of students (Invernizzi and Hayes 2004). (See the box "Five Questions to Answer *Before* Setting Up Small-Group Instruction.")

Even with training, positive support, and a skilled teacher, some students take a little longer than others to be able to work independently. A young child can sincerely want to follow directions or please a teacher but still be in the process of developing the self-control to do so. Other students need to develop the social skills to solve problems in the classroom without adult intervention. Students who have not had previous school experience are more likely to need help in developing these skills than others do. Do not give up on teaching students how to work independently, but have reasonable expectations about what this takes.

Lesson Parts

For most of the units provided, the small-group phonics lesson has five parts, but in Beyond First Words, several of the parts are not necessary. See Figure 3.2. The lesson moves logically from review to phonological awareness to decoding to spelling to text reading and, as such, actually encompasses more than *just* phonics.

FIGURE 3.2

	Lesson Part	Unit	Purpose
1	**Review-It** Practice Words and Letter Sounds	Letter Lessons First Words Beyond First Words	**Practice for automaticity (rehearse)** • Letter names and sounds • High-frequency words • Not applicable
2	**Hear-It** Phonemic Awareness	Letter Lessons First Words Beyond First Words	**Identify sounds in words orally (analyze)** • Beginning sounds • Segment sounds • Not applicable
3	**Decode-It** Read Words	Letter Lessons First Words Beyond First Words	**Use letter–sounds to decode (analyze)** • Learn letter–sounds • Decode c-v-c words • Decode vowel team words (e.g., *ee, oa*)

continues

Lesson Part	Unit	Purpose
4 **Spell-It** Write Words	Letter Lessons First Words Beyond First Words	**Use letter–sounds to spell (synthesize)** • Spell first letter–sounds • Spell c-v-c words • Spell vowel team words
5 **Read-It** Text Reading	Letter Lessons First Words Beyond First Words	**Read words in context (apply)** • Use beginning sounds in caption books • Fully sound out words in decodables • Fully sound out words in decodables

Review-It (5 minutes)

At the beginning of lessons in the Letter Lessons and First Words units is a five-minute segment to review content that must be automatic. In Letter Lessons, students practice naming and saying the sounds for letters they know. In First Words, they practice reading high-frequency and other decodable words. The idea is to practice recently learned words and letters in several different ways (e.g., games, partner activities). Usually students keep about fifteen to twenty words or letters and then "retire" those that they know. As discussed in Chapter 5, the goal is to solidify learning but not to resort to drilling the same way every time. (See "Review-It" in Chapter 5.)

WATCH

VIDEO 3.7

Review First Words

In this short clip, teacher Kelly Linkenhoker asks Zaylie, Kayleigh, and Tim to perform a word review.

Hear-It: Phonemic Awareness

In both First Words and Letter Lessons, the Hear-It lesson segment involves oral work with sounds in words to build capacity for the next lesson section, decoding. In my own practice, I have used a dedicated phonological awareness lesson section that focuses on *hearing* the discrete speech sounds in words (Mesmer 2001; Mesmer and Griffith 2005). In Letter Lessons children identify initial sounds, and in First Words they practice segmenting words first into onsets and rimes (e.g., /b/ /ig/) and then into individual sounds (e.g., /b/ /i/ /g/), often using sound boxes. (In Chapter 5, see "Elkonin (Sound) Boxes and Letter Boxes" on page 173 for specifics about how to do this.) By Beyond First Words, the phonological awareness section of the lesson is no longer necessary.

Decode-It (or Target Letter Activity): Read Words

The next section of the lesson is the longest. This section is the point at which new content is introduced, modeled, and practiced. In Letter Lessons, the goal is not really decoding words but learning new letter–sounds. During First Words, students decode simple words by fully applying their letter–sound knowledge. In the Beyond First Words lesson, students learn patterns in which more than one letter represents a vowel sound (e.g., *home*, *book*, *cart*, *team*).

Spell-It: Write Words

The fourth section of the lesson is probably one of the most challenging but also one of the most important. The teacher dictates a word or sentence and the student writes that word or sentence. This is challenging for students because they must stare down at a blank page and synthesize all that they know about letter–sounds. They must produce something. The other parts of the lesson are analytical, but this is synthesis. In this section, teachers may use Word Building (McCandliss et al. 2003) or do Making Words lessons (Cunningham and Cunningham 1992). (Note: This section of the lesson does not focus on the mechanics of handwriting, an essential skill for young learners, but one that can be taught at other times in a whole-group setting. It also does not really focus on children composing their own novel sentences. That kind of work can take place during writer's workshop, interactive writing, or journal writing. Brief periods of dictation build fluency and skill with hearing and writing sounds in words.)

WATCH

VIDEO 3.8
Word Building Activity
In this short clip, teacher Kelly Linkenhoker asks Zaylie, Kaleigh, and Tim to complete the Word Building activity.

Read-It: Text Reading (5 minutes)

The final part is connected text reading, and during this part of the lesson students practice *applying* their phonics knowledge as they read texts. Students in Letter Lessons are practicing concept of word and cannot fully decode words, but they can use their knowledge of letter–sounds to help them with beginning sounds in simple caption books and other predictable materials. (For a full description of these texts, see Chapter 4, pp. 116). In First Words, children *can* sound out simple words and they practice this in decodable texts. (See Chapter 5 for a full description of decodable texts pp. 163.) In Beyond First Words, students read decodable texts and poems with long vowels.

Word Prompting: What to Do When Students Struggle with Word Recognition

When students come to a word that they do not know or when they make a mistake, their teacher will take action to support them in pronouncing the word. I call this "word prompting." Although it is not something that is given a great deal of attention or thought, word prompting is very important because it essentially "teaches" a child how to figure out words. The things that teachers say when students struggle will be internalized by students and used in the future, perhaps when a student is reading independently. There are various approaches to word prompting, many of them rather eclectic; some people suggest that a teacher simply try a variety of approaches that are all equally valuable at any given stage of development (Brown 2003). Based on the work of Brown and my own instructional studies (e.g., Mesmer 1999, 2001; Mesmer and Lake 2010), I suggest an approach to take when a child is reading and has difficulty with a word. This is not a lockstep process, but it does include a "first step" and some differentiated "second steps," based on the child's development and the word being attempted. It is my perspective that we should direct young readers to *use* all the letter–sound information that they possess as they attempt to figure out words. On the following page is a card that sketches out the guidelines for "what to say when they struggle on a word." The very first step for all readers at all stages who are reading all types of words is surprising—don't say or do *anything*. Instead, wait. What research tells us is that, especially with struggling learners, when students have difficulty, the teacher simply provides the word to them (Allington 1980; Hoffman and Clements 1984). This is a problem because it creates learned helplessness and it gets in the way of students' self-correcting. Thus, the first step in word prompting is to wait. If you wait and a student makes a mistake, wait until the end of sentence break or phrase before providing direction. When students have finished reading a thought, they are more likely to notice that something is wrong and to self-correct the problem. Secondly, if you do say something, use the generic prompt "Something tricked you" and put your finger or sentence right *before* the place where the error was made to get the student started. This prompt can work for all students at all stages decoding any type of word.

VIDEO 3.9

Word Prompting

In this clip, I describe what word prompting is.

VIDEO 3.10

Something Tricked You

In this short clip, I use the "Something tricked you" prompt to help Micah figure out what tricked him as he read aloud.

In the clip, I ask Micah what he said originally and we talk about why his mistake was not correct. I ask him to verbalize his problem solving to encourage this behavior and to help him remember it. A general guideline for word prompting is to provide three quick prompts and then move on (and note that waiting is considered a prompt). The reason to limit yourself to three prompts is that the use of more than three transforms a book reading into a word or phonics lesson, disrupts the meaning of the text, and sends the message that "it's all about decoding."

Word Prompting:
What to Say When They Struggle on a Word

Word prompting is what teachers and parents say when children don't read a word correctly. Word prompts are important because they shape the way readers approach reading.

STEP 1

- WAIT . . . DON'T say anything until a phrase or sentence break.
- Use three quick prompts and move on.

↓

STEP 2

Generic prompt

"Something tricked you . . ." (Put your pencil at a place in the sentence before the error.)

↓

STEP 3

Holistic prompts (when word is not decodable)

- Reread.
- What makes sense?
- Fill in a placeholder ("something") and then finish the sentence.

Code-oriented prompt (when word is decodable)

- "Sound." Put your finger at the front of the word.
- "Bulldoze through the word."
- "What's the first sound?"

Reference: Brown, K. J. 2003. "What Do I Say When They Get Stuck on a Word? Aligning Teachers' Prompts with Students' Development." *Reading Teacher* 56 (8): 720-33.

The third prompt should be matched to the student's stage of development and the type of word being read, with the caveat that, in my opinion, we should always try to support students in using letter–sound information while reading. If a student is at the very beginning of development and is working on learning letter–sounds, I might use the prompt "Sound," or "What's the first sound?" and point to the beginning sound so that the child can use the beginning sound. If a child comes to a word at this stage and I know that she does not know that sound (e.g., /w/), I might say, "What makes sense?" or "What do we see in the picture?" Usually there has been a book walk before the reading and the child has had some review on the content, vocabulary, and pictures in the book. These types of prompts are typical for students working in Letter Lessons who are reading predictable caption books and gaining control over concept of word. For a child in the First Words unit who knows all the letter–sounds and might be working on decoding short vowel c-v-c words, when I come to a c-v-c word in text I will say, "Bulldoze the word" or "Sound it out." (Note: "Sound it out" is probably the second-most-popular thing that teachers say, aside from providing the word. When you ask children to "sound it out," make sure that they have been taught the information that they need to do so. Usually multisyllabic words are difficult for young learners to sound out.) As readers gain more and more information about how words work, adding vowel teams, r-controlled vowels, blends, digraphs, and diphthongs, teachers can use the "Sound it out" prompt more and more.

Finding Time

If you are like most teachers, you probably have many pressing questions: "When am I going to do this? How much time should I spend on phonics? How do I make decisions?" And the answer is "It depends." It depends on what grade you are talking about and what standards you are teaching. It depends on what unit you are doing and where kids are developmentally. And it depends on what children *need* and what your standards require. In kindergarten and first grade, phonics instruction is paired with word reading review, phonological awareness, and print concepts. This is appropriate. Both the Common Core and the standards in all states reflect that most kindergarten and first-grade students will need all these components Thus, Letter Lessons and First Words units take more time daily because they include a review of phonological awareness, words, and print concepts. However, time spent on phonics is also governed by what children *need*, which is informed by assessment through the placement test. Some children will already have mastered information that other children will need. In second grade, when most students would be in Beyond First Words, phonics instruction is usually a smaller portion of time (e.g., 15–20 minutes) because lesson sections like Review-It and Hear-It have dropped out of the phonics lesson.

Teachers also ask, "How do I do small groups? How do I get time to meet with children in smaller groups?" I encourage teachers in primary grades to do their best to organize small-group instruction. We know that small-group instruction in the primary grades is associated with better outcomes for students (Taylor et al. 2000). The units in this book can be embedded into *any* organizational framework that provides time for small-group instruction, and the majority of frameworks in the primary grades do this because it is good practice. So, for example, if you are using a workshop approach, there is a daily time for small groups. Simply do the subunit lessons (e.g., Review-It, Hear-It, Decode-It,

Spell-It, Read-It) during that time. As another example, if you are doing guided reading groups, then do the subunits at the beginning or end of the guided reading groups.

Some teachers may ask, "Well, won't this cut into time for reading books?" The books that children read during Letter Lessons and First Words, usually during kindergarten and early first grade, are the same types of materials read in many other instructional schemes. These materials are typically at the pre-primer (e.g., Fountas and Pinnell, A–E) and primer levels (F–G). Most of these books are very short, with 50–150 words, and are read in about two to five minutes. Comprehension work with these books is often relatively brief as well. Children can understand content that is much richer and more complicated than what they can read at this stage, and what advances their comprehension are rich read-alouds with in-depth stories and well-developed characters. What is holding children back at these reading levels is their lack of phonics knowledge, so the book reading in Letter Lessons and First Words helps them apply their letter–sound knowledge.

When Small Groups Are Not Needed or Possible

There are times when whole-group phonics instruction is appropriate. As discussed in Chapter 2, sometimes the placement test indicates that the group is homogenous and most of the students need the same instruction. If this is the case and small groups are not possible, then teaching in a whole group may be appropriate. Nell Duke and I have suggested a rule of thumb that when about 60 percent of the students need the same thing, it can be taught in a whole group.

Assuming that the content is appropriate for everyone, the biggest challenges in a whole-group phonics lesson are (1) keeping all the students engaged and on-task with reading words and spelling, and (2) providing feedback. Both of these challenges can be addressed (but not fully solved) in a whole-group setting. (This is why small-group instruction is preferable.)

For a whole-group phonics lesson, students will need spaces to manipulate their own word cards, magnetic letters, books, and dry erase boards. To do whole-group phonics instruction, banish the picture of a large group of children sitting on the carpet staring up at the teacher. This scenario works for read-alouds, interactive writing, or vocabulary work but not for phonics instruction. It is too passive. Unlike most whole-group lessons, where a teacher asks a question, students raise their hands, and one student answers the question, in the whole-group phonics lesson, all the students answer the questions or do activities with their *own* materials.

WATCH

VIDEO 3.11
How to Do Whole-Group Phonics

VIDEO 3.12
Dry Erase Board Activity
In these two video clips, teacher Kelly Linkenhoker and I discuss the value of whole-group instruction, and then we see Kelly do a whole-group dry erase board activity called Race where students write words they know.

So now you have a lot of "behind the scenes" information about phonics instruction, but what would you see and hear in a classroom where children *use* phonics? You would see kids writing on dry erase boards. You would see charts with a mixture of teacher writing and child writing. You would see easels with big books and pointers. You would see bins of magnetic letters and word cards. You would see rings of words. You would hear children putting word parts together, "*b-at, b-at, b-at,*" and then the aha of the real word, "*bat!*" You would hear teachers using clear language. You would hear teachers giving children word challenges to try to figure out. ("What would this word say?") You would hear reading and word solving during that reading. You would see small groups with intently focused children and teachers leaning in quietly to offer the "just right" feedback. In sum, you would see empowered children and teachers learning and growing.

What would you not see? Worksheets. Everyone doing the same thing at the same time all the time. Too much pencil and paper. Whole-group instruction all the time. What would you not hear? The same dull language over and over again. Nervous verbal clutter. Phonics instruction that has taken over the curriculum.

This chapter adds the last layer to the information that you need to teach phonics. It provides a framework for small-group instruction, a set of practices, and some support for language and choices that will affect children. The earlier layers—information about English orthography and phonics assessment—intersect with the instructional framework to put you in a good position for doing the work. The remaining chapters guide lessons in each of the units and serve as references for helping you empower young children with knowledge.

Where to Start: Using the Letter Lessons and First Words Placement Test to Identify What to Teach

This book has three units organized into a scope and sequence that matches the developmental progression. The three units (Chapters 4–6) are Letter Lessons, First Words, and Beyond First Words. Each of these units takes twenty-five to twenty-seven weeks and is broken down into four to five subunits that target specific groups of letter–sounds (e.g., short vowels, beginning blends). The Letter Lessons and First Words Placement Test has three sections that match the units and these milestones.

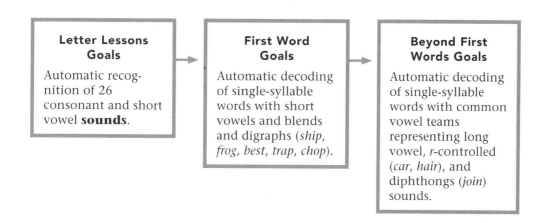

Letter Lessons Goals

Automatic recognition of 26 consonant and short vowel **sounds**.

First Word Goals

Automatic decoding of single-syllable words with short vowels and blends and digraphs (*ship, frog, best, trap, chop*).

Beyond First Words Goals

Automatic decoding of single-syllable words with common vowel teams representing long vowel, *r*-controlled (*car, hair*), and diphthongs (*join*) sounds.

The knowledge from each previous unit lays the foundation for learning in the next. The graphic shows this progression. For example, in order for a reader to efficiently decode words in First Words, she must be able to automatically recognize all consonant and short vowel letter–sounds. In order to most efficiently learn to decode vowel teams in Beyond First Words, she must be able to easily decode words with the consonant-vowel-consonant (c-v-c) pattern, including words with blends and digraphs. Thus, there are three big assessment points: (1) letter knowledge, (2) decoding c-v-c words, and (3) decoding vowel teams. The placement test checks this knowledge so that children are placed in the correct unit and subunit. As described in Chapter 2, after giving the Letter Lessons and First Words Placement Test, complete the cover sheet for each child.

Then, using that data, follow these three steps before teaching:

1. Identify the correct unit for *each* child (i.e., Letter Lessons, First Words, Beyond First Words).

2. Identify the correct subunit within the unit for *each* child (e.g., Letter Lessons Cycle 1: What's in a Name? Cycle 2: First Pass; Cycle 3: Review/Solidify; Cycle 4: Word Building). Group children together who are in the same cycle.

3. Adjustment unit and subunit placement using judgment and observation.

This section of the book will show you how to take the data from the cover sheet, analyze it, and determine the correct unit and subunit. It provides detailed guidance along with student examples that show you how to find the right subunit. There are examples for students in Letter Lessons Part A, First Words Part B, and Beyond First Words Part C. Additionally, the section illustrates how to use teacher judgment and make decisions when students are between subunits.

Where to Start: Finding the Right Subunit for Letter Lessons, First Words, and Beyond First Words

Letter Lessons

- Part A.3: Letter–Sounds score of 0–5 out of 26?
  Start with Letter Cycle 1: What's in a Name?

- Part A.3: Letter–Sounds score of 6–10 out of 26?
  Start with Letter Cycle 2: First Pass (slower pace).

- Part A.3: Letter–Sounds score of 11–20 out of 26?
  Start with Letter Cycle 3: Review/Solidify (faster pace).

- Part A.3: Letter–Sounds score of 21 or more out of 26?
  Start with Letter Cycle 4: Word Building *OR* go to First Words unit (see Chapter 2 and Figure 2.5, for guidance about which to use.)

First Words and Beyond First Words

Start at the lowest (easiest) unit in which the student misses *two or more items*, balancing this guideline with teacher judgment and observation. Subunits that are longer may require close analysis of incorrect items to locate the proper place to start.

Part B: First Words (Grades K–2)	
B.1. Short Vowels (We Are Family)	9/10
B.2. Digraphs (Two for One)	4/5
B.3. Beginning Blends	0/15
B.4. Final Blends	0/8 ← START HERE

Where to Start in Letter Lessons?

Score Part A.3: Letter–Sounds	Letter Lessons Cycle to Start	Focus
0–5 letter–sounds	Letter Cycle 1: What's in a Name?	• Introduction to letters • What are the letters in my name?
6–10 letter–sounds	Letter Cycle 2: First Pass	• Focused teaching of each letter for first time • What sounds do letters represent?
11–20 letter–sounds	Letter Cycle 3: Review/Solidify	• Focused on unknown letter–sounds based on reassessment • Review pace; less time per letter • Which letter sounds do I still need to learn?
21+ letter–sounds	Letter Cycle 4: Word Building	• Uses letter–sounds to teach high-frequency words and decodable words • How can I use what I know about letter sounds to read common words?

The guidelines for Letter Lessons are very specific, but, as always, teacher observations and knowledge of the children should be integrated with assessment data. Following are cover sheets and scores for one student, descriptions of this learner, and identification of the target letter cycle subunit.

Paul: Letter Lessons Example

Starting Unit: <u>Letter Lessons</u>   Starting Subunit: <u>Letter Cycle 2: 4</u>

Who takes it?	Part A: Letter Lessons (Pre-K–1)	Score
Prekindergarten Kindergarten First Grade	A.1. Uppercase Letter Names	14/26
	A.2. Lowercase Letter Names	9/28
	A.3. Letter–Sounds (Use this score for subunit placement.)	7/26

Paul had 7/26 on A.3. Using the guidelines, he should start on Letter Cycle 2, First Pass.

Where to Start in First Words?

A child who is ready for First Words will have a score of 21/26 on Part A.3: Letter–Sounds and should be given all sections of the First Words assessment on the Placement Test (Parts B.1–B.4). To find the right subunit in First Words, start at the *easiest unit where the student misses two or more items*, and then adjust up or down as instruction unfolds and your own observations support such moves. In the next two student examples, Tarion and Anna, have different subunit needs based on their results.

Tarion: First Words Example

Starting Unit: <u>First Words</u>   Starting Subunit: <u>We Are Family 4</u>

Part B: First Words (Grades 1–2)	
B.1. Short Vowels (We Are Family)	8/10
B.2. Consonant Digraphs (Two for One)	4/5
B.3. Beginning Blends	0/15
B.4. Final Blends and Digraphs	0/8

START HER

In this example, testing stopped with First Words Section B because Tarion had at least one part of the First Words section with two or more incorrect (i.e., B.1, B.3, B.4). He should be taught in the First Words unit. To find the proper subunit inspect his scores in section B.1–B.4. Tarion has 8/10 on Short Vowels (We Are Family), a better score of 4/5 on Digraphs (Two for One), and the lowest scores on Beginning

Blends (0/15) and Final Blends (0/8). Even though Tarion has a score of 4/5 on a harder unit, Two for One, instruction will start at the easier unit, We Are Family.

Below is another cover sheet, with scores for Anna, as well as a description of her and the identification of the target subunit in First Words. Importantly, teachers must use their own judgment and their everyday observations as they use the test data. This case with Anna shows how to do this.

Anna: First Words Example

Starting Unit: <u>First Words</u>   Starting Subunit: <u>We are Family 4 Lessons 11 and 12 then</u> <u>Beginning Blends 20</u>

Part B: First Words (Grades K–2)		*
Kindergarten First Grade Second Grade	B.1. Short Vowels (We Are Family)	_8/10
	B.2. Consonant Digraphs (Two for One)	_5/5
	B.3. Beginning Blends	_7/15
	B.4. Final Blends and Digraphs	_4/8

*Placement requires teacher's judgment

With Anna testing stopped in the First Words section B because she missed two or more on at least one section (B.1, B.3, B.4). She should be taught in the First Words unit. To find the proper subunit, inspect scores in sections B.1–B.4. Anna's Placement Test results are a little less clear-cut than Tarion's and require a bit more judgment on the part of the teacher. If we were to strictly follow the guidelines for identifying a subunit, then that would be Short Vowels (We Are Family), because that is the easiest unit in which Anna misses two or more items. However, Anna's teacher believes that her performance on Part B.1: Short Vowels (We Are Family) does not warrant doing the entire unit. She noticed that Anna got a little confused with two short *e* words, so she decided that Anna should do the last two lessons in We Are Family (11 and 12), which focus on short *e*. Then Anna will begin with Lesson 18 in Beginning Blends, skipping Two for One entirely since she already knows that.

Where to Start in Beyond First Words?

To identify the correct subunit in Beyond First Words, use the same decision point that was used with First Words. Start on the *easiest* subunit where the student missed two or more. As with First Words and other units, observations and other data points, along with teacher judgment, should be used. Following are two examples of completed cover sheets and a discussion of how this teacher used judgment in finding the right place to start.

Darren: Beyond First Words Example

Starting Unit: <u>Beyond First Words</u>   Starting Subunit: <u>Teamwork 6–7 (Long a)</u>

(Letter Lessons, First Words, Beyond First Words) (We Are Family, Two for One, etc.)

Who takes it?	Part A: Letter Lessons (Pre-K–1)	Score
Prekindergarten Kindergarten First Grade	A.1. Uppercase Letter Names	26/26
	A.2. Lowercase Letter Names	26/28
	A.3. Letter–Sounds (Use this score for subunit placement)	26/26

Decision Point

Score of 21/26 *or higher* on Part A.3: Letter–Sounds?
• Give test for Part B: First Words.

Score of 20/26 *or lower* on Part A.3: Letter–Sounds?
• STOP; IDENTIFY *Letter Lessons* subunit.

Who takes it?	Part B: First Words (Grades K–2)	Score
First Grade Second Grade	B.1. Short Vowels (We Are Family)	10/10
	B.2. Consonant Digraphs (Two for One)	5/5
	B.3. Beginning Blends	13/15
	B.4. Final Blends and Digraphs	8/8

Decision Point

Score of 0–1 *incorrect* on *any* section (B.1, B.2, B.3, B.4)?
• Give test for Part C: Beyond First Words.

Score of 2 or *more* incorrect on *any* section (B.1, B.2, B.3, B.4)?
• STOP; IDENTIFY *First Words* subunit.

Who takes it?	Part C: Beyond First Words (Grades 1–2)	Score
First Grade Second Grade	C.1. Silent *e* (Sneaky Silent *e*)	5/5
	C.2. Vowel Digraphs (Teamwork)	2/15
	C.3. *R*-Controlled (*R* the Robber)	3/10
	C.4. Diphthongs	5/5

Decision Point

Score of 0–1 *incorrect* on *each* section (C.1, C.2, C.3, C.4)?
• Student has mastered Beyond First Words content. Seek other material for phonics instruction.

Score of 2 *or more* incorrect on *any* section (C.1, C.2, C.3, C.4)?
• STOP; IDENTIFY Beyond First Words subunit.
(See Beyond First Words Teacher Record, Figure 2.9,
and section introduction "Where to Start," after Chapter 3.)

In this example, the testing should have stopped with First Words B.3 because Darren missed two or more on at least one section, Beginning Blends. Technically Darren should start on the First Words unit with Beginning Blends but teacher judgment and additional analysis suggested otherwise. In this situation, the teacher looked at the Beginning Blends section of the test and noticed that the items missed were patterns (e.g., *sn, sk*) that Darion demonstrated knowledge of in other ways. In a spelling test in the classroom, Darren spelled the *sk-* word, *skip*, with the correct letter–sounds (e.g., *scip*). This teacher also knew that Darion had already done Beginning Blends the previous year and would be bored doing it again, so she started him in the Beyond First Words unit, on the Teamwork subunit.

2. Teamwork		(Vowel Teams)
6–7	**Long *a* (ai & ay)**	**ai**
	-ain	rain, plain, chain, gain, plain, stain, train, grain, drain, brain
	-ail	trail, sail, hail, fail, mail, nail, rail, bail
	exceptions:	said, again
	-ay	hay, may, ray, tray, say, lay, day, gray, play, pay, clay, stay, slay

Samara: Beyond First Words Example

Placement Cover Sheet

Starting Unit: <u>Beyond First Words</u>   Starting Subunit: <u>Teamwork 10 (Long o)</u>

(Letter Lessons, First Words, Beyond First Words) (We Are Family, Two for One, etc.)

Part C: Beyond First Words (Grades 1–2)	Score
C.1. Silent *e* (Sneaky Silent *e*)	5/5
C.2. Vowel Digraphs (Teamwork)	10/15
C.3. *R*-Controlled (*R* the Robber)	5/10
C.4. Diphthongs	5/5

For Samara, testing stopped with the Beyond First Words Section because she had two or more incorrect on any section in Part C. Beyond First Words is the correct unit for her. To identify the correct subunit, analyze the scores in Section C. In Part C.1: Silent *e* (Sneaky Silent *e*), Samara has a score of 5/5, and she also has a 5/5 on Part C.4: Diphthongs, which shows she knows these patterns very well. In Part C.2: Vowel Digraphs (Teamwork), Samara got a score of 10/15, which shows that she has some knowledge of vowel teams but is not sure exactly how all vowel teams work. In Part C.3: R-Controlled (*R* the Robber), she got only 5/10. The easiest subunit where Samara misses one or more items is Part C.2: Vowel Digraphs (Teamwork).

To start instruction, you would thus go to the Teamwork subunit. However, it may not be appropriate to start at the beginning of the subunit, since Samara already knows over 60 percent of the patterns. After reviewing her errors in Part C.2 and reviewing her writing and oral reading accuracy, this teacher determined that Samara was fairly solid in the common long *a* and long *e* patterns found in Lessons 6–8. Samara was also fairly strong with the long *e* exception words like *steak*, *great*, *head*, and *bread*. For this reason, instead of starting at the first lesson of the subunit, Lesson 6, this teacher decided to start at Lesson 10, long *o*, because that content was new to the student. In addition, when this group gets to Diphthongs, Samara will not participate because she knows the content.

2. Teamwork			(Vowel Teams)
6–7	**Long *a*** **(ai & ay)**	**ai**	
		-ain	rain, plain, chain, gain, plain, stain, train, grain, drain, brain
		-ail	trail, sail, hail, fail, mail, nail, rail, bail
			exceptions: said, again
		-ay	hay, may, ray, tray, say, lay, day, gray, play, pay, clay, stay, slay
8	**Long *e*** **(ee & ea)**	**ee**	deep, sleep, sheep, keep, see, bee, tree, weed, seed, sheet, meet
		ea	meal, speak, leap, heal, team, east, feast, peach
		-eat	heat, meat, beat, neat, seat, wheat, feat, cheat, treat
9	***ea* exceptions**	**ea = /ĕ/**	dead, head, ahead, instead, dread, tread, bread
			(The word *read* can be pronounced with either a long *e* or a short *e*.)
		ea = /ā/	steak, great, break
			(Note: There are very few instances of *ea* = long *a*.)
			(Contrast short *e* words [e.g., *dead*] with long *e* words [e.g., *treat*, *heat*].)

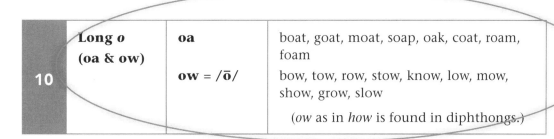

10	Long *o* (oa & ow)	oa	boat, goat, moat, soap, oak, coat, roam, foam
		ow = /ō/	bow, tow, row, stow, know, low, mow, show, grow, slow
			(*ow* as in *how* is found in diphthongs.)

After completing the cover sheet and identifying a subunit for each student, the easiest thing to do is simply group the cover sheets together to create groups. In first and second grade it is common for students to be in different places, with some doing work in First Words, a larger group working in Beyond First Words, and some students showing complete mastery of Beyond First Words content.

4

UNIT: Letter Lessons for Kindergartners and Prekindergartners

Developing Understanding of Alphabet Knowledge and the Alphabetic Principle

I WILL NEVER FORGET WORKING WITH TROY, A KINDERGARTNER, who needed some help with alphabet knowledge. "I don't understand it," said his mother. "His teachers keep telling us that he needs to learn his letters, but he knows all his letters. He can say them right here. Go ahead, Troy." As Troy proceeded to say the names of the letters in order, I realized just how much confusion there can be when we say that students "know their letters." Of course, Troy could say the names of the letters, but he did not know that the letter name labels represented speech sounds (i.e., phonemes). He did not know how to *use* that information to read words.

Like Troy's mother, many adults and even some educators do not realize that "knowing the alphabet" actually means having a diverse set of skills around the fifty-two building blocks of words in English (e.g., recognizing letters, naming letters, naming the sound or sounds commonly associated with that letter, and forming letters). What educators mean when they say that children "know their letters" is *alphabet knowledge*.

When children really know their letters, they do not hesitate when asked to name them. They rarely get confused by similar letters (e.g., *b/d*, *p/b*, *m/w*), and they are able to name letters and sounds without showing inconsistencies (i.e., they do not name a letter correctly sometimes and incorrectly other times).

Different Types of Alphabet Knowledge

A child who has alphabet knowledge can

- **Point to letters.** When a teacher names a letter, the child can point to it.

- **Name letters.** When shown an uppercase or lowercase letter, the child can give the name of the letter.

- **Say letter–sounds.** The child can automatically identify the common sound or sounds associated with each single consonant and the short vowel sounds.

- **Write letters.** The child can correctly form the uppercase and lowercase letters and write the letters fluently to produce "invented" spellings.

- **Understand the alphabetic principle.** The child demonstrates understanding that the alphabet is a set of symbols used to encode speech into a written format that can then be decoded by a reader.

It *is* common for children to reverse letters, especially *b* and *d*, at the early stages of letter learning, but this does *not* indicate dyslexia. (See the box "Letter Reversals ≠ Dyslexia—Don't Contribute to the Panic!") Children tend to reverse letters early on because letters, unlike other objects in their world, can actually change their identity when flipped, rotated, or reversed. Think about it: a cat upside down is a cat. But a lowercase *Bb* upside down is a *Pp*. When children really know their letters, they *own* letter knowledge and it cannot be taken away from them or disrupted in any way. There is no point in teaching letters and phonemes without showing children how that knowledge is useful. Yet, in the busyness of the classroom, children can seem to be getting the "big picture," or understanding the alphabetic principle, when they are really not. The box on page 80 provides specific examples of things that children will say and do when they understand the alphabetic principle and when they do not.

When Troy's teacher started to teach him the names of the letters of the alphabet, Troy was at first very confused. Because the traditional alphabet song blurs the middle letters of the alphabet, *L, M, N, O, P*, together, he thought they were actually all one letter, "ellemenopee." Most teachers have encountered this phenomenon. A good teacher can exploit this rote knowledge to develop the alphabetic principle. Troy's teacher pointed out, "Look, each of these are separate letters. Say them slowly: 'El, Em, En, Oh, Pee.' *P* stands for the /p/ sound. Here is a *P* for /p/ /p/ *peanut*." A teacher develops the alphabetic principle consistently over time by connecting these floating bits of information to the larger understanding that letters are the building blocks for words. This happens through explicit instruction in small groups, as described in this

How You Can Tell If Children Have the Alphabetic Principle

When children *do* understand the alphabetic principle, they will

- *say a word* when they are trying to spell it
- *use invented (temporary) spelling* with logical errors (e.g., *get = git*)
- *start a word* they are trying to read with the correct sound, even if they don't read the whole word correctly (e.g., *see* = say)
- *read back* writing (e.g., *trick or treat = trcrtreet*)
- *spell words* without needing to copy them from a book letter-by-letter

When children *do not* understand the alphabetic principle, they will

- *write* something but not know how to read it back because they are not using the letter–sound relationship
- *copy* words but not be able to read them back
- *write* letters without any correspondence to sounds (e.g., *I went to the store = bmlssmii*)
- *not talk or say the word* while trying to spell it
- *use* letters they know (e.g., in their own names) to write all words, regardless of sounds
- *look to the teacher* when they can't read a word
- *ask, "How do you write it?"* when they can't spell a word
- *say the name of a letter* when asked to read a word (e.g., *no = n*)

chapter, but it also occurs in the "big picture" practices described in Chapter 3 (see "Shared Reading with Print Referencing" and "Interactive Writing" on pp. 54–56).

According to the Common Core State Standards for English Language Arts (NGA and CCSSO 2012), kindergarten children should be able to name all uppercase and lowercase letter–sounds. This standard is in line with decades of work and all states' standards. In prekindergarten, agencies and researchers have recommended a range from 10 letters (either upper or lowercase) to 18 uppercase and 15 lowercase letters (Piasta, Petscher, and Justice 2012). Thus, preschoolers should learn at least 10 letters and more if possible, and, more important, they need to be developing phonological awareness and concepts of print, including concept of word, comprehension, and vocabulary knowledge.

Letter Reversals ≠ Dyslexia—Don't Contribute to the Panic!

With current emphasis on diagnosing "dyslexia" in today's young readers, it is not uncommon for parents or even misinformed teachers to believe that reversing letters is a sign that a child might be "dyslexic." A flip-flopped *s* or a *b* and *d* reversal can create all kinds of concern. In fact, there is even a PSA produced by the Disney corporation that further perpetuates this myth. But letter reversals are *very common as children learn letters*. Children often reverse *b* and *d* throughout first grade. Think of it as analogous to learning your right hand from your left hand. At some level the distinction is arbitrary and it takes practice, mnemonic devices, and time to get it right. So when young learners reverse letters during the Spell-It portion of the lesson, provide a gentle reminder or suggest using an alphabet strip, but don't call in the school psychologist.

WATCH

VIDEO 4.1

Letter Reversals Do Not Usually Mean Dyslexia
In this short clip, I explain why letter reversals are not always an indicator of dyslexia.

But What Is Dyslexia?

Dyslexia is a language-based learning disability. Dyslexia refers to a cluster of symptoms, which result in people having difficulties with specific language skills, particularly reading. Students with dyslexia usually experience difficulties with other language skills such as spelling, writing, and pronouncing words. Dyslexia affects individuals throughout their lives; however, its impact can change at different stages in a person's life. It is referred to as a learning disability because dyslexia can make it very difficult for a student to succeed academically in the typical instructional environment, and in its more severe forms, will qualify a student for special education, special accommodations, or extra support services.

continues

The problems displayed by individuals with dyslexia involve difficulties in acquiring and using written language. It is a myth that individuals with dyslexia "read backward," although spelling can look quite jumbled at times because students have trouble remembering letter symbols for sounds and forming memories for words. Other problems experienced by people with dyslexia include the following:

- Learning to speak
- Learning letters and their sounds
- Organizing written and spoken language
- Memorizing number facts
- Reading quickly enough to comprehend
- Persisting with and comprehending longer reading assignments
- Spelling
- Learning a foreign language
- Correctly doing math operations

Not all students who have difficulties with these skills have dyslexia. Formal testing of reading, language, and writing skills is the only way to confirm a diagnosis of suspected dyslexia.

Source: International Dyslexia Association, www.DyslexiaIDA.org

Development of Concept of Word in Print

Concept of word in print refers to the ability of young children to understand how words work in print, how they are configured on the page. Specifically, when children begin to try to "read" books themselves or watch a teacher point to the words in a big book, they begin to notice that the words stay the same each time, that there is a connection between print and voice, that words are made of groups of letters, and that white space separates words. Children acquire concept of word by attempting to point to words as they say them in a line of print. Although it sounds easy, it is not! In fact, children go through distinct stages as they gain control over this (Ehri and Sweet 1991; Henderson and Beers 1980; Morris 1983; Morris et al. 2003).

Different Phases of Concept of Word

Full Concept of Word

In the example in Figure 4.1, the child is reading the line "Come again another day" from the nursery rhyme "Rain, Rain, Go Away." As she recites the words, she points exactly to the word that she is saying at the time, as indicated by the ✓marks.

FIGURE 4.1

Text:	*Come*	*again*	*another*	*day.*
Child Reciting:	"Come	again	another	day."
Child Pointing:	✓	✓	✓	✓

No Concept of Word

In the examples in Figures 4.2 and 4.3, two other children are pointing to the same line of print from the nursery rhyme. As these examples show, they are not showing any insight about words. Both of these children know that print carries meaning and that what is said can be printed, but they do not know where words begin and end. They don't really know what the system is. In the example in Figure 4.2, the child simply points to the first word, *Come*, and says the entire line.

FIGURE 4.2

Text:	*Come*	*again*	*another*	*day.*
Child Reciting:	"Come again another day."			
Child Pointing:	✓			

In the example in Figure 4.3, the child quickly runs his finger quickly under the print while reciting the words without pausing.

FIGURE 4.3

Text:	*Come*	*again*	*another*	*day.*
Child Reciting:	"Come again another day."			
Child Pointing:	✓——————————→			

continues

Developing Concept of Word

In between full acquisition of concept of word and none, is a second stage where a reader can point to some words accurately but not others. Usually a reader has difficulty handling multisyllabic words. In the example in Figure 4.4, the reader points to each of the words in the line until encountering a multisyllabic word. Then the learner inaccurately points to the word *another* while saying the second syllable of *a-gain*. You can see that she "runs out of words" to point to. Syllables are very prominent in the speech stream and it is not uncommon for an inexperienced child to think that a spoken syllable represents a printed word on the page.

FIGURE 4.4

Text:	*Come*	*again*	*another*	*day.*		
Child Reciting:	"Come	a-	gain	a-	nother	day."
Child Pointing:	✓	✓	✓	✓	?	?

Letter Names *and* Letter–Sounds

The following statement has resulted in some confusion, so let's unpack it:

> *The best predictor of beginning reading achievement is a child's knowledge of letter names. (Adams 1990)*

This statement is probably one of the most frequently cited bits of reading research. And like many excerpted statements from research, this one seems to suggest a clear, easy solution, a veritable cure—teach children to name letters and they will learn to read.

While research supports that letter naming *is* critical for learning to read, it is not a straight path to learning to read (Bond and Dykstra 1967; Chall 1967; Lonigan and Shanahan 2009). Invernizzi and Buckrop (2018) facetiously explain that letter naming has become like a "Ouija board" of literacy achievement: find out how many letter names children have and you can peer into their futures. Yet *naming* letters is only one facet of letter knowledge and probably not the most important one. It is the *use of* and *application of* letter knowledge that advances children.

Children use letter knowledge to read and spell. However, possessing letter knowledge will not guarantee future literacy success. Simply put, you cannot become a skilled reader without letter knowledge, but you need many other skills as well (Lonigan and Shanahan 2009).

Letter naming predicts future literacy success because it is highly related to other important factors that also have a relationship with success in literacy (Share 1995). For example, Jasmin entered kindergarten able to name all twenty-six uppercase letters, but she also sat with her parents every evening reading books, engaged in many activities in the community (e.g., visiting museums, going on guided nature walks) that built world knowledge, and attended a small preschool that focused heavily on social skills and oral language in addition to more conventional content like letters. These experiences developed her vocabulary knowledge, her print awareness, her world knowledge, her phonological awareness (e.g., rhyming and beginning sounds), and her abilities to negotiate classrooms and peers. Her ability to name letters was simply the tip of the iceberg, an easily measured indicator of a set of rich early literacy (and other) experiences.

Knowing letter–sounds is different from knowing letter names. If a child knows the name of the letter *Tt*, he will say "Tee," but if he knows the sound, he will say /t/. In most US schools, children are taught letter names and letter–sounds, but in Great Britain and in some schools in the United States, such as those following a Montessori approach, only letter–sounds are emphasized (Ellefson, Treiman, and Kessler 2009). In order to decode words, children need to know letter–sounds; this is the essential information, but teaching both letter names and sounds gives better results (Piasta, Purpura, and Wagner 2010; Piasta and Wagner 2010). It appears that with some level of phonemic awareness children use letters names to help them extract sounds (Share 2004).

When children are taught letter names they will typically learn letter names first, and usually first those at the beginning of the alphabet (e.g., *A*, *B*, *C*), then those with salient forms (e.g., *O*, *X*), and then those in their names (Drouin, Horner, and Sondergeld 2012; Justice et al. 2006; Piasta, Petscher, and Justice 2012). If you are working with a four-year-old who knows one to five letters, these letters are probably among them. The last letter names to be learned are typically *U*, *V*, *N*, and *Q*. However, these generalizations will vary based on various factors, such as the letters in the child's name, which are typically learned earlier, and other letters that may have personal significance to the child (e.g., the first letter of a sibling's name). The last skill to come is associating letters with sounds, and there is a clear pattern to how these associations typically emerge as well (Pence et al. 2009; Treiman and Kessler 2004). However, this may be a function of the greater emphasis on letter names in the preschool years. I recommend teaching names and sounds simultaneously in prekindergarten and kindergarten classrooms.

For children who learn letter names, the letter–sounds tend to be learned in a sequence that is connected to whether and how the sound of the letter is included in the letter's name (Evans et al. 2006; McBride-Chang 1999; Huang, Tortorelli, and

Invernizzi 2014; Jones and Reutzel 2012; Share 2004; Treiman and Kessler 2003). I use three labels to describe three types of letter–sounds based on letter names:

- *transparent* (also called *acrophonic*): letter names with the target sound of the letter at the beginning of the name (e.g., *b, v, t, d*); these often have a c-v structure

- *opaque*: letter names with the sound at the end of the name (e.g., *l, m, n, s*)

- *no-information*: letter names that provide no link to the sound (e.g., *w, x, h*).

Ever wonder why a child will tell you that the sound for *Yy* is /w/? Children will use information from the letter names to remember letter–sounds. Sometimes this information helps, but sometimes it does not (e.g., *Yy*'s name begins with the /w/ sound). Children typically learn the sounds for letters with *transparent* names before they learn the sounds for letters with *opaque* names, and they learn both of those prior to the *no-information* names (Treiman and Kessler 2003; Treiman et al. 1998). For example, the letter–sounds for transparent names like *Bb* are easier to learn because the name for the letter, "bee," starts with the target sound, /b/. The letter–sounds for *Yy* is learned later because the name does not match with the /y/ sound (Treiman, Weatherston, and Berch 1994). A researcher tested this pattern and found a direct, causal connection between names of letters and their sounds but only if children had some level of phonemic awareness (Share 2004). In other words, without the ability to hear sound similarities in words (e.g., *l*emon and *l*ady), children could not use the letter names information to help them. What this reinforces is that phonemic awareness activities that focus on identifying, contrasting, and matching beginning sounds help children learn letter–sounds.

Targeted Small Groups Instead of Whole-Group "Letter of the Week"

When I was growing up in the 1970s, I learned letters one at a time sitting in my kindergarten chair with the entire class. A recently published book, *No More Teaching a Letter a Week* (McKay and Teale 2015), describes why this traditional approach is ineffective:

- Teaching a letter a week does not assume mastery from week to week. Instead, the teacher moves on to the next letter each week, regardless of whether or not everyone has learned the letter.

- There is no differentiation in instruction based on the letter (*U, V* vs. *A, B, C*) and individual student knowledge is not addressed.

- The pacing of instruction does not provide the repetition and practice that it takes to learn all the elements of letters (e.g., letter–sounds, writing). With twenty-six letters and about thirty-six weeks of school for most districts, children would not be taught all the letters until the school year was almost three-quarters done. The instruction typically focuses only on naming letters even though the research tells us that phonemic awareness, letter–sounds instruction, and development of the alphabetic principle are essential (Piasta and Wagner 2010; Share 2008).

Sometimes letters are even used as the primary theme for class work—in *D* week, for example, everything revolves around *D*. Such a theme, however, is not likely to be as compelling and educative for children as a unit on fairy tales or jobs in the community or animal life cycles, for example.

Whole-group letter lessons, as the only structure for letter lessons, are often not effective. Children in kindergarten are often the most diverse in their literacy knowledge because some have had multiple years of preschool while others are experiencing their first year in a formal school setting. In one study, at the *beginning* of the year, kindergartners ranged in the number of uppercase and lowercase letters they knew (prior to any instruction) from 0 letters to 52 (Piasta 2014). Unfortunately, in many, many kindergartens everyone in the entire class gets the same letter instruction, day after day after day, on the carpet in the middle of the room.

Small-group instruction is also particularly beneficial for letter learners due to their age, maturity, and development. Young children can get distracted, zone out, or daydream. As Nancy, a kindergarten teacher, explains, "Oh yeah, I was the best teacher around when I only taught in large groups. Everyone knew everything. They were nodding and chiming in and smiling. But when I get them in a small group, I really figure out who really understands." In fact, small-group instruction actually adds value over and above *individual* instruction (Piasta and Wagner 2010). Perhaps children are learning from each other or benefiting from the feedback provided to others in the small group.

Letter Lessons Unit: Scope and Sequence

The Letter Lessons unit scope and sequence allows teachers to deliver the amount of letter instruction *based on what students need*. Teachers *use* initial assessment information to start instruction and then conduct a quick assessment at the midpoint to continue to direct instruction. The subunits in Letter Lessons are called "cycles" because the instruction keeps "cycling" back to letter–sound instruction, *based on what a student needs*. The term *cycle* most accurately captures what current research suggests about learning letters: that it is not a "one-shot deal" but rather content that should be reviewed in successive sweeps for children who need it (Jones, Clark, and Reutzel 2013).

From start to finish, the Letter Lessons unit is twenty-seven weeks, but many kindergartners start midway through. The scope and sequence covers an initial subunit for children will almost no entering letter knowledge, two subunits to teach the letter sounds, and a final subunit in which children use their knowledge to read a collection of high-frequency words. See Figure 4.5. After this unit, students should be ready for First Words with word families. In most kindergartens, this will occur by the last half of the school year, if not before.

FIGURE 4.5

Week of Instruction	Content	Notes
Letter Cycle 1: What's in a Name?		
• Children who know 0–5 letter–sounds		
1	Name (own)	Write name, read name, name letters, cut up names
2	Names (class)	Sort by first letter, sign in, find a word that starts with _____
3 optional	Names story (class)	LEA (language experience approach): stories with each person's name, "read" your own sentence with accurate pointing
Letter Cycle 2: First Pass		
• Children who know 6–10 letter–sounds (if Letter Cycle 1 is not done)		
• Slower pace, more time per letter		
4	m, a	Note: This sequence is *suggested* only. Although there are many different considerations in presenting letters (e.g., letter frequency, visual contrast, transparent letter name, sonority), there is not at this time a clear evidence-based sequence for teaching letter names and sounds together.
5	t, s	
6	e, b	
7	o, l	
8	f, g	
9	n, p	
10	r, d, i	
11	j, u, k	
12	c, v, y	
13	h, q, z	
14	w, x, h	

After Letter Cycle 2, *assess* all letter–sounds.

- Children with 21+ letter–sounds should do Letter Cycle: 4 Word Building
- Children with 11–20 letter–sounds should do Letter Cycle 3: Review/Solidify

Letter Cycle 3: Review/Solidify

- Children who know 11–20 letter–sounds
- Faster pace, less time per letter
- More focus on harder letter–sounds
- Note: Six weeks is suggested, but cycle length will depend on assessment.

15	Letter sounds that are *somewhat* challenging l, m, s	Letters taught in this six-week unit are based on the assessment taken after Letter Cycle 2 or the placement test.
16	f, n	Content should prioritize ***letter–sounds not known***.
17	g, h, q, e	The sequence on the left can be used if it matches student knowledge.
18	Letter sounds that are *most* challenging	
19	r, w, o,	
20	y, x, i, u	

Letter Cycle 4: Word Building

- Children who know 21+ letter–sounds
- Use letter–sounds to teach high-frequency words and related decodable words

21	so, no, go, + [the]	
22	we, me, he, be, + [said]	
23	up, not + [look]	*-ot* word family
24	it, in, is, his + [for]	*-it* word family
25	to, do, you + [and]	*-in* word family
26	can, man, ran + [little]	*-an* word family
27	Review	

Letter Cycle 1: What's in a Name? (0–5 Letter–Sounds)

Letter Cycle 1: What's in a Name? is a light introduction to letters based on children's names and it is based on Cunningham's (1988) brilliant work. This two- to three-week subunit is for children who truly know very few, if any, letter–sounds (0–5). Often this may mean children who are English language learners, children in prekindergarten, or children for whom kindergarten is their first formal schooling experience. During this subunit, the goal is for children to learn how to recognize their own name, write their own name, and understand, if possible, the target letter–sounds for the first letter in their name. (Note: Sometimes target sounds for first names can be complex.) In this whole-class subunit, the teacher will work with the class to analyze each child's name, count the number of letters, focus on the beginning sound, and/or group names with similar sounds together.

A few words about the length of the subunit: If the class is mostly beginners or if the class is large, then this unit could actually be closer to four weeks long. Twenty days would allow analysis of twenty different names. If the class has a lot of students who already know letter–sounds, it should not go for longer than three weeks, since most children will get bored and instructional time should be maximized with more instructionally appropriate activities.

Sometimes a child's name will not match to the typical sound that we think of when we have the letter. For example, *Juan* has a *Jj*, but the initial sound is not /j/. In these cases, it's best to simply acknowledge that the sound that the *Jj* represents in the name *Juan* is unique and special, just like people, and that it reflects the child's home, family, and culture.

Sometimes a teacher will actually do this subunit with everyone in the class. This subunit is unlike any of the other letter cycles, and its goals are simple. Children should be able to

- **Recognize and write their own names.** One of the very first real applications of letter knowledge to which children are exposed is their own name. Many kindergartners can recognize their own names, but they may not know how to write their names, put the letters in their names in order, or identify their names without context. For kindergartners, practicing spelling their names is both a highly pragmatic and exciting activity. At the very least, this subunit should address writing *first names*; if 60 percent or more of the kindergartners can write their first name, this unit can also address *last names*.

- **Identify an increased number of uppercase and lowercase letter names.** Children at this very early stage are still learning letter names, and the activities in What's in a Name? will help them add more letter names to their knowledge.

- **Distinguish a word from a letter and practice concept of word.** During this subunit, children begin to see how letters and words are related to each other. Through activities such as counting letters and doing word puzzles, they acquire the insight that letters are the building blocks of words. Words are groups of letters. As children "read" their sentences with *their* name and *their* ideas, they point to each word as they say it, practicing this essential starting point for the alphabetic principle. They use letter names and letter–sounds as they point to words in these sentences.

What's in a Name? Lesson Framework with Activities

Unlike all other subunits in this book—which follow the sequence of Review-It, Hear-It, Decode-It, Spell-It, Read-It—What's in a Name? has *three* lesson parts:

1. alphabet review
2. names with the whole group and
3. names with an individual or partner.

See Figure 4.6 for activities in weeks 1, 2, and 3 for each lesson part (review, whole group, small group, or individual).

FIGURE 4.6

1. Alphabet Review	2. Names Whole Group	3. Names Individual or Partner Activities
Every day, the teacher models pointing to letters and naming them using an alphabet arc or a letter strip. *Children* sing and point to letters once they have watched the teacher enough to handle their own manipulatives. Always remind them, "Look at the letters when you say them!"	**Week 1**	
	Put each name on a sentence strip. Stack the names up in a column and compare them. • Which is longest? Which is shortest? • Which start with the same letter? • How many letters do they have? • What words rhyme with *Tate*?	Name Card: Child traces name card. Child uses a dry erase marker to write name using name card as a guide.
	Hold up each name and ask the child to come up and "claim it."	
	Play the "In My Name?" game. Draw a line on a dry erase board with one side labeled "Letters in my name" and the other side labeled "Letters not in my name." Pull out a child's name card and grab a handful of magnetic letters. Hold up a letter, and ask the child to decide if it is "in my name." Put the letter in the correct column.	Child plays the "In My Name?" game.

1. Alphabet Review	2. Names Whole Group	3. Names Individual or Partner Activities
	Week 2	
	Compare names using a Venn diagram. Pull out two name cards. Draw a Venn diagram. Write the names at the top of the diagram. Place the letters in proper places.	Child plays Venn diagram game with a partner.
	Cut off the beginning sound of a name and then put it back on the name.	Name Puzzle: Child has a name card and name puzzle (cut-up letters of the name). Child puts the letters of the name in the correct order using the name card. Later in the unit, take the name card away and have the child do this from memory.
	Cut up the entire name and then use another copy of the name to match the cut-up pieces back.	Magnetic Letters: Same as name puzzle but with magnetic letters.
	Star Child (Cunningham 1988): Put all the name cards into a basket and randomly choose one each day. Pull it out. Analyze the name.	

continues

1. Alphabet Review	2. Names Whole Group	3. Names Individual or Partner Activities
	Week 3	
	Create a sentence for each child in this format: _____ likes to _____. (e.g., *Katie likes to ride her bike.*) Point to the words and read. Ask the child to point and read.	Sentence: Child illustrates sentence. Child reads sentence.
	Make a class book with all the LEA sentences. Read each sentence each day. Have each child illustrate their page.	LEA Book: Create a small version of the sentences in the LEA book and let children work together with buddies to read the LEA book.

Letter Cycle 2: First Pass (6–10 Letter–Sounds)

Letter Cycle 2 is the first powerful dose of instruction and presents all the letter–sounds across eleven weeks. It is for students who know 6–10 letter–sounds. Most kindergarten students will start here. Depending on the school calendar, Letter Cycles 1 and 2 will be completed after three and a half months, at least by the winter holidays in mid-December. After Letter Cycle 2, teachers reassess and identify students who know 21 or more letter–sounds or 20 or fewer letter–sounds.

Letter Cycle 3: Review/Solidify (11–20 Letter–Sounds)

Letter Cycle 3 is a second pass of Letter Cycle 2 for students who know 20 or fewer letter–sounds. It is a review for children who need it. Both letter names and letter–sounds are emphasized, with particular focus given to letter–sounds because that is the information needed for reading. Pictures are used to help children listen for sounds, and alphabet strips or alphabet arcs are used to review naming the letters every day. Simple "caption" books with one to three words per page help students acquire concept of word and use their burgeoning letter–sounds knowledge in authentic print experiences.

The specific sequence for the letter–sounds in Letter Cycles 2 and 3 is simply a suggestion. There are probably about as many different sequences for teaching letters as there are teachers, and research has yet to establish one perfect sequence. (Note, however, that children learn certain letter–sounds more easily than they learn others, as discussed earlier.) In general, the order and groupings of letter–sounds were identified by considering the frequency of a letter (how often it appears in print), the sound of a letter (whether it can easily be stretched, e.g., *s*, *m*), the difficulty of the letter–sound in relationship to its name (*b* vs. *h*), and visual properties (*b* vs. *p* vs. *d*).

Letter Cycle 3 is a faster-paced six-week subunit to review and solidify letter–sounds. It is for children who have 11–20 letter–sounds. Instruction in Letter Cycle 3 is based on the letters that a group of children do not know. Thus, the content cannot be listed specifically. If Letter Cycle 3 starts at the beginning of the year, the placement test results are used to identify the letters taught. If Letter Cycle 3 follows Letter Cycle 2, then the teacher gives the test for Part A.3: Letter–Sounds again, after Cycle 2, and uses this information to guide the content.

Even though the content is specific to assessment data, it is likely that many children in this cycle will need the same letters. As described above, there is research that indicates the letter–sounds that tend to take longer to learn. In Figure 4.5, the section for Letter Cycle 3 lists letter–sounds that are most challenging and those that are somewhat challenging. Of course, children can have gaps in their knowledge and it is common for some of the "easier" letters to be taught in this review cycle.

Although six weeks are dedicated to this cycle, it is possible that it might only take three. Letter Cycles 2 and 3 do not vary in the content and in many respects the lesson activities will be very similar. Each lesson has a brisk, engaging format with five predictable parts:

1. All-Alphabet Review and Letter Banks (5 minutes)

2. Hear-It (phonemic awareness) (5 minutes)

3. Target Letter Activity (7–9 minutes)

4. Spell-It (5 minutes)

5. Read-It (text reading) (5 minutes)

For Letter Lessons, each child should have

- a laminated alphabet strip with their name clearly written on it as a model

- their own "letter bank"—a ring of cards with the letters on it

- a dry erase board and marker, and

- the text that is being read.

Letter Lessons usually take place in small groups for about twenty to twenty-five minutes, five times per week. Letter Cycles 2 and 3 both focus on helping children to become automatic with letter–sounds knowledge and use that knowledge as they attempt to spell words. The primary difference between these two cycles is that Letter Cycle 3 is often a review for children who need more work or a subunit for children who enter kindergarten with 11 or more letter–sounds. Thus, the pace is a bit faster in Letter Cycle 3 and the content of the cycle is shaped by what the assessments tell us children need to learn. Usually more emphasis is given to the harder, later-developing sounds (e.g., *y*, *w*, *h*, *g*, *x*, *qu*). Figure 4.7 shows the goals for Letter Cycles 2 and 3. For some children these will be met with only one letter cycle, but for others it may take two.

- **Say all single-consonant letter–sounds and short vowel letter–sounds fluently.** In order to *use* letter–sound knowledge in their future decoding and writing, students need to gain command of all consonant letter–sounds. The Common Core State Standards require this to be obtained by the end of kindergarten.

- **Identify the sound at the beginning of a spoken word.** Research shows that letter instruction that combines with phonemic awareness will result in better letter–sounds and letter name learning (Piasta and Wagner 2010). As letter instruction takes place, a simple series of oral activities builds capacity for hearing sounds at the beginning of words.

- **Use letter–sound knowledge to spell and read words.** One of the best ways to gain fluidity with letter–sounds is to practice spelling dictated words or words of students' own choosing that begin with the target letter–sounds. Even if students cannot spell the word fully and include the vowels, the practice of pushing themselves to use invented (or temporary) spellings is very powerful.

- **Develop concept of word.** Concept of word is developed in a small-group lesson by allowing children to "read" memorized simple books. What is most important during these readings is that the child say the words and point to them at the same time. A coordination between print and voice should be occurring. This is not reading in the traditional sense because children are not sounding out words or using all the patterns.

Lesson Framework with Activities for Letter Cycles 2 and 3

The lesson framework for Letter Cycles 2 and 3 is shown in Figure 4.7.

FIGURE 4.7

		Lesson Part	Content	Sample Language	Activity Choices
1	5 minutes	**All-Alphabet Review** (Rehearse)	Say the names and sounds of letters.	Teacher: Watch me as I sing this song and point to each letter. I am making sure that my finger matches the letter that I am saying in the song.	Sing and point the alphabet with an alphabet strip. Easier: Name the letters on a letter ring. Harder: Alphabet Arc: 1. Name each letter. 2. Say its sound. 3. Place it on the arc. Other games you might try: Find It!, Reverse Bingo, Slap It! Pick Up.
2	5 minutes	**Hear-It** (Analyze) Phonemic Awareness (Beginning Sounds)	Orally identify two words that have the same beginning sound or identify the beginning sound in a word.	Teacher: This is Larry. Larry Lion. Larry likes *lemons*. Larry likes *limes*. Larry likes *lollipops*. Teacher: Same or different? I am going to say two words. You tell me if they start the same. *Ffffish, ffffish, ffffish, ffffun*. Do they start the same? Yes, /f/ and /f/ are the same.	Picture Sorts Same or Different? Silly Sentences

continues

FIGURE 4.7 (continued)

		Lesson Part	Content	Sample Language	Activity Choices
3	7–9 minutes	**Target Letter** Activity (Analyze)	Identify the letter–sounds for each letter.	We have these two letters Nn and Pp. What are their sounds? /p/ and /n/. Let's draw a sound. /p/ what could I draw that starts with the /p/ sound? Oh I know! Pillow. I will draw a pillow and write the letter p next to it.	Matching Games Letter Scavenger Hunt Letter Dominoes Bingo Letter Sound Match Draw a Sound Turn It
4	5 minutes	**Spell-It** (Synthesize)	Write the beginning sound (or more) in dictated words.	Teacher: I am going to start to write the word *happy.* Let's see, how would I start this word? /h/. Oh, h. Now let me keep saying this word, *hhhaaapy.* I hear p, p. I think there's more: *hhhhhapppy.* I hear e, e. [At the earliest stages it really helps for teachers to model invented (nonperfect) spelling that matches a reasonable approximation that a child might make.]	Magnetic Letters Dry Erase Boards

	Lesson Part	Content	Sample Language	Activity Choices
5 minutes	**Read-It** (Apply)	Develop concept of word: accurately point to words while saying them in a simple book using beginning sounds.	Teacher: Before reading this book, let's do a book walk. Look, this little girl is getting dressed. What is she putting on? What's this? Child: A shirt. Teacher: Yes, there it says, "my shirt." Teacher: Watch me as I read and point. [Read and point without looking at the words.] Is that right? Do I need to look at the words? Okay, I'll try again. I'll be very specific, and when I point to a word, that's when I'll say it.	Caption Books (1–2 words per page) Predictable Books (1 repetitive sentence per page) Routine: 1. Book Walk (teacher led) 2. First Reading (teacher led) 3. Second Reading (individual readings of the book *with accurate pointing and teacher feedback and correction*)

5

How to Choose a Good Alphabet Strip

Alphabet Strip

Why is an alphabet strip so important?

The alphabet strip provides a clear example of each uppercase and lowercase letter and a picture mnemonic for the target sound for each letter. Alphabet strips are important because they are the first "go-to" for primary learners when they need help with letters and sounds. Students are going to look at that alphabet strip when they want to remember which way the *b* goes or cannot quite remember what sound /v/ makes. It's easy to simply glance over an image on a computer or in a catalog and think, "Oh, that's cute. It's colorful. The kids will love it," but I strongly suggest reviewing each picture and each letter on the strip to make sure that the images and letter forms are accurate and helpful. Without careful attention to details, a teacher may be paying the price all year (e.g., "No, that's a *jaguar*, not a lion. Remember *J* makes the /j/ sound. No, we don't make the *a* that way. We just use a ball and a short stick."). Know that many commercially made alphabet strips contain images that do not connect to the learning purposes for those images.

When choosing an alphabet strip, ask:

Are the letters clear and simple? Do they match the way you want children to *write* letters?

The letters should be perfect models of the manuscript system. Avoid alphabet strips that include letters with cursive-like embellishments or that obscure the letter's shape or distract from it.

Do the pictures serve as good exemplars for the target sound?

The purpose of the picture is to provide an easily recognizable cue that will help the children remember the sound represented by the letter.

- **Vowels:** We want children to learn both the long vowel sounds and the short vowel sounds, but because the vowel name automatically teaches the long vowel sounds (e.g., the name *Aa* [ay] *is* the long vowel sound), we typically picture the hardest vowel sound to learn, the short sound (e.g., /a/ as in *apple.*). For short vowels, make sure that the target picture begins with a clear short vowel sound. For example, a picture of an orange for the letter *O* is not a good idea because it starts with the /or/ sound and not the /o/ sound.

- **Consonants:** Make sure that for consonants the pictures begin with a clean consonant sound, not a digraph (e.g., *sh, ch, th, ph*) or blend (e.g., *br-, gr-, bl-*). For example, a picture of a shirt for the letter *S* is a problem because it does not start with the /s/ sound but starts with /sh/. In addition, pictures with blends at the beginning (e.g., *grapes, float*) are difficult because it is very challenging to say only the consonant sound in the blend (e.g., it is difficult to say /g/ and not /gr/ in the word *grapes*.)

- **Beginning sound is not a letter name:** Sometimes the beginning sound of a word is actually the same as the name of a letter. For example, *elephant* begins with the sound of the letter name *Ll*, a fact that could confuse a child in learning letters.

Are the pictures in the children's spoken vocabulary?

If children do not know the words represented by the picture, then the picture cannot help them (e.g., *yacht*). Pictures should represent very common words, with age-of-acquisition levels that are lower than five years, to account for the many young children who enter primary grades with less than optimal vocabulary knowledge.

Are the pictures unambiguous?

The pictures should not be easily confused with something else. When a child looks at a picture of what is supposed to be a carpet and thinks *rug*, then the picture is not helpful for cueing the letter–sound. Another example is a picture of a puzzle piece under the letter *J* for which a child is supposed to think *jigsaw*.

continues

Do pictures represent a holiday or event that is offensive to a particular group?

Things like jack-o-lanterns, birthday cakes, or Christmas trees are not good choices because they may offend a group of people. On an alphabet strip that is going to be seen and used almost every day, this can be a particular problem.

Are the pictures realistic?

The pictures should not be fantastical renderings of the target item, animal, or person (e.g., an cat in pajamas). The pictures should be realistic interpretations that cue the letter–sounds. The easiest items for children to interpret are simple, high-quality photographs of items.

Some Pictures for Letter–Sounds (Duke 2016)

Short *A* is for *Apple*, long *A* is for *Acorn*

B is for *Ball*

C is for *Cat*

D is for *Dog*

Short *E* is for *Egg*

F is for *Fish*

G is for *Goat*

G is for *Giraffe*

H is for *Hat*

Short *I* is for *Iguana*

J is for *Jump rope*

K is for *Key*

L is for *Leaf*

M is for *Moon*

N is for *Nose*

Short *O* is for *Octopus*

P is for *Pumpkin*

Q is for *Queen*

R is for *Rainbow*

S is for *Sock*

T is for *Toothbrush*

Short *U* is for *Umbrella*

V is for *Violin*

X is for *X-ray* (or you might want to do *Exit* or *Fox*—this is a hard one to deal with; I do suggest avoiding *X* is for *Xylophone*, as that sound for *X* is so rare)

Y is for *Yo-yo*

Z is for *Zebra*

Letter Lesson Template

The lesson template in Figure 4.8 can be used to plan lessons for all the subunits in Letter Lessons.

FIGURE 4.8

Letter Lessons Cycles 2 and 3 Weekly Lesson Template

Subunit: _____   Lesson #: _____   Letter/Sound Focus: _____

	All Alphabet Review *(Rehearse) 5 min.*	Hear-It *(Analyze) 5 min.*	Target Letter Activity *(Analyze) 7–9 min.*	Spell-It *(Synthesize) 5 min.*	Read-It *(Apply) 5 min.*
Monday	Activity:[1] / List New Letters	Activity:[2] / Words/Notes:	Activity:[3] / Words/Notes:	Activity:[4] / Words/Notes:	Title:[5] / Pattern & Content Words:
Tuesday	Activity:	Activity: / Words/Notes:	Activity: / Words/Notes:	Activity: / Words/Notes:	Title: / Pattern & Content Words:
Wednesday	Activity:	Activity: / Words/Notes:	Activity: / Words/Notes:	Activity: / Words/Notes:	Title: / Pattern & Content Words:

	All Alphabet Review *(Practice) 5 min.*	Hear-It *(Analyze) 5 min.*	Decode-It *(Analyze) 10 min.*	Spell-It *(Synthesize) 5 min.*	Read-It *(Apply) 5 min.*
Thursday	Activity:	Activity: / Words/Notes:	Activity: / Words/Notes:	Activity: / Words/Notes:	Title: / Pattern & Content Words:
Friday	Activity:	Activity: / Words/Notes:	Activity: / Words/Notes:	Activity: / Words/Notes:	Title: / Pattern & Content Words:

1 All ABC Review Activities: ABC Rings, Bingo, Go Fish! Find-It, Alphabet Arc, Sing and Point with Alphabet Chart

2 Hear-It Activities: Silly Sentences, Tommy Tiger, Breaking Pictures, Picture Sorts, Which One? Share a Sound, Mother May?

3 Target Letter Activities: Matching, Scavenger Hunt, Letter Dominoes, Draw a Sound, Picture Sorts, Letter Sound Match, Pick-up, Hopscotch, Slap-It

4 Spell-It Activities: Tracing letters, Air writing, Letter Bank, Dictation with Dry-Erase

5 Read-It Routine: Book Walk, First Read (Teacher, I read/you read, Choral), Second Read (Independently), Praise and Practice, Reread—POINTING IS THE POINT.

For a downloadable PDF of this template, go to http://hein.pub/letterlessons-login.

What follows are a series of activities organized as they would appear in each section of the lesson. For example, after the All-Alphabet Review description are games like Find It! and activities like Sing and Point. The activities listed in Figure 4.9 are all routines that can be used during All-Alphabet Review.

All-Alphabet Review Depending on the skills of the learners, teachers can use different review techniques, including singing the alphabet and pointing to letters on an alphabet strip, games with the alphabet strip, letter banks, or alphabet arcs. Keep in mind that these review activities and routines should not be conducted the same way every time. When you use the same activities every time, the lesson turns into a "drill." As described in Chapter 3, students do need to practice beyond the point of mastery. However, remember that the key is multiple exposures in multiple contexts, meaning that students should see letters on an alphabet chart and a ring of cards and an alphabet arc.

When I have done All-Alphabet Review, I have noticed that some children look around the room as they are pointing or get a little sloppy toward the middle, where they don't know the letters. During the All-Alphabet Review, it is very important for the teacher to make sure that the pointing and singing or talking are matching *exactly* and that each child's eyes are on the letter being pointed to. Without attention to these two details, children are not getting anything from the activity.

Sing It One of the easiest alphabet activities is singing the alphabet using an alphabet strip to point to letters. Once the children have become skilled at accurately pointing to the letters and naming the letters, the teacher can play games like Find It!

Letter Bank The second activity is Letter Bank and it requires students to name each letter or sound. A letter bank is a collection of letters that the child knows and is learning, a bit like a word bank. After assessing each child, the teacher identifies some of the letters that the child can name (both uppercase and lowercase) and puts them on a ring. As the small group learns new letters, the teacher adds them to the letter bank ring. During the Letter Bank part of the lesson, each student simply names the letters while the teacher provides feedback. This part of the lesson is the most differentiated portion because each child is practicing the letters that they need to know. Teachers will frequently extend the Letter Bank activity and have the children take it home to practice.

In some homes, finding the time to practice the Letter Bank activity is a struggle. When Hunter, a child whose single mom worked two jobs, was not retaining his letters, his teacher decided on a different approach. She had him go to a different "special teacher" in the building every morning to "show off" his letter bank. The guidance teacher, art teacher, assistant principal, and cafeteria manager all listened to him name his letters and signed a laminated card on the ring. On Friday, Hunter was rewarded with time "helping" each of these people for ten minutes before school. This worked because Hunter really needed adults in his life to practice the letters with him and he also needed adult attention and affection.

Alphabet Arc The Alphabet Arc is the most difficult activity for students, but it is a great challenge for students in Letter Cycle 3. The arc is a mat with outlines of uppercase or lowercase letters in an arc. Students place plastic letters in each space on the mat. Students name, sound, and place each letter on the mat (e.g., a student picks up an *F*, says "*F*, /fff/," and then places it in the *F* space). After the letters are placed, students check their work by touching and saying each letter. In the beginning, the routine is untimed, with the focus on all three essential parts of the routine: naming, sounding, and placing. Students start with an uppercase arc and then move to a lowercase arc. Once students can successfully place all the letters, teachers can time them. Most children can name, place, and sound the letters in two minutes.

FIGURE 4.9

Activities for All-Alphabet Review (Easier)	
Sing and Point—Alphabet Tune Alternative (to "Mary Had a Little Lamb")	
A, B, C, D, E, F, G	Mary had a little lamb,
H, I, J	little lamb,
K, L, M	little lamb.
N, O, P, Q, R, S, T	Mary had a little lamb,
U, V, W,	His fleece was
X, Y, Z	White as snow.

Find It! (Alphabet Strip)

After students can sing, point, and name the alphabet during All-Alphabet Review, play Find It! Ask the children to point to different letters on the strip.

   "Find *B*."

Make it more complicated by asking children to find an uppercase or lowercase letter.

   "Find uppercase *J*. Find lowercase *t*."

Turn the game over to the children and let them call out letters for the group to find.

continues

Pick Up! (Letter Bank)

The teacher tells the students to pick up different letters.

"Pick up *x*."

Reverse Bingo (Letter Bank)

Using the letter bank cards and a three-by-three grid, students place their cards face down on the grid. The teacher identifies the bingo pattern (straight line, diagonal, X, or blackout). Each child turns over a card and names the letter. If the answer is correct, then the letter can stay turned over. The student to first make the pattern wins.

Name It! (Alphabet Strip)

Once students can point to letters that the teacher names, ask them to name the letters that the teacher points to.

"Name this letter" (point to *f*).

Activities for All-Alphabet Review (More Difficult)

These activities are designed to practice quickly saying the letter–sounds of known letters and those being learned.

Alphabet Arc

Alphabet arcs, letters, and activity books are available from Neuhaus Education (neuhaus.org). Give students a set of alphabet letters and ask them to match the letters to the outlines on the arc. For this to work, students *must* follow this routine:

1. Name it. (Student says the name.)

2. Sound it. (Student says the sound.)

3. Place it.

4. Check after placing all the letters.

Caution: Handing a student in the early phase a pile of twenty-six plastic letters and an arc will result in a lot of confusion and distraction. Students in the early phase can use letter cards (also available from Neuhaus) that include only five letters on a card.

Slap It!

Slap It! is a card game that is played with a deck of letter cards. Pairs of students play this game. A deck of cards is placed between them. One player flips the card and the first player to slap the card and correctly name the sound gets to keep the card. The student with the most cards at the end of the game wins. In order to validate their "win," students must recite the letter–sounds of all the cards they are holding.

Caution: Some children really do slap and some children never get a chance to name a sound because their partner is too fast. If this is the case, simply change the game so that each person gets a turn. One person flips the card and counts quietly ("1, 2, 3"). If the other player can name the sound in three seconds, then that player gets to keep the card.

Letter–Sounds Hopscotch

This game is a bit like regular hopscotch, but not exactly. Students simply practice hopping to different letters and saying the sound of each letter landed on. Use a large shower curtain liner to re-create an alphabet mat. This is a favorite "reward" activity that can be done on Friday.

S	F	U	A	G	R
E		L	T		U
B	N	O	P	A	X
M	L	A	W	O	J
D		K	J		H
C	Y	I	Q	V	Z

Hear-It (Phonemic Awareness) The goal of this part of the lesson is for students to say the sound at the beginning of a pictured or spoken word (e.g., "What sound do you hear at the beginning of fffffish?"). The sounds that students will recognize in this part of the lesson will match the target letters for the week. Remember that phonemic awareness concentrates on oral and aural (listening) work. If a manipulative is used, then it is usually a picture or item that represents the sound.

Because phonemic awareness usually develops in very predictable ways (Anthony et al. 2003), activities should move from the least difficult to the most difficult, following this sequence:

Easiest: Discriminating Between Different Sounds

- Same sound?

  Student can tell you if words begin with the same sound.

  > "Do *boy* and *cat* begin the same way? Do *boy*, *ball*, and *bib* start the same way?" (Start by contrasting two words, and then move to three.)

  Student can tell if two to three sounds are the same.

  > "Are these the same? /s/ /s/. Are these the same? /f/ /f/ /l/." (Pause between sounds.)

- Same or different sound?

  Student can tell you which sounds or words are the same and which ones are different.

  > "Are these sounds the same? /f/ /f/ /l/. Which one is different?"

  > "Do these words begin the same way? *Cat, keep, sip*. Which one is different?"

Harder: Matching First Sounds in Oral Words

- Student can group/sort pictures or items by sound.
- Student can categorize or sort pictures by initial sound.

  > "Here are some pictures. *Cat, bag, kite, boy, bowl*. Does *bbbbbag* go with *ccccccat* or *bbbbboy*?"

Hardest: Saying the First Sounds in Words

- Student says the beginning sound of a word or picture.

  > "What sound is at the beginning of *late*?"

FIGURE 4.10 Teacher Language That Helps Children Focus in Letter Lessons

When reviewing the alphabet	Look at the letters when you say them.
After writing a word	What does that say? Ask the child to read the word they wrote, pointing to the letter–sounds.
When "reading" a caption text	Point to each word as you say it. Insist on accurate pointing.

Following are activity ideas for Hear-It (Figure 4.11). There are three important things to do when planning and conducting Hear-It:

1. Keep the activities very simple. Many times, the subunit is only oral.

2. Think carefully about the words that will be used and look through pictures before starting. At the very beginning of this type of work, single-consonant sounds are easiest (i.e., *not* consonant blends such as *tr*, *sl*, *str*). In addition, *continuant* sounds, those that can be continued or stretched out, should be used (e.g., *f*, *l*, *m*, *n*, *r*, *s*, *v*, *z*). When using pictures, teachers should name the pictures up front and be ready to take out any one that students chronically mislabel.

3. Remind students to *say* each word or sound. Speech sounds have both physical and aural (heard) components, and when children say the sound, they learn how the sound feels in their mouth.

FIGURE 4.11

Activities for Phonemic Awareness

Same or Different? (Discriminating Sounds)

Using pictures or just oral words, the teacher names words, emphasizing the first sound, and asks students if the sounds are the same or different.

"Listen to these two words: *mat, mike*. Same or different? Listen again: *mmmmmmmat, mmmmike*."

Extensions: Once students can contrast two words or sounds, add a third.

If the sounds are different, ask the student to identify a word or a sound that is the *same* as the target.

"Yes, *bbbbballl* and *ssssssip* are different. What word sounds like *bbbbball*?"

Silly Sentences (Identifying a Word with the Same Beginning Sound)

This light and playful game is adored by kindergartners, who find making up silly words and sentences hilarious. It is based on children's intuitive, semiconscious awareness of sounds. The teacher says a silly sentence with words that begin with a target sound. Children complete the sentence.

"Silly Sara sang songs in [on/at] her _____."

continues

Picture Sorts (Identifying Words with the Same Starting Sounds)

Students sort pictures with either two or three different sounds (e.g., *b*, *l*, *m*) into groups. Select pictures that are easy to interpret and that represent contrasting sounds. *Words Their Way: Letter and Picture Sorts for Emerging Readers* has over thirty sorts with pictures already selected. Use the following routine:

Routine for Picture Sorting

1. *Name* each picture.

2. *Set up* the anchor pictures. (Use pictures that match the target sound, e.g., a ball, a leaf, and a mop.)

3. *Say* each picture and compare it to the key letter/words/pictures by *saying the picture name*. For example:

   "This picture is a *log*. Ball/log? Leaf/log? Mop/log? [A student answers.] Yes, *leaf* and *log* start the same. I will put the leaf here, under the log."

4. *Check* for mistakes.

   Take the anchor picture and hold it beside each picture that was placed in the group, saying the anchor and the words.

   "*Ball/box, ball/bag, ball/bear.* Do they all match?"

5. *Reflect.*

   "These pictures are in this column <u>because they all start with /l/.</u>"

Breaking Pictures / Blending Pictures (Blending and Segmenting Onsets and Rimes)

The goal of this game is to have students practice orally breaking words into onsets and rimes (e.g., *b-at*) or blending an onset and rime together (e.g., *bat*). Start with blending, and then move to segmenting.

Use a set of pictures that are single-syllable words and cut them in half. Sometimes it is even fun to do this as you break the word.

"Did you know that words have parts and that we can break them up? Watch me, I am going to cut this bee in half and say the first sound. *B-ee* [cut as you are speaking]. *B-ee.* Two parts, *b-ee.*"

"Look at the picture. I am going to say the parts and you are going to put the parts together like this. I would say '*b-ee*' and you would answer '*bee!*'"
Give each child a picture. Say the word in parts and ask them to say the word back to you.

After several days, once the children have become skilled with blending, reverse the task.

"Now I am going to give you a picture and you are going to break the first sound off for me. So if I gave you this picture [show a picture of a peach cut in half], you would say '*p-each.*'"

Follow the same routine, giving each child a practice item and rotating items as you move from child to child.

Caution: This is not as easy as it sounds. Children frequently need a lot of practice and a lot of modeling. Do not give up if this does not come easily. The activity is really quite powerful.

Target Letter Activity The Target Letter Activity is at the heart of the lesson. The goal of the Target Letter Activity is for the student to name and provide the sound for both uppercase and lowercase letters. It would be close to impossible to enumerate the many different activities that could take place. The activities in Figure 4.12 provide some ideas. There are, however, certain principles to keep in mind in choosing activities.

Early in Letter Cycle 2, children need to visually discriminate the letter shapes and attend to the most salient features of each letter's shape. Visual matching activities help with visually discriminating letters (e.g. What makes an *Nn* different from an *Mm*?). Examples might include games with letter cards, or letter clip games where students use clothespins on a letter wheel.

As students move into the middle of Letter Cycle 2 and into Letter Cycle 3, they should do activities that focus on letter–sounds, saying the sound that matches the letter, or finding objects that start with a letter's sound. These are the most challenging activities because they require students to call up the letter–sounds themselves, which is necessary to read words. Simple card games where students turn over and then name the letter and its sound are great. Follow-the-path games where students move to a space and name the letter and sound are also good.

In essence, the activities in the Target Letter Activity part of the lesson will consistently target the same skills. The content of the activities will be repetitive, but they should be creative, fun, engaging, and brisk. They should not feel boring to the children (see Figure 4.12).

FIGURE 4.12

Activities for Target Letters

Early Phase (Letter Naming, Recognition, Visual Discrimination)
Students name letters and match letters that are the same (uppercase to uppercase, uppercase to lowercase).

Matching Games

Students match letters at two levels. In the first level of matching games children match the uppercase forms (e.g., *A* to *A*, *B* to *B*), and in the second level they match the lowercase forms to the uppercase forms (e.g., *A* to *a*, *B* to *b*).

It is also possible to match lettered clothespins to letters on a wheel.

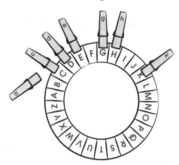

Font Sort/Match

One activity that helps children generalize the visual features of letters is to do a font sort. Letters written in different fonts are provided and children group them together.

Letter Scavenger Hunt

To reinforce the alphabetic principle and the purpose of letters, have children go on an alphabet scavenger hunt. Each child takes a magnetic letter and a dry erase board and tallies the number of times they find their letter in the classroom, the hall, a walk around the school, or a big book.

Letter Dominoes

Students match letter dominoes with the target letter. Dominoes with all uppercase letters, all lowercase letters, or a mix can be created for different levels of matching.

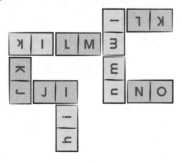

Activities for Target Letters

Later Phase (Naming Letter–Sounds)
Students identify the sound that connects with a letter.

Matching Items or Pictures to the Correct Letter

Items or pictures that begin with the target sounds are laid out on the table. Near them are bags or just the letters (*Bb*, *Ss*).

Students find the items or pictures that begin with the sounds and put them in the corresponding bags.

Letter–Sounds Match

Students have a group of cards with the target letters and a group of pictures. They match the letters to the pictures that begin with that sound.

Letter–Sounds Dominoes

Students have dominoes with both pictures and letters. They match the pictures on the dominoes with the letters that match the beginning sound.

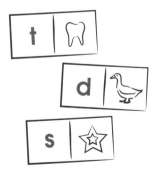

continues

Activities for Target Letters

Draw a Sound

Students create a table, with two to three letters at the top. Then, they draw items that have the first sound that matches the letters.

Nn	Pp

Bingo or Turn It

The teacher has a pile of pictures that begin with the target sounds. Students have letter cards with the target letters or a bingo board with the target letters. The teacher flips the card with the picture, say the name of the picture, and students identify the letter that matches the picture by turning the letter card over or removing it. Three-in-a-row wins the game.

Gg	Rr	Gg
Rr	Nn	Nn
Nn	Gg	Rr

Spin a Letter

The teacher has a bag full of letters or a spinner with the target letters. Students have pictures that match the target sound. The teacher spins the letter, says the letter name only, and the students must know the letter–sound and choose the right picture.

Spell-It

In Letter Lessons this part of the lesson amounts to writing letters, first to learn the general shapes and then later to begin "spelling" by thinking about letter–sounds. Children use a dry erase board and marker to complete a number of different activities. Early in Letter Cycle 2, when children are first learning the letters, Spell-It is about simply making the letters. The teacher models how to write a letter and the children repeat it on their boards. Large dry erase markers are fine-motor-skills-friendly for little hands. When showing children how to make letters, don't get too bogged down in handwriting, which can be done later as a whole group. The idea is to simply practice once or twice the letter form. In the Spell-It portion of the lesson in Letter Cycle 3, the child writes to match a dictated word. See Figure 4.13.

FIGURE 4.13

Activities for Spell-It
Tracing Letters (Easier)
Children trace letter cards with the target letters on them after the teacher models where to start each letter and how to make it.
Air Write (Easier)
After the teacher models how to write a letter, the children and teacher together "air write" the letter. A fun game is "guess my air write," where a child or the teacher air writes a letter and the others have to name the letter.
Letter Bank Writing (Easier)
After some practice writing letters, students use their letter banks and practice writing letters that they know on a dry erase board.
Dictation (Harder)
The teacher says a word that matches a target sound and students write the first letter (and any other letters that they hear) on a dry erase board. In earlier lessons, when students need support, an alphabet strip is displayed. In later lessons, students write the letter without the alphabet strip reminder.

Read-It Letter Cycles 2 and 3 finish with text "reading," an authentic application of letter knowledge. When people hear about "book reading" with kindergartners, they either think of a read-aloud, where the teacher is doing the reading, or they think of a developmentally inappropriate activity, because most kindergartners are not really reading. In Letter Lessons, what is called "text reading" focuses on concepts of print and concept of word practice. It has two goals: (1) accurate pointing to words while saying them and (2) using letter–sounds to ground pointing.

Children each have a simple book, they hold that book *themselves*, and point to the repeating words as they say them. It's the very first step. Children are not really blending and decoding full words. In many cases, they would not know the words in text without the pictures. But they are *using* letter–sounds at the beginning of words in a very exciting way.

Two types of books are used during Read-It in Letter Cycles 2 and 3. One type is simple repetitive caption books, which literally label the pictures with one to two words (e.g., "My pants."). When children "read" these texts, they are practicing differentiating words from pictures, pointing to words, and differentiating two words from each other. In order to point to the words in the caption in the figure, the learner does use the pictures and memory but must pay even closer attention to each word because there are two. To read "My pants," the child must distinguish the word *my* from *pants* in a more technical approach.

Caption Book

My pants. My shirt.

- One or two words per page in a repetitive sequence.
- All print on one line.
- Minimal multisyllabic words.
- Interchanged word is directly pictured.

The other text type is a slightly more complex, "predictable" text where a sentence stem is repeated (e.g., "This is my hat. This is my jacket."). The text design, with the repetition and the close match to the picture, helps children memorize the text so that they can coordinate their pointing.

Predictable Text

This is my hat.

- Predictable one-line sentence.
- One repetitive sentence per page.
- All on one line.
- Minimal multisyllabic words.
- Interchanged word is directly pictured.
- The child uses the repetitive structure ("This is my _____ ,") memory, pictures, and letter–sounds to support word recognition. The interchanging last word may encourage more attention to letter–sounds.

Often at this stage children are impulsive or careless with their pointing. Text reading must be carefully monitored. I like to remind children, "Eyes on the page. Fingers ready." By reminding them that they must point to the word that they are saying, we are helping them learn that using letter–sound knowledge is a very precise endeavor.

Figure 4.14 shows the routine for Read-It.

FIGURE 4.14

Read-It Routine

Before the Lesson: Preview the Book

Never use a book in a lesson without first previewing it.

Before using any book, preview it and find the sentence pattern (e.g., "This is my _____.") or the category (e.g., fruit, clothing, toys). Review the content words and pictures. Look to see how closely the target content words match the pictures or if the content words are likely to be in a child's vocabulary.

For example, if a book has a word like *iguana*, which children are not likely to know, you have to teach that vocabulary prior to reading.

Step 1: Book Walk

In a book walk, I hand the children the book and we talk about the content and story, flipping the pages. I ask them what they see in the pictures. This helps them remember the target content words (e.g., *hat*).

If there is a content word that I don't think they know, I tell them the word and define it (e.g., *tower*).

Step 2: First Reading—Teacher Guided

At this stage I rarely ask children to "read" these books without practice. We do that together for the first time. There are three options:
• Teacher read (easiest): I read the whole book and they point. Sometimes we do this two times.

• I read / you read: I read and point a page and then they do. "'This is my hat.' Now you do it."

• Choral read (hardest): We read and point the book all together. This is for the easiest books.

Step 3: Second Reading—Child Reads *and Points*

The *pointing* is the *point*, so make sure it happens.

After one or two times with me, the child reads and points to the print alone. I watch, looking for accurate pointing and helping when it gets off track.

Step 4: Praise and Practice

At the end of the book, I find something the child did well.

"When you came to *hat*, you weren't sure. You paused and looked at the word, then you said '/h/' and I think that you remembered *hat*. You used your letter–sounds."

I also might return to a place that caused trouble and review or reteach.

"Let's look at this part again. It said, 'This is my belt,' but you said 'This is my pants.' Could that be *pants*? Watch me point to that word. My mouth says '/ppp/,' but I am pointing to this word [*belt*]. Is that right?"

continues

> **Step 5: Reread**
>
> After the children have read the book once by themselves, I ask them to reread the book to other teachers, cafeteria staff, counselors, family members, and friends. I like to say, "If you read it once, you should read it six more times!"

What Is a Book Walk?

A book walk is a preview of the book that a teacher does with a student *before* the student reads. The purpose of the book walk is to practice reading words, give the student a sense of what the story will be about, and also to review, front-load, or preteach words in the book that might be challenging. Book walks should be different at different stages of development. In Letter Lessons, when students are using predictable or caption books and beginning sounds to read, the book walk focuses on introducing the pattern in the book (e.g., "I like green grapes. I like yellow pears.") and the content words (e.g., *grapes*, *pears*). These words are usually pictured and they cannot really be sounded out. During the book walk, the teacher points out the pictures and might also note the colors, since they are part of the pattern. Sometimes the teacher also points out high-frequency words that the child knows. After the book walk, the teacher and child read the book.

A book walk for a decodable text, which contains words that the child can sound out, will get a different kind of book walk. In this kind of book walk, the teacher identifies words that have patterns that the child knows (e.g., "Do you see any words with *-ap*?"). This gives the students a chance to practice sounding out those words prior to reading them in the text and draws their attention to known letter–sound patterns.

VIDEO 4.2

Book Walk Explanation

This clip explains what a book walk is and why it needs to be different with different types of books.

VIDEO 4.3

Book Walk for a Predictable Text

See this video for an example of a book walk for a pre-dictable text.

WATCH

VIDEO 4.4

Example of Why a Book Walk Is Necessary

See this video for an example of why a book walk is necessary. (The student did not know the word *pears*.)

Letter Cycle 4: Word Building (21+ Letter–Sounds)

Because the need for review is increasingly not common, Letter Cycle 4: Word Building bypasses a second dose of letter instruction and introduces students to the first 25 high-frequency words by helping them *use* their newfound letter–sounds knowledge to read words. As discussed in detail in Chapter 5, high-frequency words are those that occur a great deal in English and must be learned early because they are so important to text reading (e.g., *the, said, you*).

The Word Building subunit, Letter Cycle 4, is for students who know 21 or more letter–sounds, and it focuses on learning 25 words on the preprimer Dolch list and applying letter–sounds knowledge to read these. What we know is that children will retain high-frequency "sight words" best if they use letter–sounds (Ehri, Satlow, and Gaskins 2009; Steacy et al. 2017; Wang et al. 2013). Based on research, instead of having children memorize these "sight words" holistically, teachers should not give high-frequency sight words heavy instructional attention until solid letter–sounds knowledge (as well as concept of word and initial phonemic segmentation) is established. (Note: Some high-frequency words can and should be taught while children are acquiring letter–sounds. In the course of reading charts, doing interactive writing, and engaging in print referencing activities, it makes sense to teach a handful of useful words like *the*. However, systematic instruction using high-frequency lists is best given once students have solid letter knowledge.)

Each week usually has a group of words that are very similar (e.g., *so, no, go*) and then one additional word that is less predictable (e.g., *said*). See Figure 4.15. In the first weeks, most of the words have two sounds and usually two letters (e.g., *so, no, go, we, me, the, in, it, is, to*). In later weeks, word families are introduced that can be built from known high-frequency words. Three-sound / three-letter words are added (e.g., *can, man, ran*). Beginning in the third week of the unit or Lesson 23, students can learn c-v-c words in families that match a taught high-frequency word. For example, the students learn the word *not* and build words with the *-ot* family (e.g., *hot, pot, got*). (See Chapter 5 for word family strategies.) When you encounter patterns that the children have not learned, for example, the *th* digraph in *the*, show them how to map the sound to the two letters, without overteaching or worrying too much about the complexities. Take the same approach with the *ou* in *you* and the *ai* in *said*.

FIGURE 4.15

Lesson	Week	Content	Extra Word Families
21	1	so, no, go, + [the]	
22	2	we, me, he, be, + [said]	
23	3	up, not + [look]	*-ot* word family
24	4	it, in, is, his + [for]	*-it* word family
25	5	to, do, you + [and]	*-in* word family
26	6	can, man, ran + [little]	*-an* word family
27	7	Review	

The goals of the Word Building subunit are to

- **Read and spell 25 high-frequency words both in isolation and in text.** Although there is nothing unique about teaching kindergartners high-frequency "sight words," focusing on the letter–sounds in these words *is* unique. Often we try to tell students that these words are so irregular that you could not possibly learn the letter–sounds, but this is not true.

- **Orally blend and segment the words.** What we know is that both reading words and spelling words require students to blend and segment sounds. In this subunit, children begin to do that with the simplest of words, those that have two sounds. During this part of the lesson Elkonin boxes are used to segment the word, and this provides an important practice for decoding later in the First Words unit.

- **Use high-frequency words to build c-v-c word families.** In most of the units, the students use one of the high-frequency words to build new words with word families.

- **Read high-frequency words in books.** Students practice applying their knowledge of words by reading predictable and caption books.

Word Building Lesson Framework with Activities

Children in kindergarten usually get really excited when the focus of lessons moves to "real words." The lesson format is similar in many respects to First Words lessons but with a few differences. The review section of the lesson in Letter Cycle 4: Word Building involves mostly the high-frequency words that are being learned, but since children still need to solidify a few letters, there are some letters in the review. See Figures 4.16 and 4.17. The word ring will have letters and words, usually letters like *Vv*, *Ww*, and *Yy*, which are typically the last to be learned. During the review section, students will most often simply read the words, since this is time efficient. However, some games are included in Figures 4.16 and 4.17 to add interest. It's ideal if the words can come off of a word ring so that students can sort the words or play other games.

FIGURE 4.16

		Lesson Part	Content	Sample Language	Activity Choices
1	5 minutes	**Review-It** (Rehearse) Practice reading individual high-frequency words.	High-frequency words from scope and sequence and previous lessons.	Teacher: Please get out your word ring and whisper read each word.	Word Rings or Cards, Matching Games (Pick Up, Concentration, I'm Thinking)—see video: **WATCH** **VIDEO 4.5** **Word Card Practice** Watch this video to see children practicing words in a whole group lesson.
2	5 minutes	**Hear-It** (Analyze) Phonemic Segmentation and Blending	Orally break a word into each sound (*go* = /g/ /o/, *you* = /y/ /ou/). Orally blend words together (/g/ /o/ = *go*).	Teacher: I am going to break this word into its sounds. Here I go. /s/ /o/. Now watch me push my finger into a box for each sound. /s/ /o/, *so*. I'll do it again. /s/ /o/, *so*. Now you do it.	Elkonin Boxes Unifix Cubes Secret Word Secret Word—see video: **WATCH** **VIDEO 4.6** **Secret Word Activity** In this video the teacher is playing Secret Word with the whole class.

continues

		Lesson Part	Content	Sample Language	Activity Choices
3	7–9 minutes	**Decode-It** (Analyze) Decode high-frequency and related decodable words.	Decode each sound in a word.	Teacher: Take the words off your rings. [*I, a, so, no, go, we, me, the, in, it, is.*] Now I am going to put these in two groups. Here's a group with *o—so, no, go,* here's a group with *e—we, me,* and here's a group with *i—in, it, is.* so me in go we it no is	Word Sort Read the Words Cut up Words Unifix Cubes
4	5 minutes	**Spell-It** (Synthesize) Spell high-frequency and related decodable words.	Write words letter-by-letter, paying attention to sequence.	Teacher: Now we are going to start with the word *go.* /g/ /o/. Spell that word. Touch the part that makes the /g/ sound. Pull that down. Now spell *so.* /sssss/ /o/. Teacher: This word is hard. It has the sounds /th/ /u/. The first sound is tricky; it has two letters. Spell /th/.	Magnetic Letters Dry Erase Boards Word Building Making Words

		Lesson Part	Content	Sample Language	Activity Choices
5	5 minutes	**Read-It** (Apply) Read in text	Practice reading high-frequency words in connected text.	Teacher: Before reading this book, let's do a book walk [see videos 4.2, 4.3, and 4.4 to look for words that we know. Do you see *no*? What about *the*? Teacher: Watch me read this and point. "I go. You go. We go. Go, go, go. Yipppeee!"	Predictable or Caption Text Routine: (1) Book Walk (teacher led); (2) First Reading (teacher led); (3) Second Reading (individual readings of the book *with accurate pointing* and teacher feedback and correction).

FIGURE 4.17

Activities for Word Review

Read the Words

The most frequent activity in this section of the lesson is simply reading the words. Students can do this alone or with a partner.

Slap It!, Find It, and **Reverse Bingo** are all great games for word review, and they were described earlier on pages 105–107.

Sample Language for Find It

Find the words that

• have an *o*
• have three letters
• have two letters
• have the sound /e/

Hear-It

This section of the lesson is all oral. There are no word cards and no letters. The purpose of this part of the lesson is to analyze the *sounds* in the new words that are being taught for that week (e.g., *in, it, is* | *so, no, go*). So children will analyze one of the high-frequency words listed in this unit. At this stage, children break words into two sound parts, either the onset and rime (e.g., *c-at*, *b-ig*) or the phoneme if the word has only two sounds (e.g., *g-o*, *th-e*, *s-ee*). The harder activity is breaking a word into parts or segmenting. The easier activity is blending parts together into a word. A variety of activities present this content to children through games (see Figure 4.18); examples include Robot Talk, Sit Down, and Unifix Cubes (Figure 4.18). (Note: Pay attention to the number of *sounds* in a word, not the number of letters. Many two-phoneme words have more than two letters [e.g., *see*, *the*]. In this section, words are broken down by sound.)

FIGURE 4.18

Activities for Hear-It: Orally breaking words into two parts
Unifix Cubes (Onset-Rime)
In this activity, each cube represents a sound and children move them together, saying the sounds and then blending the word together. ("/g/ /o/, /g/ /o/, /g/ /o/, *go!*")
Elkonin Boxes (for Two-Phoneme Words)
Boxes is a technique for breaking down words or segmenting them. It is fully described on pages 173–175.
Secret Word
Secret Word is a game where the teacher says the "secret word," broken into parts. For words with more than two phonemes, the parts are onset and rime. For words with two phonemes, the parts are the sounds. The teacher says the secret word and then the children whisper the fully blended word to a partner. (Blending is easier than breaking words down.) Once children can blend words together, then the teacher lets them say the secret word for the group, in parts. (For a demonstration, see the "Secret Word Activity" video on page 121.)

Decode-It

During this section of the lesson, students practice decoding the high-frequency Word Building words and related decodable words, using the techniques listed in Figure 4.19. Starting in Week 3 of the subunit with the *–ot* family as in *not*, students can build new words (e.g., *hot*, *pot*, *not*). Thus, the Decode-it portion of the lesson will include both the high-frequency words and those words that can be built from them. Remember, high-frequency words should be taught by using letter–sounds. Do not encourage a holistic, memory-based approach. All the strategies in Figure 4.19 are based on using letter–sounds.

FIGURE 4.19

Activities for Decode-It: Accurately reading the 25 words in the Word Building unit and related decodable words

Read the Words

When a new word is being introduced, children can simply be taught to read the new word. The following questions can guide analysis:

• What does this word start with?

• How many letters does this word have?

• What does this word end with?

• Does this look like another word we know?

• Which sounds do you here?

Word Sort

Word sorting is an activity in which children put words in groups based on similarities. Usually the teacher sets the categories (e.g., all the words with *i*) in what is called a "closed sort." With kindergartners and for the Word Building unit, create sorts in which there are two categories: words that *do* (e.g., have two letters, have *a*, have *e*) and words that *do not*. This is easier for the young child.

Words that do have *e*	Words that do not
me	i
we	it
be	it

After successful closed sorts, once the children understand sorting, ask them to do their own "open sort," in which they create categories. This is really useful for understanding what they are seeing in words.

continues

Activities for Decode-It:
Accurately reading the 25 words
in the Word Building unit and related decodable words

Cut-Up Words

A very simple activity to help children think about word architecture is this little game where you give children words written on cards and scissors.

1. Read the word.

2. Cut off the first sound.

3. Scramble the two parts.

4. Put the word back together.

5. Read the word again.

Optional Additional Steps

6. Cut apart all the letters. (For words with more than two letters.)

7. Scramble the word.

8. Put the word back together.

Match

Using their word rings and books with high-frequency words, students match word cards to high-frequency words that they see in their books.

Building on a high-frequency word

Using the high-frequency word as a base, show students how to add consonants to make new words. For example, show students how to decode *in* and then add consonants to it (e.g., *p-in, f-in, b-in*). (See Figure 5.7, pp. 153–155.)

Spell-It

In Letter Cycle 4: Word Building, the spelling activities are ones in which the teacher says the word and the children build the word. See Figure 4.20. The expectation is that children spell each word accurately, with the letters in the correct order. More than any other activity, this one solidifies the knowledge of these high-frequency words. Do you remember, in the Introduction, when we discussed the idea of "word architecture"? This is the start. Children take words apart, and then build them back to solidify and properly store those words cognitively. Because the Word Building unit is focused on learning 20 words, children are held accountable for correctly spelling these words. When a word is not spelled correctly, it is corrected and rewritten, with a gentle reminder (e.g., "Hmm you have *o* and *n*. Does that say *no*? */nnnnn/* is at the beginning. Can you fix that?")

FIGURE 4.20

Activities for Spell-It: **Accurately spelling the 25 words** **that are the Word Building unit focus**
Making Words or Word Building
Using a dry erase board, magnetic letters, or letter cards, children start with a word and then change one letter to make a new word. This is a great strategy to show how groups of words are related. (See "Making Words or Word Building Lesson" on page 63.)
Dictation
The teacher says a word that matches a target sound and students write the word on a dry erase board.

Chapter Summary

This chapter started with Troy, a joyful student who came to our reading clinic needing to learn the alphabet. Like many adults in the United States (and even some teachers), his mother was unclear about exactly what it means to learn letters. It means not simply singing a song and naming letters but, more importantly, learning the *sounds*. The letter–sounds help children move to the next essential phase and decode words. Another important principle to remember is that letter lessons must accompany rich teaching of the alphabetic principle throughout the day. Without this, the motivation, meaning, and critical *use* of letter–sounds information is lost and children will acquire a rote, inert collection of letter–sounds that are meaningless to them. The chapter focuses mostly on the contents of letter lessons, but the first part of the activities section describes a number of parallel practices that must take place within early childhood classrooms if letter knowledge is going to be useful and stick. Use these joyful and meaningful practices throughout the day to keep instruction meaning centered and balanced.

5

UNIT: First Words

Decoding

TAYLOR CAME INTO OUR READING CLINIC AS AN EAGER FIRST grader. She could proudly name any letter–sound we gave her in seconds. But sitting at the table trying to decode the word *cat* went something like this:

Text:	*This*	*is*	*my*	*cat.*
Taylor:	This	is	my	/c/ /aaaa/ /t/,
				/c/ /aaaa/ /t/,
				/c/ /aaaa/ /t/,
				/c/ /aaaa/ /t/.

Tutor: Okay, now say it faster, Taylor. Put them together. Bulldoze them.

Taylor: /c/ /aaaa/ /t/,

                       /c/ /aaaa/ /t/.

Tutor: What does it say?

Taylor   *Take*?

Perhaps you have seen a student like Taylor grasp onto the ending sound in a word and take a stab? The situation can be maddening, but as with all instruction, the problem is in the instruction, not the student. Taylor didn't have the necessary knowledge to fully blend a word like *cat* together, so that interaction gave us the information we needed to provide some targeted explicit instruction.

We started with showing her how to take a simple two-phoneme word like *at* and put the sounds together (/a/ /t/, *at*). This was easier because the word started with an open mouth (as all vowels do) and there were only two sounds to put together. She could "bite down" on that word as she opened her mouth to say the vowel and then close down on the consonant. After she got the *at* word chunk, we started having her add initial consonants to it to build words like *cat*, *bat*, *hat*, and *fat*, a research-supported approach to reading first words (Treiman and Kessler 2005; Ziegler and Goswami 2005).

Four weeks later, Taylor was reading a book and this is what happened:

Text:	*The*	*cat*	*ran*	*away.*
Taylor:	The	c|c-at|cat	run	away.
Tutor:	Almost. Something tricked you [points to *run*].			
Taylor:	The	cat	/r/ /u/ /a/,	
			/r/ /a/ /n/ ran	away.

"I got it!" Taylor beamed. This was it! The oh-so-cool-to-be-a-teacher moment when the lightbulb goes on and you know that if you had not been there it would not have happened. This moment had cost four weeks of focused, purposeful instruction and support, but it was well worth it. Taylor now really understood something new, something that would take her to the next level.

Learning to fully decode words is a game changer. When students can do it, they can reliably read words without a sentence context or teacher telling them the word. They can attack a word with no prior exposure. Seemingly overnight they can unlock literally hundreds of new words (e.g., *got*, *hot*, *rot*, *in*, *pin*, *fin*, *tin*, *win*) because they possess a reliable new strategy that differentiates them from readers guessing at words, memorizing idiosyncratic word features, or using only the beginning sounds. For the child, decoding is liberating but it doesn't happen by just telling kids to "say it faster" or "sound it out." It doesn't happen with flash cards or worksheets. It doesn't happen by rereading texts over and over. It happens when teachers observe students and then bring them "just right" instruction with plenty of practice. This chapter focuses on how to bring students joyfully to this literacy milestone.

Decoding Cements a Word in Memory

"Words? Reading words?" remarked one kindergarten teacher near the end of the year. "They already know words, a bunch of them. Their names, some high-frequency words, environmental words. They know words." This is true. Children like Taylor, even when they struggle to decode, do learn to recognize words very early, and it is very rare to encounter even the most novice learner who cannot read at least *some* words. However, often children at this stage will have word knowledge that is insecure. One day they know the word; the next day they don't. Sometimes they might know the word in one context (e.g., a big book) but not in another (e.g., a word card). At times they may seem to know a word but then confuse it with another (e.g., *took/look*, *it/in/is*). This insecure knowledge is due to the way that the early learner is storing and retrieving information. Remember when I talked in the Introduction about phonics instruction being about setting up a file system? When learners have insecure word knowledge, their file system is unsophisticated and imprecise, so they are not storing information as well as they could be. Since there are actually several ways to recognize words, readers might be able to pronounce them but might not retain critical details. In order to properly store, retrieve, and eventually automatize words, readers need to be able to decode.

In the very early stages, children recognize words holistically, using idiosyncratic features and prediction. When they know some consonant sounds, they will also use that knowledge. How does the transition from memorizing whole words to decoding happen? To the unobservant (or the observer of a child to whom this comes unusually easily), it seems like one day a child is learning letter–sounds and the next the child is reading words in what appears to be a natural progression. Oh, that this were true!

For most readers, there is a developmental progression that occurs depending on a child's knowledge and application of alphabetic knowledge.

- In the **pre-alphabetic phase**, children do not use letter–sound information to recognize words. These students are learners who need Letter Lessons.

- In the **partial alphabetic phase**, during the Letter Lessons units, children use beginning sounds, often in combination with pictures, to recognize words.

- Once children learn vowels, they can fully decode simple words with the consonant-vowel-consonant (c-v-c) pattern in the **full alphabetic phase** (Ehri 2005). The First Words unit is focused on this essential phase.

- After mastering mostly one-to-one correspondences, children consolidate multi-letter units in the **consolidated alphabetic phase**. They learn relationships with two-to-one patterns (e.g., *sh*, *str*, *ea*). Students learn these in the Beyond First Words unit.

Eventually words become cemented into memory once student have decoded them repeatedly. Then the words are accessed via automatic recognition without conscious attention. Think about it: As a skilled reader, how many words do you stop and decode? Automatization of word recognition is essential so that the reader can devote the lion's share of attention to the meaning of a text as passage lengths increase and ideas and stories become more complex.

Phases of Alphabetic Knowledge

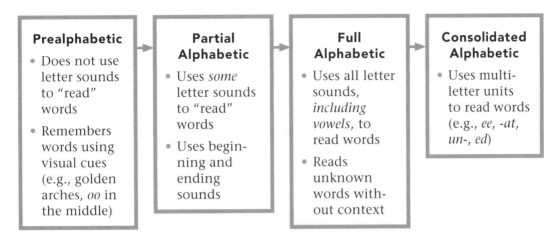

Prealphabetic	Partial Alphabetic	Full Alphabetic	Consolidated Alphabetic
• Does not use letter sounds to "read" words • Remembers words using visual cues (e.g., golden arches, *oo* in the middle)	• Uses *some* letter sounds to "read" words • Uses beginning and ending sounds	• Uses all letter sounds, *including vowels*, to read words • Reads unknown words without context	• Uses multi-letter units to read words (e.g., *ee*, *-at*, *un-*, *ed*)

Research tells us that when learners *decode*, they store and retrieve words more easily (Share 1995). This is because the learner has used a very precise, letter-by-letter "filing" system. Words like *look, took, book*, and *hook* will not be confused when stored letter-by-letter nor will a reader require a picture to "read" a word. In fact, decoding activates a "self-teaching" mechanism that supports students in more quickly acquiring new words during text reading, even when a teacher is not present (Share 1995).

How Should I Teach High-Frequency Words?

"But what about sight words?" Elva, an experienced teacher at a workshop asked me. "You've got to teach those Dolch words and those are not easy to sound out. You've just got to memorize them." Elva was partially right. Children do need to learn the very common, frequently occurring words that may have complex patterns (e.g., *the, go, to, for*). However, memorizing them using visual memory and rote approaches is not recommended.

High-frequency words are those that occur a great deal across all texts, no matter what grade level or content (Dolch 1936; Fry 2004). They are the most frequently occurring words in the English language, and scientists have determined this by sampling words in books and putting them in order from those that occur the most (e.g., *the, of, and, to, in, is*) to those that occur the least (e.g., *evaporation, mammal*). High-frequency words kick-start book reading. In order for beginners to read books of any sort, they need to learn a handful of words like *the, of, and, to, in, is, you, that, it, he, was, for, on, are*, and *with*.

In many classrooms, people call these high-frequency words "sight words" and teach them differently than other words. Reasoning that these words must be learned "visually" and "by sight" due to their irregularities, teachers encourage rote memorization or visual learning without attention to letter–sounds. Sometimes these words are taught in prekindergarten or kindergarten before children have solid letter–sound knowledge or understanding of the alphabetic principle. However, this is not effective. Using the term "sight word" for high-frequency words is not accurate. Technically, "sight words" are any words that a reader can read automatically, not just high-frequency words (Ehri 2005; LaBerge and Samuels 1974). Once a reader has decoded a word multiple times and properly stored it, the reader will access that word by *sight* without conscious attention.

In this book, high-frequency words are not introduced in a systematic way until readers know about 21/26 letter–sounds, because without letter–sound knowledge, storing words is difficult. The final unit in Letter Lessons, Word Building, introduces these words.

Essential Principles for Teaching High-Frequency Words

- **Teach high-frequency words along with phonemic awareness, individual letter–sound relationships, and concept of word.** High-frequency word instruction should not be given a great deal of attention until the child has a concept of word, some phonemic awareness at the beginning sound level, and knows *most* letter–sounds. Without these basics, storage and retrieval of words will be unsystematic and inefficient.

- **Ask students to use letter–sound knowledge to read high-frequency words** (Ehri 2005). At every possible turn, ask children to apply all their letter–sound knowledge when reading these words. For example, a child who is solidifying consonant sounds can at least use the initial sounds, using the /g/ in *go*. Many high-frequency words are very easy to sound out (e.g., *at, in, can*). Even for words that are not spelled using common letter–sound correspondences, teachers should still tell children the letter–sounds. For example, for the word *was*, teach that *w* says /w/, say *a* say /ă/.

- **Teach high-frequency words in groups that have similar patterns.** Try to group words with similar patterns together. In Word Building in Chapter 4, for example, the words *go, so,* and *no* are taught together. Even words that are thought of as "rule breakers" can be taught together (e.g., *some, come, above, love*).

- **Use high-frequency words to help children learn to decode new words.** A child who has learned *at*, for example, can use the part to build other words. In one study, children were taught high-frequency words with little attention to the letter–sounds or with extensive attention to letter–sounds (Ehri, Satlow, and Gaskins 2009). Children taught the words with letter–sound analysis could more easily apply their knowledge of word parts to new words (e.g., *strong, long*).

- **Practice reading high-frequency words in sentences and books.** High-frequency words are most applicable in book reading. Children should analyze these words individually, but they must also practice them in sentences and books.

Organize Instruction Around Patterns in Words

When teaching high-frequency words or even when teaching letter–sounds, there is a tendency for teachers to use random, unrelated words. Instead, let a clear developmental scope and sequence be the *driver* of phonics content, rather than using a serendipitous approach. Use teachable moments for emphasizing *learned* patterns found in books, poems, stories, and charts, not as a way to introduce new patterns. In some schools it can feel a little taboo to teach phonics with words explicitly and individually. However, analyzing isolated words is important. Do not excerpt random words in a random order from books as a way to teach phonics. For example, do not pull the word *cat* from a book on Tuesday and then pull *it* from a book on Wednesday and then *pen* on Thursday. This will not lead to learning, because information will be disjointed, unpracticed, and disorganized to the child. Children need time over many days to practice sounding out words. Below are some "dos."

- Use teachable moments to call attention to known patterns as you are reading: "Wow, look, I see an *-at* word right on this page. Can you see it?"

- List words in groups on charts (e.g., "*-an* Words We Found While Reading").

- Use a whole-part-whole approach. Using a scope and sequence, find books with target patterns. Introduce the target pattern (e.g., *-at*) in a text and then teach the pattern in isolation, returning to the book to read and apply.

- Use decodable texts or phonics readers.

First Words Unit: Scope and Sequence

The First Words unit is about the pivotal transition from partial alphabetic word reading to really sounding out words in the full alphabetic stage. How does a teacher know when readers are ready to "sound out" words by themselves? Children who are ready for the First Words unit can easily name 21/26 letter–sounds within five seconds.

The scope of First Words is short vowel sounds in single-syllable words as well as consonant blends and digraphs. See Figure 5.1. In addition, the unit embeds 50 high-frequency words from the pre-primer and primer levels of the Dolch list. The base of the unit is learning how to read a word with a short vowel sound, and then consonant blends and digraphs are added.

Subunit 1: Letter–Sound Review

The First Words unit takes twenty-four to twenty-six weeks depending on whether or not you do the Letter–Sound Review. It is usually a good fit for children in mid to late kindergarten or the beginning of first grade, but this will depend on how you differentiate. If the unit starts at the beginning of the year, the first subunit, Letter-Sound Review, targets specific letter–sounds that children need to solidify after a long break from school. The content is based on the specific letter–sounds that are unknown, as assessed on the Placement Test. This unit is entirely optional based on the students. If after two weeks, a student is not automatic with nearly all the letter–sounds, it may be necessary to go back to the Letter Lessons: Letter Cycle 3 subunit.

Subunit 2: We Are Family (Short Vowel Word Families)

The next subunit, We Are Family, presents first words using short vowel c-v-c word families or rimes in a ten-week unit. Children learn how to blend the two-sound word family (e.g., *-at*, *-ig*) and then add initial consonants to the word family (e.g., *cat*, *bat*, *rat*). This word family approach is especially useful at the beginning of sounding out words because children have to retain only two sound units. In Weeks 8 and 11, short *e* and short *i* words that have the double *ll* at the end are added.

For different groups of students, the We Are Family ten-week subunit might require extension or compression. Some children catch on to short vowel sounds very quickly. If that happens, you can shorten the two weeks allocated for each short vowel sound to one, but *make sure to teach the common rimes* marked with an asterisk in Figure 5.1. For some groups, the unit might need to take twelve weeks, with tougher patterns reviewed. If a long holiday break comes in the middle of this unit, add a week or two. Always let the responses of the students and your professional judgment be the driver. Use the *sequence*, but speed up or slow down as necessary.

The order of the sounds (i.e., *a*, *i*, *o*, *u*, *e*) separates those that are really similar so they are not taught adjacently (e.g., /e/ vs. /i/). As defined in Chapter 1, a word family or rime is the vowel in a word and all that comes after it (*-at*, *-og*, *-ick*). Instead of asking a child to sound out a word sound-by-sound (e.g., *g-o-t*), we introduce decoding by showing students how to blend the two sounds in the word family (e.g., *-ot*) and then add a consonant to that unit (e.g., *g-ot*). However, after that first step, students will also practice sound-by-sound decoding; fully segmenting and blending short vowel words letter-by-letter requires full analysis, and this firmly impresses each letter of the pattern into memory (Ehri 2005; Hulme et al. 2002; Muter et al. 1998).

The word family starts things off for three reasons:

1. *It's easier at first.* The easiest way to decode first words is to have children retain the word family "chunk" (e.g., *-og*) and then change the initial consonant (i.e., *hog*, *dog*, *fog*). Changing the beginning sound in a word family (e.g., *f-an*, *t-an*, *r-an*) is easier than blending three sounds together (e.g., *f-a-n*).

2. *It matches how children develop awareness of sounds (phonology).* Children can hear the word family unit more easily than they can hear individual sounds. The ability to hear larger units (e.g., words, syllables, rimes / word families) develops before the ability to hear smaller ones (e.g., individual sounds) (Lonigan and Shanahan 2009).

3. *It is more natural.* When it comes to the parts of words, children can more naturally *break down* the parts of a rime / word family (*b-et*) but must receive more instruction to break down the separate sounds (e.g., *b-e-t*) (Carroll et al. 2003). When decoding instruction builds on rimes, it is more successful initially (Treiman and Kessler 2005; Ziegler and Goswami 2005).

In each week, the first activity is to blend the sounds in a word family and add a consonant (e.g., *b-at, c-at, f-at, h-at*). Word wheels or flip books (see Figure 5.7) are good strategies for this stage. For word families with an asterisk (see Figure 5.1), using word wheels is a good idea because you know that there will be a lot of words to make with a wheel.

A great activity to do at this stage is Word Building, where you start with a word family and then go up the ladder changing sounds (McCandliss et al. 2003).

In the second week, additional word families are added (*-ap, -ad, -am,*) and the instruction should move to letter-by-letter decoding. Word families are a great first step, but they are not enough. Children must move on to fully segmenting and blending all letter–sounds in words, not just a beginning sound and a rime. They must understand that *hog* has three units represented by three sounds—/h/ /o/ /g/—and not two units (e.g., *h-og*). If decoding and spelling instruction does not go beyond word families, children will confuse units that end with the same letters, like *-ag* and *-og*. In fact, if children learn the first 3,000 words in their reading books using *only* word families, they will actually have to learn *more* information, not less. There are 400 different word families / rimes in those first 3,000 words rather than 44–45 sounds (Ziegler and Goswami 2005). So breaking words down by individual *sound* and corresponding *grapheme* is essential.

Starting in Lesson 6, the second week of a word family introduces a contrast where words all have the same last letter but different middle vowels (e.g., *-um* vs. *-am*, *-it* vs. *-at*, *-ot* vs. *-it*). After teaching the word families for the week, you should have children read words from previous lessons *along with* a word family of the week. When children practice reading words like *sit, sat, bit,* and *bat*, they must pay attention to the middle sound and fully decode the word. Comparison activities can include sound and letter boxes in which students hear sounds and then spell them in the boxes. Word sorts are also useful. Dictation, Word Building, and Making Words are other activities that help students spell words letter-by-letter. (For descriptions, see the "Activities" section on pages 104–127.) These activities will help children retain information and transfer their knowledge to new word families (Hines et al. 2007).

FIGURE 5.1

Week	Letter–Sound Pattern	Example Words	High-Frequency Words
1. Letter–Sound Review			
1	**Missed letter–sounds**	The content in this section is letter–sounds students did not know. Use assessments to identify letter–sounds for review.	
2	**Missed letter–sounds**		
2. We Are Family (Short Vowel Word Families)			

3	**Short *a* (-at*, -an*)**	Step 1: Blend together /a/ /t/, then add consonants to the -at family.
		  -at* bat, cat, fat, hat, mat, pat, rat, sat
		Step 2: Do Step 1 with -the -an word family, then compare to -at words.
		  -an* can, fan, **man**, pan, ran, tan
			two

4	**Short *a* (-ap*, -ad, -am)**	**-ap*** cap, lap, map, rap, sap, tap **-ad** bad, dad, **had**, mad, pad, sad **-am** ham, ram, jam	have

5	**Short *i* (-ip*, -in*)**	Step 1: Blend together /i/ /p/, then add consonants to the -ip family.
		  -ip* hip, lip, rip, sip, tip, dip, nip, zip
		Step 2: Do Step 1 with -in family, then compare to -ip words.
		  -in* bin, fin, kin, pin, sin, tin, win
			into

6	**Short *i* (-it*, -ig, -ill*, id)**	**-it*** bit, fit, hit, kit, lit, pit, sit, wit, zit **-ig big**, dig, fig, gig, pig, rig, wig **-ill*** bill, fill, gill, pill, sill, **will** **-id** bid, did, hid, kid, lid, rid Contrast: -it vs. -at bat, cat, fat, hat, mat, pat, rat, sat	saw, was

Week	Letter–Sound Pattern	Example Words	High-Frequency Words

7	**Short o** (-op*, -ot*)	Step 1: Blend together /o/ /p/, then add consonants to the -op family.
		  -op* cop, hop, mop, pop, top
		Step 2: Do Step 1 with -ot word family, then compare to -op words.
		  -ot dot, got, hot, lot, **not**, pot, rot
			my

8	**Short o** (-ob, -og)	**-ob** cob, job, mob, rob, sob **-og** hog, jog, log, fog, dog Contrast: -ot vs. -it **-it** bit, fit, hit, kit, lit, pit, sit, wit, zit	on, all

9	**Short u** (-ug,* -un)	Step 1: Blend together /u/ /g/, then add consonants to the -ug family.
		  -ug* bug, hug, jug, mug, pug, rug, tug
		Step 2: Do Step 1 with -un word family, then compare to -ug words.
		  -un run, fun, sun, bun
			are, for

10	**Short u** (-ub, -ut, -um)	**-ub** cub, nub, rub, sub, tub **-ut but**, cut, gut, hut, nut **-um** gum, hum, sum Contrast: -um vs. -am **-am** ham, ram, jam	pretty, what

11	**Short e** (-et, -eg)	Step 1: Add a consonant to the -et word family.
		  -et bet, **get**, **let**, jet, met, net, pet, **set**, wet, vet, yet
		Step 2: Add a consonant to the -eg word family, then compare to -et.
		  -eg beg, leg, peg
			help, yes

12	**Short e** (-ed, -en, -ell*)	**-ed** bed, fed, led, **red**, wed
		-en men, hen, den, pen, **when**
		-ell* bell, sell, **well**, **tell**, Nell, fell
		Contrast: -eg vs. -ig vs -og
		  dig, fig, gig, pig, rig, wig
		  hog, jog, log, fog, dog
			out, our

continues

Week	Letter–Sound Pattern	Example Words	High-Frequency Words
3. Two for One (Consonant Digraphs)			
13	**sh- (at the beginning)**	**sh-** shed, ship, shack, shut, shin, shock	she, see
14	**-sh (at the end)**	**-sh**, fish, dish, wish **-ash*** dash, cash, rash, mash, hash, lash	one, come
15	**th-**	**th- that**, **this**, **then**, thin, thick	with, three
16	**ch-**	**ch-** chat, chin, chip, chill, chop, chum	there, where
17	**-ck**	**-ack*** back, jack, pack, rack, sack, tack **-eck** deck, neck, peck **-ick*** kick, lick, pick, sick, tick, wick **-ock*** dock, lock, mock, rock, sock **-uck*** buck, duck, luck, muck, suck, tuck	they, here
4. Beginning Blends (Consonant Blends at the Beginning)			
18	*r*-blends (**fr-, br-, cr-, dr-**)	**fr-** frog, fresh, frill, fret **br-** brim, brag **cr-** crab, crash, crop, cross, crib **dr-** drum, drip, drill, drop, dress	brown, down, now
19	*r*-blends (**gr-, pr-, tr-**)	**gr-** grab, grip, grass, grill **pr-** prom, prop, press **tr-** trap, track, trick, trim, trash	soon, too
20	*l*-blends (**bl-, cl-, fl-, gl-, pl-**)	**bl-** blot, bled, blush, bless, **black** **cl-** clap, clip, club, class, clock, club, clam **fl-** flag, flat, flap, flop, flip, fled, floss, flash, flush **gl-** glad, gloss, glass, glob **pl-** plan, plot, plum, plug, plus	say, play, away
21	*s*-blends (**sc-, sk-, sl-, sm-**)	**sc-** scab, scan **sk-** skip, skim, skin, skit, skill **sl-** slam, slap, slip, slim, slop, slip **sm-** smack, small, smell, smash	please, who

Week	Letter–Sound Pattern	Example Words	High-Frequency Words
22	*s*-blends (sn-, sp-, st-, sw-)	**sn-** snap, snob, snug, snack, sniff **sp-** spot, spell, spit, spat, span, sped **st-** stack, stem, step, stop, stuck **sw-** swam, swan, swell, swim, swat	yellow, funny

5. Final Blends and Digraphs (Consonant blends at the End)

Week	Letter–Sound Pattern	Example Words	High-Frequency Words
23	-st	**-est*** best, rest, test, nest, west, pest, chest, vest **-st** fist, list, mist, mast, fast, cast, last, **just**, **must**, dust, bust, rust, gust, crust, trust, past, blast, mast	new, blue
24	-ing* -ng	**-ing*** ring, sing, bring, thing, wing, sting, sling, fling, swing, **-ng** rang, rung, hung, bang, sang, slang	good, find
25	-nk	**-ank*** bank, tank, Hank, prank, crank, blank **-unk*** bunk, hunk, trunk, spunk, junk, stunk, sunk, plunk **-ink*** think, mink, sink, link, pink, rink, stink, drink, wink, blink	ate, came, make
26	-nt -mp	**-nt** bent, rent, tent, dent, **went**, hint, mint, lint, hunt, punt, runt, rant, pant, **want**, chant **-mp** stamp, **jump**, camp, ramp, chimp, limp, chomp, stomp **-ump* jump**, bump, lump, mumps, hump, dump, stump, pump, plump, slump	ride, white, like

Notes: Example words have been carefully chosen as optimal "teaching words." They include *only* target letter–sounds or letter–sounds previously taught in this scope and sequence. Use these words in Decode-It and Spell-It lesson sections. The lists are not exhaustive.

High-frequency words are specifically chosen to be taught alongside the subunit. Often (but not always), these match a letter–sound pattern being taught. Sometimes these words are grouped together by pattern (e.g., *ate, came, make | ride, white, like*), but sometimes they have been chosen to match previously taught patterns.

Bold words in the "Example Words" section are also high-frequency words.

* Word families marked by the * are in the list "37 Most Common Rimes" by Wylie and Durrell (1970). These will generate many new words and are essential to teach. First Words covers 21 of the 37.

Subunit 3: Two for One (Consonant Digraphs)

The Two for One subunit teaches common consonant digraphs (e.g., *th*, *sh*, *ch*), two letter–sounds that represent one sound, in a five-week subunit. In this subunit, these sounds are added to the beginning or ending of words with short vowels. The *sh* sound and *ch* sound can be difficult to distinguish. Say those two sounds and you can hear how close they are. It can be helpful with these two sounds to show the children how the *ch* sound creates a burst of air and the *sh* does not. I like to say that *ch* ch-ch-chugs and the *shhhhhhhh* is quiet. (Note: In the First Words unit, some of the words include double consonants that retain the same sounds [e.g., *-ll*, *-ss*]. These are not explicitly taught in the book, so you may have to slow down and do a little extra teaching.)

Often this subunit goes very fast because many children already know these digraphs and simply need to add them to word families. Also, these letters become unitized and quickly applied. After teaching traditional consonant digraphs, the subunit presents, in the last lesson, a series of short vowel words with *-ck* at the end. Students usually learn this pattern very quickly. In this collection are 4 of the 37 most common rimes (i.e., *-ack*, *-ick*, *-ock*, *-uck*).

Subunit 4: Beginning Blends (Consonant Blends at the Beginning)

The next subunit, Beginning Blends, provides a six-week focus on consonant blends at the beginning of short vowel words. The *r*-blends (e.g., *fr*, *tr*, *br*) and the *s*-blends (e.g., *st*, *sl*, *sk*) get the most attention. For many children, especially for blends at the beginning of words, the insight about how these patterns work can come very quickly. Often if a child gets one *r*-blend, for example, *fr*-, and then others almost do not need to be taught—the insight just comes.

Subunit 5: Final Blends and Digraphs (Consonant Blends at the End)

The last subunit addresses final blends (e.g., *-st*, *-ng*, *-nt*, *-mp*) in a four-week period. The patterns in this subunit are very important because several are useful rimes that will generate many new words (e.g., *-est*, *-ing*, *-ank*, *-unk*, *-ink*). The *-st* lesson also includes the common rime *-est*, which will generate a great number of words. Other lessons include the common rimes *-ing* and *-ank*. Note that for *-ing* and *-ank* the vowel sound is not really a short sound. For the *i* in *-ing* the sound is more of a long *e* sound, and the *a* in *-ank* also takes more of a long sound. These two patterns, however, are important and really accelerate the word learning that will support text reading.

Lesson Framework and Activities

The lesson framework includes the following five parts: Letter or Word Practice, Hear-It, Decode-It, Spell-It, and Read-It. Here is a brief explanation of the specific goals for each part of the lesson.

Letter or Word Practice

- **Review letter sounds or words.** Children review challenging letter–sounds (e.g., *h*, *y*, *w*), words from previous lessons (e.g., *-at* words), and high-frequency words.

Hear-It

- **Identify rhyming words (orally).** As part of the early work with word families, students practice hearing words that rhyme and generating both real and silly rhyming words. This primes them for understanding word family decoding.

- **Segment and blend words into two parts: beginning (onset) and word family (rime).** Students segment and blend words using onset and rime parts. For this section, the reader should be able to segment a word into a beginning sound and rime (e.g., *t-ip*) and then should be able to blend that word together (e.g., *g-ot = got*).

- **Fully segment a word into each sound.** Beginning at Lesson 6 in We Are Family, phonemic awareness moves from hearing the larger sound unit in the word family unit to fully segmenting words into *each* sound (e.g., *b-a-g* vs. *b-ag*). This skill builds capacity for decoding (Nation, Allen, and Hulme 2001; Muter et al. 1998).

- **Identify the two to three sounds in a consonant blend.** When consonant blends are the focus, phonemic awareness moves toward identifying the sounds in consonant blends (e.g., *gr-*, *str-*, *gl-*), often using pictures. When students can hear these sounds, they can usually access them to read and spell words.

Decode-It

- **Blend the sounds in a c-v-c word family and add consonants to the family.** The child first blends the sounds together in a word family unit (e.g., *-og*) and then adds consonants to the beginning (e.g., *h-og*, *b-og*).

- **Blend individual sounds in c-v-c words with single consonants or consonant blends.** Beginning with Lesson 6, where contrasts are introduced, decoding focuses on blending all three sounds in a short vowel word together. Students are given words with different medial vowel sounds so that they must pay close attention to each vowel and correctly pronounce that sound. This is challenging.

Spell-It

- **Accurately spell words with short vowels, blends, and digraphs.** This task requires synthesis. The teacher dictates a word from the family and the child assembles the letter–sounds to spell it. In order to do this, the student must get each sound in the word family in the correct order.

Read-It

- **Read words in decodable books.** Students practice reading texts containing taught short vowel word families. The text reading supports transfer of knowledge. Students are held responsible for fully decoding words.

The lesson framework for First Words applies to all subunits and is shown in Figure 5.2. Note that for Hear-It and Decode-It there are two options. The boxes that are shaded identify content that is taught later in First Words (after Lesson 6). In the Hear-It section, early lessons focus on onset-rime and rhyming, and later lessons focus on fully breaking a word (see shaded part). In the early lessons for Decode-It, the focus is blending a c-v word family (e.g., *a-t*) and then adding a consonant to it (e.g., *m-at*). In Lesson 6 and later lessons, Decode-It focuses on fully sounding out individual sounds (e.g., /m/ /a/ /t/) (see shaded part). Figure 5.2 provides an overview of the parts of the lesson with content, sample language, and activity choices. Following the figure is a more detailed discussion of each part with a description of specific activities. For several very powerful activities (i.e., Unifix cubes, word sorting, Word Building, and Elkonin boxes), detailed directions are provided in the "Activities" section (see pp. 173–175).

FIGURE 5.2

		Lesson Part	Content	Sample Language	Activity Choices
1	5 minutes	**Letter and Word Review** (Practice)	Read words. Practice difficult letter–sounds.	Teacher: Please get out your word ring and whisper read each word.	Word Rings or Cards Games (Bingo, Go Fish!) I'm Thinking (see page 121 for a link to a video of children playing this game)
2	5 minutes	**Hear-It Early (Onset-Rime)** (Analyze) Rhyming Onset-Rime Segmentation	Say rhyming words. Say beginning sounds + word families. b-ag c-an b-ig ch-ug d-ish th-at	*Orally* identify words that rhyme. Teacher: *Bag*, /b/ / ag/. What rhymes with *bag*? *Gag*? Yes! *Lag*? Yes! *Hag*? Yes, *-ag, -ag, -ag. Bag, gag, lag, hag*, they all have *-ag*. What rhymes with *fig*?" Student: *Dig*. ———— *Orally* blend words using onset and rime (e.g., *c-at = cat*). Teacher: *N-ap, n-ap*. What word is that? Put the sounds together. Student: *Nap*. ———— *Orally* break words into onset and rime (e.g., *c-at, d-ig*). Teacher: *Bet*. How can you break the word *bet* into two parts? Student: *B-et*.	Chugging Sounds Unifix Cubes Rhyming Words Secret Word Note: This is *all oral*. Manipulatives can be used such as blocks or markers, but letters are not used.

continues

		Lesson Part	Content	Sample Language	Activity Choices
2	5 minutes	**Hear-It Later (Segment Fully)** (Analyze) Phonemic Segmentation	Orally break a word into each sound (*lit* = /l/ /i/ /t/). Orally blend *each* sound in a word together (e.g., /s/ /a/ /t/ = *sat*).	(Early) Teacher: *Ship*. How can you break the word *ship* into three sounds? Student: /sh/ /i/ /p/. _____ (Later) Teacher: *Grin*. What sounds make up the /gr/ part of *grin*? Student: /g/ /r/. Teacher: Which of these pictures start with *gr*? *Gate* or *grill*? Student: *Grill*.	Elkonin Boxes Order: • two-phoneme words with vowel at beginning (*at, in*) • two-phoneme words with vowel at end (*go, no, see*) • three-phoneme words with continuants (*sssssit, mmmman*) • three-phoneme words with stops (*tttip*) Picture Sorts for Blends

		Lesson Part	Content	Sample Language	Activity Choices
3	10 minutes	**Decode-It Early (Word Family)** (Analyze) Decode	Read word families. pit sit	*Sound out* the word family. Teacher: Let's build this word family, /a/ /g/. Put it together. /a/ /g/? What does it say? -*ag*. You do it. Student: /a/ /g/, -*ag*. *Sound out* a whole word. Teacher: Here's a cube that has -*ag*. Here's a cube with /w/. Push them together and say the sounds. /w/ /ag/ | /w/ /ag/ | /w/ /ag/. What is it? It says *wag*. You do it. Student: *W-ag. Wag.* ――――――― *Compare* two word families. The teacher displays the words in two columns: *hog hot* *fog got* *log lot* Teacher: Read the -*og* words and put them together. Read the -*ot* words. How are they different?	Unifix Cubes with Word Families Word Building Silly Words Follow-the-Path Games Word Sorts Picture-Word Matching Word Wheels Flip Books Note: Make sure to blend the two-letter word family first, then add consonants.

continues

		Lesson Part	Content	Sample Language	Activity Choices
3	10 minutes	**Decode-It (Later, Individual Sounds)** (Analyze)	Decode each sound in a word.	Teacher: Let's sound out two different words, one with *a* and one with *e*. Pay attention and see if you can get that middle sound. Here's one word [*sat*] and another one [*set*]. [Teacher does not pronounce the words.] Student: /s/ /a/ /t/, *sat*. /s/ /e/ /t/, *set*.	Options are the same as above with emphasis on decoding each sound.
4	5 minutes	**Spell-It** (Synthesize) Dictation	Spell words letter-by-letter.	Teacher: I want you to write the word *hit*. /h/ /it/. *It*. That's my family, /i/ /t/. I will write that first. Here I'll write an *i* and now /t/, *t*. Now *h-it*. What sound do I hear at the beginning of *h-it*? Oh, /h/, *h*. I'll write *h*. Student: [Uses pen or letters to spell word.]	Alphabet Arcs Word Building Change words at the beginning (*bat, hat, cat*). Change words at the end (*fan, fat*). Magnetic Letters Dry Erase Boards
5	5 minutes	**Read-It** (Apply)	Read a connected text with some patterns	Teacher: Let's do a book walk [see video on p. 118] and find words that have short *e*. Here's one [*red*]. Can you read it? Student: *Red*. [Reads the book independently.]	Decodables

First Words Lesson Template

The First Words lesson template in Figure 5.3 can be used to plan lesson for all the subunits in First Words.

FIGURE 5.3 **First Words Lesson Template**

First Words Weekly Lesson Template

Subunit: _____   Lesson #: _____   Letter/Sound Focus: _____

	Word Review (Practice) 5 min.	Hear-It (Analyze) 5 min.	Decode-It (Analyze) 10 min.	Spell-It (Synthesize) 5 min.	Read-It (Apply) 5 min.
Monday	Activity:[1]	Activity:[2]	Activity:[3]	Activity:[4]	Title:
	List new high-frequency words:	Words/Notes:	Words/Notes:	Words/Notes:	Decodable words: High-frequency and content words:
Tuesday	Activity:	Activity:	Activity:	Activity:	Title:
	List new high-frequency words:	Words/Notes:	Words/Notes:	Words/Notes:	Decodable words: High-frequency and content words:
Wednesday	Activity:	Activity:	Activity:	Activity:	Title:
		Words/Notes:	Words/Notes:	Words/Notes:	Decodable words: High-frequency and content words:

	Word Review (Practice) 5 min.	Hear-It (Analyze) 5 min.	Decode-It (Analyze) 10 min.	Spell-It (Synthesize) 5 min.	Read-It (Apply) 5 min.
Thursday	Activity:	Activity:	Activity:	Activity:	Title:
		Words/Notes:	Words/Notes:	Words/Notes:	Decodable words: High-frequency and content words:
Friday	Activity:	Activity:	Activity:	Activity:	Title:
		Words/Notes:	Words/Notes:	Words/Notes:	Decodable words: High-frequency and content words:

1 Word Review Activities: Word Rings, Bingo, Go Fish! Find It

2 Hear-It Activities: Rhyming Circle, Unifix cubes, Sit Down, Secret Word, Tapping Sounds, Chugging Words, Picture Sorts, Tommy Tiger, Which One? Share a Sound, Robot Talk, Mother May I?

3 Decode-It Activities: Unifix cubes, Silly Words, Word Sorts, Word Match, Word Wheels/Flip Books, Side-by-Side, Cutting Up Words

4 Spell-It Activities: Dictation with Dry-Erase, Word Building, Making Words, Alphabet Arc

For a downloadable PDF of this template, go to http://hein.pub/letterlessons-login.

Now that you have a basic understanding of the parts of the lesson and the goals for each part, the following sections provide details about what to do in each lesson part, including a series of activities and games to use.

Letter or Word Practice

During this section of the lesson, children practice reading 15–20 words that are new to them. The purpose is to review recently learned words that children know but have not yet securely stored cognitively. The practice section gives the teacher a quick moment to remind children what they learned and solidify learning (e.g., "Now, that word has a part from last week. Look, /i/ /t/. Remember that? *It*?"). The sources for these practice words are

- patterns from previous lessons (e.g., *it*: *sit, hit, fit*)
- high-frequency words from previous lessons (e.g., *the, she, he*) (see the Dolch pre-primer through second-grade list in Figure 5.4)
- words from books
- words that children themselves identify.

At the beginning of the lesson, children practice reading these words, play games like Go Fish! or other games to participate in group activities. In the group game I'm Thinking, all children have the same words on cards out and the teacher gives "clues" to help the children find the word that the teacher is thinking about. For example, "I'm thinking of a word with two letters. It has the sound /a/ at the beginning. It has the sound /t/ at the end." This game is engaging because it naturally employs inductive tension (see p. 50 for a video of this game). There are literally dozens of fun games for practicing words, many at Sightwords.com (which is misnamed but does reflect some research on high-frequency word learning). But do not turn this part of the lesson into a mindless drill in which you do the same thing every time with fifty word cards. Remember our emphasis on multiple exposures in multiple contexts. Repeat the words but not always in the same context. This will support overlearning and transfer.

Two of the most important questions that teachers have are "How many words?" and "When do I retire words?" Fifteen to twenty words at a time is sufficient. Children do not need to practice reading, for the one hundredth time, a word that they know very well. Each week add in about five words, including the week's two to three high-frequency words and two to three words representing a previously taught word family. Try to make the word family words the more challenging ones (e.g., *mat* instead of *cat*).

To tame the beast of a mountain of needlessly drilled words, build a routine to "retire words." Set up a criterion for "owning" a word (e.g., read correctly five times). You can ask students to have a partner, parent, teacher, or friend "check off" a word on the back of the card when it has been read correctly. After five check marks, it's ready to be retired. (Some teachers like to do a final check and have children read their retired words before officially retiring them.) Retiring a word can actually be a fun routine in which children display a sense of accomplishment. They can put the retired words into a big transparent container or jar labeled "Words We Own!"

FIGURE 5.4   **Dolch Words by Level (Pre-primer–Second Grade)**

Pre-primer Most Frequent		Primer		First Grade		Second Grade	
a	look	all	out	after	let	always	or
and	make	am	please	again	live	around	pull
away	me	are	pretty	an	may	because	read
big	my	at	ran	any	of	been	right
blue	not	ate	ride	as	old	before	sing
can	one	be	saw	ask	once	best	sit
come	play	black	say	by	open	both	sleep
down	red	brown	she	could	over	buy	tell
find	run	but	so	every	put	call	their
for	said	came	soon	fly	round	cold	these
funny	see	did	that	from	some	does	those
go	the	do	there	give	stop	don't	upon
help	three	eat	they	going	take	fast	us
here	to	four	this	had	thank	first	use
I	two	get	too	has	them	five	very
in	up	good	under	her	then	found	wash
is	we	have	want	him	think	gave	which
it	where	he	was	his	walk	goes	why
jump	yellow	into	well	how	were	green	wish
little	you	like	went	just	when	its	work
		must	what	know		made	would
		new	white			many	write
		no	who			off	your
		now	will				
		on	with				
		our	yes				

Adapted from "A Basic Sight Word Vocabulary," Dolch 1936.

Hear-It (Early, Onset-Rime): Rhyming and Onset-Rime Phonemic Awareness

This section of the lesson is all oral. The goal is to practice hearing rhymes and then breaking words into onsets and rimes (e.g., *b-ag*, *p-it*). Keep in mind, as well, that rhyming and breaking words apart will be part of the ongoing whole-group, teacher-guided practices. These are described in Chapter 3 in "Shared Reading with Print Referencing," "Interactive Writing," and "Language Play for Developing Phonological Awareness". In early Hear-It lessons, a teacher says words, emphasizes their word families, and then helps children say more rhyming words (e.g., *cat*, *bat*, *fat*). As children work to say rhymes, the goal is fluency, so calling out is okay! Even silly words are okay, because the idea is to *hear* rhyme and it can be hard to find a real word quickly that rhymes with a target. In fact, silly words are helpful in that they tell us that the child is really rhyming rather than having simply memorized various rhyming pairs or series. There are literally hundreds of rhyming word games and rhyming. Do choose words with the * on the scope and sequence (see Figure 5.1). Remember, these are some of the most frequently used rimes, and they will generate a lot of rhyming words.

After children can hear and produce rhyming words, Hear-It moves to onset and rime. The easier activity is to blend, or take two parts and put them together (e.g., /g/-/ot/ = *got*). The harder activity is breaking a word into parts (/g/ /ot/). A variety of activities present this content to children through games. See Figure 5.5. Examples are Unifix Word Parts, Chugging Sounds, Sit Down, and Secret Word (all described in Figure 5.5) and Robot Talk. When children analyze sounds without letters, they can focus on the "sound" part of the letter–sound relationship first. I find that when children struggle with letter–sounds, decoding, or spelling, it always helps to *back up* and just work with the sounds.

FIGURE 5.5

Activities for Hear-It: Orally breaking words into two parts (Early, Onset-Rime)
Rhyming Circle
Have the children sit in a circle. Say a word and then invite each child to say a word that rhymes with it, going around the circle. (Silly words are okay!) Build fluency with rhyming. Choose words that have one of the 37 most common rimes, from the word families marked with the * on the scope and sequence (see Figure 5.1). This will ensure a lot of possible words for the game.
Unifix Word Parts (Onset-Rime)
Use two cubes, one to represent the onset and the other to represent the rime. Children move the cubes together, saying the sounds and then blending them together (e.g., /c/-/at/, /c/-/at/, *cat*).

Which One?

Children use their fists to represent the two parts of the word. They make a gesture for each part of the word (e.g., /g/-/et/, g/-/et/), bringing their fists closer and closer together until they touch, and they blend the word (e.g., *get*).

Sit Down

Have two children stand in front of two empty chairs. They each say a part of the word and sit down as they say it (e.g., /c/ /at/).

Secret Word

The teacher says the secret word in parts (e.g., /b/ /ig/) and then the children blend the word. (Blending is easier than breaking words down.) Once children can blend words together, they can take turns "being the teacher" and breaking down a secret word for their peers. (See the video on p. 121.)

Which One?, Tommy Tiger Likes to Eat, Share a Sound, Mother May I?, Robot Talk?, Beginning Sounds Bingo

See Chapter 3, p. 42.

Hear-It (Later, Segment Fully)

After Lesson 6, the Hear-It part of the lesson, especially when there are contrasts, focuses on breaking words into *each separate sound* and blending them back again. See Figure 5.6. Robust research indicates that the two phonemic skills that are most closely associated with success in reading are (1) the ability to identify the initial sound in a spoken word and (2) the ability to break a word into individual sounds or phonemes (Hulme et al. 2002; Muter et al. 1998).

One of the best activities for this is Elkonin boxes. The directions for Elkonin boxes (see p. 173) provide a list of words and a sequence to use. The easiest way to start boxes is to use two-letter words, first those beginning with a vowel (e.g., *at, it, in*) and then those beginning with a consonant (e.g., *so, see, me*). After two-letter words, use three-letter words. Caution: Boxes seem deceptively easy, but they are not easy. The approach takes time and practice but pays off in big dividends.

FIGURE 5.6

Activities for Hear-It: Orally breaking words into two parts (Later, Fully Segment)
Orally Segmenting Each Sound in a Word
Elkonin Boxes
See directions on page 173.
Unifix Word Parts (Each Sound)
Use three cubes, with *each* cube representing *each* sound in a word (e.g., *b-e-t*). This activity is described in detail on page 168.
Tapping Sounds with Fingers
Children use their fingers to represent *each sound in the word*. They tap for each part of the word (e.g., *g-e-t, g-e-t*).

Decode-It (Early, Word Family)

In this lesson section, the focus is reading first words by adding a consonant sound to a word family (e.g., *-at, -in*). See the box "Three Ways to Sound out a C-V-C Word." In the scope and sequence for We Are Family (see Figure 5.1) are two lessons for each sound (two for short *a* families, two for short *o* families, etc.). In the first of the two lessons, the first step is to blend a short vowel family together (e.g., /o/ /p/ = *op*) and the second step is to add a consonant (e.g., *mop, pop, top*). Below are the details of these steps:

1. **Blend the two sounds of the word family together.** The teacher shows how to put the vowel sound and ending consonant together (e.g., *-oooooop, op*). This first step is very important (and rarely taught as part of word family work). When you teach a child to sound out the word family, you draw attention to each part of the word family: the vowel and the ending consonant. It is easier to decode a vowel-consonant pattern because your mouth starts out open with the vowel and then closes down when saying the consonant. (Note that this is the first step in Method 1: Three ways to sound out a c-v-c word.)

2. **Add consonant sounds to the word family.** Once the word family is built, then the child can add consonants to it, pronouncing the word family as a unit (e.g., *-op*) and then adding consonants (e.g., *p-op, m-op*). Word wheels can be used as well as flip books. If the child gets confused about the word family, then redirect the child to Step 1.

After children learn how to read words with word families, they will compare words with the same short vowel but different ending (e.g., -*op* vs. -*og*). This comparison is very important because it challenges the reader to pay attention to each part of the word's architecture. Let's say a child has learned -*op* words and -*og* words, but when she comes to *hog*, she says "*hop*." She is not paying attention to the last part of the word, the -*g*. When students have to compare words, they have to pay attention to that last part.

Activities for the early part of Read-It are shown in Figure 5.7.

FIGURE 5.7

Activities for Decode-It: Decoding words (Early, Word Family)

Reading Words

Word Wheel

Word wheels have a word family that stays the same in the center and initial consonants that "spin" around the word family to make new words. They are an easy and fun way to practice reading words. Be careful which consonants you put on the outside of the wheel. Some consonants create silly words and others may create words that aren't appropriate for school.

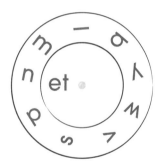

Flip Books

Flip books are easier to make than word wheels and operate on the same principle that word wheels do. A series of beginning consonants are put on the front of a word family and students practice reading words.

continues

Activities for Decode-It: Decoding words (Early, Word Family)

Matching Words in Text

After students read decodables with the target sound, they can find words in their decodables that match. Many teachers will ask students to keep a list and then tally how many times they find a word.

Boxes

Elkonin Boxes and a variation, word boxes, is another great way to practice reading words with word families. (See Elkonin (Sound) Boxes and Letter Boxes). In the *First Words* subunit, divide words into two parts, onset and rime. Let one box represent the consonant at the beginning and

Comparing Words

Word Sort

Students compare two words with the same middle vowel sound (e.g., *ug-ub-un*).

bug	tub	sun
hug	rub	fun
tug	sub	gun
pug		run
rug		

Side by Side

Place two words side by side and ask students to whisper read each word to themselves and then to the teacher. To get the most out of the activity, teachers pair up words ahead of time. Below are different levels of the game.

Same word family	rug	hug
Different word family/different first sound	tug	run
Different word family/same first sound	tub	tug

If students are having a difficult time, ask them to highlight the word family at the end to cue them to pay attention to the vowel.

Activities for Decode-It: Decoding words (Early, Word Family)

Cutting Up Words

Give each child a set of word family words. Ask the children to cut off the first sound of each. Then the children put the words back together and read them. To make this activity more complex, the entire word can be cut apart and reassembled.

b	ag
r	an

Decode-It (Later Individual Sounds)

In the later parts of We Are Family and in other subunits decoding moves toward reading three-phoneme words by blending the sounds together. This is an important step, because as mentioned, using word families is only a first step. Using a variety of strategies readers blend real words and "silly words." Once readers can reliably blend three sounds together, they are ready to read words with blends. Usually the acquisition of consonant blends is fairly speedy in comparison to learning to blend a short vowel word, because once a reader understands one *r*-blend like *tr-*, adding others (e.g., *gr-*, *br-*) is easier.

FIGURE 5.8

Activities for Decode-It: Decoding words (Later, Individual Sounds)

Word Sort

In Lessons 6, 8, and 10 students compare two words with different middle vowel sounds (e.g., *-et*, *-it*). Do word sorts with different middle sounds (see p. 169). Make sure to stretch the word and then hold it in the middle (e.g., *beeeeeeet*) to help hear the sounds.

bet	**hit**
get	bit
net	sit
met	lit
wet	fit

continues

Activities for Decode-It: Decoding words (Later, Individual Sounds)

Side by Side

Place two words side by side that have the same beginning sound and the same ending sound but different middle sounds. Ask students to whisper read each word to themselves. (Start with words that contain one of the 37 most frequent rimes; see the word families marked with the * in Figure 5.1.) Below are examples of words:

run ran

fun fan

tun tan

Ask students to highlight the word family at the end to cue them to pay attention to the vowel.

Cutting Up Words

Give each child a set of cards and scissors. Ask the children to cut the words into individual letters and then put them back together.

b	a	g
b	u	g

Three Ways to Sound Out a C-V-C Word

Method 1: Take off the beginning sound. See Figure 5.9.

FIGURE 5.9

Word	Actions	Teacher Language
sit	Cover the first sound. *sit* Blend the remaining sounds. /iiiiiiiiiiit/ *it*	"Cover the first sound in the word. What do you have? An *i* and a *t*." "Let's put those two sounds together. What do we get? /iiiiiit/, *it*. The word family *it*."
	Add the first sound back. /s/ /it/	"So we have *it*. Now let's put the sound /s/ on *it*. /s/ /it/."
	Decode the full word. *sit*	"/s/ /it/. The word is *sit*."

Method 2: Take off the last sound. See Figure 5.10.

FIGURE 5.10

Word	Actions	Teacher Language
sit	Cover the last sound. *sit* Blend the remaining sounds. /siiiiiiiiiii/	"Cover the last sound in the word. What do you have? An *s* and an *i*." "Let's put those two sounds together. What do we get? /sssssiiiiii/."
	Add the last sound back. /siiiiii/ /t/	"Put the last sound back on the word and put the sounds together. So we have */ssssit/*. Now let's put the last sound with that t/t/."
	Decode the full word *sit*	"/siiiii/ /t/, *sit*. The word is *sit*."

continues

Method 3: Figure the word out sound-by-sound. See Figure 5.11.

FIGURE 5.11

Word	Actions	Teacher Language
sit	Point to the first sound. Point to the second sound. Point to the third sound. Blend all sounds.	"Let's say each sound. /s/." "/iiii/." "/t/." "Together, /ssssssiiiiiit/."
	Decode the full word. *sit*	"/siiiiitt/, *sit*. The word is *sit*."

Spell-It

This is one of the most important and challenging parts of the lessons. During this section, children spell words with families that they have been learning. As discussed in the Introduction and in Chapter 3, phonics instruction is about word architecture, understanding how a word is built. By manipulating the letter–sounds in a word— putting it together and taking it apart—learners solidify their knowledge. Students are expected to spell the words completely correctly because they have been taught the letter–sounds. To help, the teacher should model how to say the words slowly, hearing each sound, and then write the letter–sounds. We like to say to children, "To spell a word, say it!" The box "To Spell a Word, *Say* the Word" (on p. 160) explains why. There are different ways to do the spelling section, including writing words on dry erase boards, using magnetic letters, or doing word building. See Figure 5.12.

The spelling section is very diagnostic because often a child will be able to read a word or even hear parts but not spell it accurately. In one classroom, we watched a girl easily read -*ag* words, but when she was asked to spell them, she had letter order issues (e.g., *bga* for *bag*). Without doing the spelling we would have never known that she was confused. (See the box "Letters Out of Order? Here's What to Do," p. 160.)

FIGURE 5.12

Activities for Spell-It: Spelling words
Dictation
Identify two to three words from the lesson to dictate. Children should correctly spell each word.

Making Words and Word Building

Making Words and Word Building are two activities for spelling. (See p. 171 for more information.) In a Making Words lesson, children use five to seven magnetic letters or letter cards to spell words.

Word Building is similar, but the format is a "ladder" where one letter in a word is changed each time. For *early lessons*, change letters at the beginning and end.

c	a	t
f	a	t
f	a	n

For *later lessons*, change letters in the middle or change single consonants to blends at the beginning or end.

c	a	t	
c	o	t	
c	o	s	t

Don't wing it. Plan the words that your students will spell. (See "Making Words or Word Building Lesson" on p. 171.)

Pulling Down Letters from the Alphabet Arc

Children "pull down" lowercase letters from an alphabet arc to spell words. To keep this activity organized and efficient, ask children to place letters on the arc within two minutes.

To Spell a Word, *Say* the Word

When children are spelling words, they must say those words to themselves as they are writing. Why? There are three reasons. First, spelling is the process of taking speech sounds and putting each into a visual/written code. It is natural in the beginning stages to say each sound of the word, search for the correct letter, and then write it down. This is the rich and challenging process that really helps children internalize phonics. Second, spelling is so hard for young children that they need a process to use when they have to do it. The process is to say the sounds and then write them. Without this process, children will flounder, often randomly writing down letters that they remember, frequently in the wrong place (e.g., a student might write "*bga*" and explain, "That word *bag* had a *b* and a *g* and an *a*. I put those down."). Teachers must remind them, "Say the word. Slow it down. What sounds do you hear? Say it." Third, children must do the work of saying the word or else they will not own or use the strategy when they are writing independently. Teachers sometimes do this part of the spelling for children, not realizing that they are doing half the work of spelling. A teacher might need to model saying the word at first, but eventually the children must do it.

Letters Out of Order? Here's What to Do

In the early stages of reading, students often write a word and produce a spelling with the correct letters in the incorrect order. This provides a great chance to emphasize the alphabetic principle and how letters work. When students create a disordered spelling, first ask them, "What does that say?" Sometimes a student will look at the spelling and see that the letter–sounds are not in the correct order. If this does not work, it might be useful to point to the letters in the student's disordered word and say the word, asking "Does this say *cat*?" If that doesn't do the trick, you can say, "Pretty close but listen to me read what you have written. /c/ /t/ /a/. This says /c/ /t/ /a/. It doesn't say *cat*. The word *cat* has /c/, but listen, then it has /aaaaaa/ and then /ttt/. It is /c/ /aaaaaa/ /tttt/. Where is the /a/ part in *ccccccaaaaaat*?"

Read-It

After listening for sounds, reading words, and spelling words, the final activity is reading the words within the context of a book. During First Words, use books with some level of decodability with multiple examples of words taught in lessons as well as high-frequency words. (See the box "Fear Not the Decodable: Why? When? How?")

The routine for Read-It is very similar to the routines used for book reading in Letter Lessons. As shown in Figure 5.13, the steps are preview (teacher planning), book walk, first reading, second reading, praise and practice, and rereading. The key differences in reading at this stage are the expectations around decoding and the focus of the book walk.

FIGURE 5.13

Read-It Routine

Before the Lesson: Preview the Book

Never use a book without previewing it.

To preview, check to see that *the majority* of words in the book would be "decodable" to the children, usually following the c-v-c or c-c-v-c pattern. These should be words that have word families taught in the current lesson *or earlier*. I also look for words that are taught as high-frequency words as well as decodable words that might have unknown meanings (e.g., *figs, hag*). Ask yourself, "Does the book have taught word families? Does the book have taught high-frequency words?" In addition, look for difficult-to-decode content words. If there are difficult-to-decode content words, such as *iguana*, preteach them and do not expect independent decoding. Hold children responsible only for sounding out patterns they know.

Don't expect 100 percent of the words to meet these criteria. Watch for books that sound like tongue twisters (e.g. Thad had a rad wag).

Step 1: Book Walk

The purpose of the book walk is to quickly review a few tricky decodable, content, or high-frequency words in the book *before* reading. It usually takes about three minutes.

During the book walk, call students' attention to target families: "Oh look, here's a word with the *-og* family. Let's practice reading that word. Here's another one on the next page."

Call attention to high-frequency words.

Define decodable words with unknown meanings. For example, "Look at this word [*hag*]. How would we read that? *Hag*? Do you know what a hag is? It's usually a name for a witch or mean woman."

WATCH

VIDEO 5.1

Book Walk with a Decodable

See the video for a book walk with a decodable.

continues

Step 1: Book Walk

Note: A book walk is not a picture walk. A picture walk is a review of all the pages in the book focusing on the pictures and the story. A book walk alerts the readers to high-frequency or decodable words and gives them a chance to practice those words. With hard words, the picture might be used, but the focus is not reviewing *all* the pictures and retelling the story.

Caution: Don't feel the need to go through every page and every picture in a book, especially if it's a long book. Doing so gives the story or information away. This provides less reason to read the book. According to K. A. D. Stahl (2004), picture walks may not support comprehension as much as we think.

Step 2: First Reading

In the Word Building subunit in Chapter 4, I described three ways to do a first read. When books are decodable, there is a fourth: student independent reading.

• Teacher read (hardest books): Read the whole book to the students as they point.

• I read / you read: Read and point to a page and then ask the students to do it. Try to hang back and pause and allow the students to decode if they can.

• Choral read (easier books): Read and point the book all together. The teacher's voice stays in the mix and scaffolds through harder words.

• Independent read (easiest books): This method is for books with words that students can decode very easily. The students read on their own without the teacher's voice.

Step 3: Second Reading

Each child reads independently.

Decoding words is the point, so make sure it happens. Watch and listen for accurate decoding and help when a student is struggling to decode.

Use the methods described in the box "Three Ways to Sound Out a C-V-C Word," p. 157.

Don't turn Read-It into a phonics lesson. If the child cannot decode the word fairly quickly, provide three quick prompts and then move on. (See "Word Prompting: What to Say When They Struggle on a Word," page 64.) The first prompt is pausing and waiting; the second prompt is saying, "Something tricked you"; and the third prompt is based on the child's letter–sound knowledge. If these three prompts don't get the child to the word, model the word and move on.

Step 4: Praise and Practice

At the end of the book, praise something the students have done well.

"When you came to the word *had*, you stopped and were not sure. Then you said the first sound and put that word together. Good job! What is that word [*had*]? [Pointing to word.]"

Then practice something that was difficult.

"When you came to *hat*, you said '*ham*.' Then you stopped and you reread the sentence and you said '_____' [let the child fill in the correct word]. You used your letter–sounds to read that word."

> **Step 5: Reread**
>
> After the children have read the book once by themselves, I ask them to reread the book to other teachers, cafeteria staff, counselors, family members, and friends. I like to say, "If you read it once, you should read it six more times!"

When choosing texts with some level of decodability, remember that it is not decodable *to children* if they do not know the letter–sounds. Make sure to choose decodables by coordinating with the scope and sequence. Many texts will tell you the focal pattern. The box below provides insight about decodability.

Fear Not the Decodable: Why? When? How?

"Ugh! Are you kidding? Figs, pigs, wigs, and jigs! No, thank you! Reading is about meaning!" protested one first-grade teacher when asked about decodable texts. "What good is it to teach kids to 'sound things out' if there are not words to sound out in a text?" countered another teacher. And so goes the typical conversation about decodable text, a worn-out love/hate debate that seems to swing back and forth with the early literacy pendulum. But dwelling in hyperbole almost never helps kids, so I would like to suggest that we step back from extreme responses to take a more measured, middle-ground approach with respect to decodables. Decodable text can be a limited but useful tool. To properly use decodables, a teacher must know why, when, and how to use decodables.

Why?

Decodable text is a type of beginning reading material in which the words have been controlled to contain letter–sounds and high-frequency words *that the learner has been taught*, a feature called lesson-to-text-match (Mesmer 2001). The reason to use decodables is that they allow the reader to apply letter–sound knowledge or automatic word recognition to *independently* decode or recognize words in text. Although there has been some attempt to ensure that decodable texts match 80 percent of the words that have been taught, close analysis has proved this percentage to be unattainable in the most "decodable" materials (Foorman et al. 2004).

If you are like the first teacher quoted earlier, you might be wondering why anyone would use decodable texts. There are three reasons—to bridge an important developmental transition in word reading, to provide a field for the transfer of letter–sound knowledge to reading, and to encourage beginning readers to decode. You might also be wondering what research support there is for the benefits of decodables. What the research tells us is that texts with some level of decodability encourage students to use letter–sounds to decode,

continues

help them read words more accurately, and enable them to better read words they have not seen before (Cheatham and Allor 2012; Compton, Appleton, and Hosp 2004; Juel and Roper 1985; Mesmer 2001, 2003; Vadasy, Sanders, and Peyton 2005).

When?

One of the reasons that people have questions about decodable texts is that the issue of *when* has not really been well addressed. When to use decodables is based on development, not grade. I see decodable sets with hundreds of sequential books that stretch over an entire year! I do not think that is necessary at all.

I first discovered this material in working with a second grader who, after a year in a one-on-one tutoring program, was still reading at the very lowest levels. Despite having letter–sound knowledge, the child was actually using a "partial alphabetic" approach to reading words in books (Ehri 2005; Mesmer 1999). She would use beginning sounds along with pictures and memory to guess at words. The approach would have been fine in early first grade or late kindergarten, but it was not appropriate in second grade. She needed to move into "full alphabetic" reading, or fully sounding out words, including the vowels. I soon realized that the books I was using did not support this transition. She would come to words in text like *hair* and *grouchy*, and she did not have the knowledge to decode these. When I used texts with a greater degree of decodability, she began to *use* what she knew about letter–sounds to sound out words in text. It was empowering and amazing to see the "I can do it!" smile spread across her face when she would pause at a tough word and work it out. Use decodables when students need to practice their phonics skills in connected texts.

How?

I offer the following directions about how to use decodables.

Use at the right developmental point.
Decodables should be used once children are extremely solid with all letter–sounds and are ready to fully decode. They should have a solid concept of word and be able to accurately point to both single-syllable and multisyllabic words in a predictable text, using beginning sounds to help them. Children should know about 20 high-frequency words so that they can power through the words in text that are not as regular. Children should be able to decode a simple c-v-c word *prior* to using decodables. (Don't use the decodable as a *way* to teach letter–sound relationships or decoding. That work needs to be done with isolated words. Decodables provide a place to apply and practice.)

Use after a phonics lesson to practice the target word family or sound.
The most obvious time to ask children to read a decodable is right after a lesson in which they have had instruction on a specific pattern. When children see words that they have decoded in text, they understand that the work they are doing has a real application. Put the book in children's hands, and let them do it! You can also have children use decodables to find words that match patterns.

Do not use exclusively.
I do not recommend using highly decodable texts exclusively for two reasons. First, the sounding out that children have to do in a decodable is substantial and can be tiring. Second, there are other types of books that children benefit from—in particular, texts that integrate decodability with engagingness, natural language, and a paced repetition of words, often called multiple-criterion texts. (Note: The feature that is overwhelmingly missing from today's beginning reading texts is programmatic repetition of words [Hiebert 2005; Foorman et al. 2004]. In 2000, programs presented between 32 and 95 new words per week compared to 15 new words per week in 1980 [Hiebert 2002].)

Pay attention to the level of decodability.
I believe that instead of thinking of books as "decodable" or "not decodable," we should simply think of "decodability" as a continuum, with some books having words that are more or less decodable to some readers depending on the scope and sequence used. In *more decodable* books there is a really tight level of control with many words having specific letter–sound patterns. For example, here is some text from a Bob Book:

Dot had a dog. The dog is Mag.

Mag took the bag. Dot got Mag.

Notice that the -*ot*, -*og*, and -*ag* families are all represented *throughout each line.* To decode the first line of print, the reader has to shift between several word families, first -*ot* (*Dot*), then -*og* (*dog*), then -*og* again (*dog*), and then -*ag* (*Mag*). I like to use books like this *near the end* of short vowel instruction, when readers have gotten fluent with decoding short vowels and can handle these shifts pretty seamlessly (in the Beginning Blends subunit). These books are a challenge. If you are using a decodable and the reader is slowing down at every third word to sound it out, the book is likely not quite right. At the beginning of decoding instruction, when the focus is on word families and adding a beginning sound to a family, I like to use books that I call *somewhat decodable.* Below is an example:

I like to win.

I like to pin.

I like to sip.

I like to dip.

continues

I like to hop.

I like to pop.

This is me!

All I can be!

In this example, there are decodable words, but they are at the end of each sentence. In order to read this book, the reader can use the repeated sentence and the high-frequency word *like*, and then do the decoding work at the end of the sentence. The decoding work is not too overwhelming, and the reader can apply letter–sound knowledge without taking too long. I like to use this type of book in the early stages of decoding instruction, when students may not know all the short vowels. Further into instruction, I like "multi-criterion" texts, which have some level of decodability (Menon and Hiebert 2005). These texts also have a paced introduction of high-frequency words. Below is an example of a text like this. Note that decodable words are in different positions in this text, not just at the end of sentences.

Text with Some Decodability

Tim has a fan.

His fan is big.

- Simple words with taught letter–sound patterns (e.g., *Tim*, *fan*, *big*)
- Words with different letter–sounds (e.g., *big* vs. *fan* vs. *has*)
- Words clustered and repeated within a story
- Decodable words in different parts of the sentence to discourage memorizing
- Words match what the reader knows about letter–sounds
- High-frequency words (e.g., *is*, *his*)

Know when to stop.
I believe that decodables are most useful for propelling children through the period in which they are learning to decode words or blend sounds together. They should be used when single-syllable word decoding is the goal. Once a child can quickly and easily blend words with taught patterns, decodables may not be necessary.

Catchphrases for First Words throughout this unit:

- *Use your letters. Use your sounds.*
  What sound goes with that [letter]?

- *(Move away from asking for letter names.*
  Don't ask, "What letter is that?" Go straight to the sound.)

- *How would you say that word?*
  (Resist decoding for the child.)

- *Look at this [letter / word part].*
  What is the sound?

When spelling a word:

- *Say that word.*

- *What sounds do you hear?*

- *What letter would you use?*

To decode a new c-v-c word:

- *Take off the first sound. Now add it back.*
                          or
- *Take off the last sound. Now add it back.*

Chapter Summary

This chapter started with Taylor, a student who at first struggled to use letter–sounds for word reading but, with focused instruction, persevered and became an empowered reader. All the details and steps introduced in this chapter can be a little bit over-whelming. Take it step by step and stay the course and your students will be able to do amazing things once they finish the First Words unit. They will surprise and delight you and actually surpass your expectations. Students who read their first words become "word monsters," as first-grade teacher Carol calls them. She explains, "I tell them they are word monsters because they are unstoppable and kind of crazy. They like that! But they do just devour words all around them. They are like little beasts. Like the other day, a little girl came up to me while I was passing out papers and said, 'That word on your paper says *camp*!' Another one said to me, 'I know how to write *grub* and you didn't even teach me.'"

The First Words unit, perhaps more than any other unit, will unlock reading for your students. This unit really shows students how to *apply* letter–sound knowledge. They really need instruction in how to use that information because most kids just will not figure this out on their own. But once they have completed the unit, they will have confirmation that they are indeed *real* readers. They will know that they have what it takes to unlock words. They will feel lit. Success and knowledge are incredibly exciting. What's really important for teachers at this stage is to realize that some children will get it really quickly and others will need more practice and rehearsal. Do not give up. A child who is not figuring it out right away usually needs a patient teacher and more practice. Learning to sound out words is an essential developmental step on the path to becoming a good reader.

Activities

Note: This section has detailed instructions for a handful of powerful strategies that can be used across most subunits. These pages can be used by an instructional coach or reading specialist to support teacher professional development on a specific strategy.

Using Unifix® Cubes for Hearing Sounds and Decoding Words

Why It Works Unifix cubes are not just for math. They are useful for reading too! Cubes make the parts of words concrete and children can manipulate them. They can be taken apart and put together. Use cubes to show children how to put sounds together or how to bring letters together to decode. Use plain colored cubes without letters when hearing sounds in words and use cubes with letters written on them when decoding words. The Unifix cubes pictured have preprinted letters, but teachers can use a permanent marker to write letters on existing cubes.

Phonological Awareness The Hear-It part of the lesson focuses on orally breaking words into onset and rime or individual phonemes. Have children move cubes to show sounds in words being segmented (e.g., *c-a-t*) or blended (*cat*). Use different colors to reflect each different sound. The three cubes below might be used to break down a three-phoneme word or put them back together.

When the focus of the lesson is onsets and rimes, teachers can use two cubes, one to represent the onset (*c-*) and one to represent the rime (*-at*). Break the cubes apart as you segment and say the sounds. Move the cubes together as you blend or combine the sounds into a word.

Decoding Onsets and Rimes In Read-It, children practicing decoding words. Use a cube with a word family and a beginning sound, and show the reader how to put a beginning sound on the word. Move the two word parts closer to each other while saying the sounds until they are snapped together and the full word is blended (see pictures below).

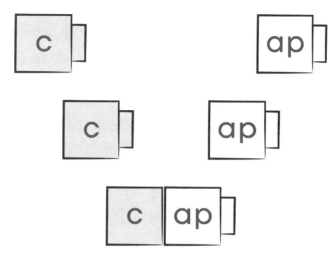

Decoding All Three Sounds To blend three sounds, use color-coded cubes, like the ones below, to draw the reader's attention to the vowel. Use the cubes as you show the three ways to sound out a word, as described in the box on p. 157.

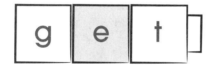

How to Do a Word Sort

Source: *Words Their Way* (Bear et al. 2000)

Why It Works Word sorting mimics the way that the human brain makes sense of information by sorting and categorizing. When students compare two or more patterns, they pay close attention to the letters in them.

Steps

Preparation

Choose at least two patterns to contrast (e.g., *-ug, -ub, -un*). Prepare word cards with these patterns. Identify anchor words for each pattern, using well-known and easily read words (e.g., *bug, tub, sun*). See Figure 5.14. Create different numbers of words for each category. (This prevents students from guessing at the end of the sort.)

FIGURE 5.14

bug	tub	sun
hug	rub	fun
tug	sub	gun
pug		run
rug		

Step 1: Read the Words

Word sorts are done with *known* words. Ask students to read each word. Put aside the words that cannot be *easily* read.

Step 2: Model the Sort

See the routine for word sorting, which appears at the end of this step. To model the sort, use a different set of words than those that the students have. For example, model with *dug*, *cub*, and *bun*. Set up the key words at the top of each column; in this example, the key words are *bug*, *tub*, and *sun*, as shown in Figure 5.15.

FIGURE 5.15

bug	tub	sun

Turn over the first card to be sorted and *say the word and each anchor*. (This is *critical*.)

Think aloud: "*Cub, bug*? No, *cub* has *-ub* at the end and *bug* has *-ug*. *Cub, tub*? Yes, they both have *-ub*. But I am going to check this last one. *Cub, sun*? No. *Cub, tub* is right." Perform the last two actions in the routine for word sorting (shown below): check for mistakes and reflect.

Routine for Word Sorting

- Read each word out loud. Pull the unknown words out of the pile. Set up the anchor words.

- Say each word and compare it to the anchor words.

- Check for mistakes.

- **Reflect:** These words go in the *-ug* group because _____ .

Step 3: Practice

Either individually within a small group or with partners, have students sort their sets of words.

Important Reminders

Learners *must*

- be able to read the words
- understand what it means to sort
- say the words as they sort
- check for mistakes
- reflect.

When children say the words, they benefit from hearing the sound and feeling the way that sound works in their mouths. Without saying the word, children will simply sort visually, which they could do without even reading the words. Train students to check for mistakes, and resist the urge to jump in and immediately correct a mistake. Make sure children use the mistake-checking strategy—they should say the anchor word and compare it to each word in the sort. There is amazing learning that takes place when children find their own mistakes.

Learners must state why the words go in different groups. This is important because it allows the teacher to understand what the student notices about the words. For instance, if the student notices that all the -*ug* words end in *g*, this would not be exactly the goal because the word family unit is both *u* and *g*.

Making Words or Word Building Lesson

Why It Works Word Building and Making Words work because they require students to pay attention to each letter–sound in a word. These are excellent activities for solidifying a pattern and making sure that students really "own" that pattern because students must pay attention to letter order (Cunningham and Cunningham 1992; McCandliss et al. 2003). For both students use a set of specific letters (*i, s, r, n, g*). These letters can be magnetic, on cards, or written on a small dry erase board. The teacher dictates words and the students spell the words, usually changing one letter at a time or adding letters (e.g., *in, pin, pig, rig*). In Word Building students create words in a column like a ladder leaving the previous word visible (McCandliss et al. 2003). In a Making Words, the newly spelled word replaces the old one and at the end of the lesson, students use all the letters to make a "secret word (e.g., *spring*)."

This description is geared toward a Word Building lesson with guidance for Making Words offered at the end. Because the Making Words lesson is usually built around a "secret word," the letter choices may be constrained and the words constructed are limited. You must create words using only the letters in *spring*, for example. Word Building does not have these constraints. You can pick a few word families and select consonants without the additional planning around a "secret word." Word Building can be used when students are just learning new short vowels. Making Words works best once the students have a large repertoire of many different vowel sounds, including long vowels.

Steps

Preparation

For Word Building, identify one or more high-frequency rime or word family, one of those starred in the scope and sequence, Figure 5.1. For example, -*ick* and -*ock*. Then brainstorm 5–7 consonants that could be added to both word families to make words (e.g., *h-*, *s-*, *t-*, *l-*, *m-*). Then plan the sequence (e.g., *lick, lock, sock, sick, thick, stick, stock, mock, smock, smocks, socks, shocks, shock*). Do not wing it! It seems simpler than it actually is.

For a Making Words lesson, start with the "secret word" that the students will make at the end. Then brainstorm additional words that the students can make with the letters in that word. Make sure that the word has the vowels that the student has been taught. Try to identify between ten and fifteen words. If possible, find words that can be rearranged to make a new word (e.g., *tip/pit, was/saw*).

Step 1: Review the Letters

Review the letters and sounds for each letter by having students touch each letter and say the sound.

Step 2: Call the Words

Tell the students the number of letters in the word. Dictate the first word and then ask the students to hold up their ladders, boards with magnetic letters, or dry erase boards Tell the where the letter–sound will be changed in the word:

- The first word has two letters in it. Listen to the word, *in*. I went *in* the house. Spell the word and hold it up.

- Now we are going to add a letter so that our word has three letters. Make the word *pin*. At the beginning of the word, add *pppp* to *in*. She put a *pin* in her dress where it had ripped.

- Now we are going to change that word at the beginning again. We are going to make the word *pin* into *fin*, like a fish has, a *fin*.

Step 3: Find the Secret Words (in a Making Words Lesson)

If the lesson is a Making Words lesson, ask the students to make the secret word. Make sure to have two to three hints that might help the students think about that word (e.g., "This is a season. It is usually a warm season. It is the season that comes after winter."). Do not give any hints at first; see if the students can come up with the word on their own.

Important Reminders

Pay attention to the words. There are a number of teacher resource books with premade word ladders or Making Words lessons. These are very convenient, but it's very important to look closely at the words. A word ladder might start with simple one-to-one correspondences (e.g., *bat*, *bag*) and then move to harder ones that are not appropriate (e.g., *beat*). The activity defeats its purpose if students are being asked to write words that they do not know.

Elkonin (Sound) Boxes and Letter Boxes

Why It Works Elkonin boxes, or "sound boxes," support phonemic awareness, spelling, and decoding. This phonemic awareness strategy helps readers break up words into sounds. It can also be extended to support spelling and decoding. The teacher uses a square box to show each sound in a word. The reader says each sound and at the same time pushes a counter into each box while saying the sounds (Elkonin 1963; Griffith and Olson 1992; Murray and Lesniak 1999; Yopp and Yopp 2000). Because sound boxes have empty squares, the reader is not overwhelmed by trying to remember which letters go with which sounds and instead can simply focus on saying the sound parts and moving counters into each box. After doing sound boxes, readers can do letter boxes by pushing letters into the boxes or by putting letters in the boxes to spell the words.

Steps

Preparation

Making Sound Boxes To make a sound box, glue a picture representing a two- or three-phoneme word on a sheet of paper. (Some two-phoneme words are not easily depicted in a picture.) Under the picture draw a box for each sound in the word. (Note: Pay attention to the *sounds*. Sometimes a word might have three letters but two sounds, like *see*. Some words have four letters but only three sounds, like *ship*.)

Choosing Words Start with two-phoneme words that begin with vowels. Then move to two-phoneme words that start with continuant consonants that can be stretched and held (e.g., *s*, *m*, *n*). After students can segment two-phoneme words, have them move to three-phoneme words, first with continuants and then with other consonant sounds. See Figure 5.16.

FIGURE 5.16

2-Phoneme Words (easiest to hardest)	• Beginning with a vowel: *at, add, am, an, as, at, egg, ed, in, if, it, is, on, odd, up, of* • Beginning with a continuant consonant: *low, lie, lay, my, may, me, no, sew/so, say, see, zoo, hi, hay, fee, row, ray* • Beginning with other consonants: *to, toe, tie, who, boo, do, go, no, row, day, doe, die, do, Joe, pay, pie* (Note: Many words with two phonemes have long vowels in them. Some with patterns like *-ow, -ie,* and *oe* would not be good candidates for *letter boxes,* but they are great for helping students hear the sounds in words.)
3-Phoneme Words (easiest to hardest)	• Beginning with a continuant consonant: *fan, fin, hat, ham, hot, hut, jam, jog, lit, lip, leg, mad, mud, mat, map, man, nap, nut, net, neck, red, rat, rug, rip, sit, sad, sack, sat, sub, sun, van, wet, whip, win, wag* • Beginning with other consonants: *bag, back, bat, cat, cab, can, cap, dog, dig, dad, dot, duck, gun, gas, pat, pan, pig, pod, pick, pit, tap, top, tag, tin, ten* (Note: All these three phoneme words have some type of picture that could be generated. These words could be used for the extensions to letter boxes in Step 4.)

Step 1: Stretch the Words

First, practice stretching words orally. The sound boxes activity breaks down when students are not practiced enough in stretching the words and hearing sound differences—a skill that this strategy presumes.

Model how to stretch words: "Let's stretch out the word *sat*, /sssssssaaaaaaaattttttt/. I made those sounds longer. Let's try *meat* together, /mmmmmmeeeeeeeaaatt/. See, I can say each of these words the normal way or I can stretch it." (Note that these words both start with continuants.)

Then give each student a word to stretch.

Step 2: Model Pushing the Counters

Once students can stretch words, bring out the sound boxes and the counters and model pushing the counters into boxes while saying each sound. After modeling pushing the counters and saying the sounds, ask the *students* to say the sounds while you push the counters.

Step 3: Students Use Sound Boxes and Push the Counters

After modeling the process, give each student their own sound box. Ask each to first stretch the word and then push the counters in the boxes. Sometimes, students struggle with matching their voices to pushing the counters. Teachers can simplify the task by asking the student to do only one of the behaviors (i.e., pushing counters or saying the sounds). Another way to handle this is modeling the correct procedure with corrective feedback about what went wrong, like this: "When you pushed the counters, you pushed a counter for the sound /ff/, but on the last part, /an/, there were two sounds and you pushed only one counter. On /aaaaan/ you went like this. [Push one counter into the box while saying '/aaaaan/.'] There are two sounds in /aaan/. /aaaaa/ /nnnnn/. Watch me do all three sounds."

If the student cannot do it after the correction, tell the student, "Follow my finger," and put your finger above each box as you are also saying the sound.

Step 4: Letter Boxes

There are two extensions of letter boxes. In the first, students push magnetic letters into the boxes while saying the sounds and then blend the words back together. This approach is used to decode an unknown word. With this approach, the student is given a word without a picture; the student pushes the letters into the box while saying the sounds and then blends the sounds to read the words.

In the second extension, the student does the sound box and then writes the letters in the boxes after using the counters to push and say the sounds.

chapter 6

UNIT: Beyond First Words

Learning Long Vowels and Other Patterns

KAYLA WAS A THRIVING FIRST GRADER SOARING INTO THE end of the year and zipping through every book she was given. Her teacher had done a masterful job. When Kayla entered second grade after a long summer, she struggled a bit. Dale, her second grade teacher explained, "Kayla loved to read and she could get through most books, but she stumbled a lot. She could sound out simple words and she used context, but when words got a little more complicated and the pictures weren't there, she didn't have a lot in her arsenal." After looking at Kayla's writing and giving a decoding test, Dale started to understand.

"Kayla would write every word with a long vowel using a silent *e*," Dale explained. "So *boat* was *bote* and *beat* was *bete*. It was like she knew that you couldn't just put a vowel by itself, but she didn't know exactly what to put. When she was reading, words like *harm*, *noise*, *shook*, or *sight* were difficult. I knew that she needed some type of focused instruction on vowels." When Kayla struggled with the word *meat*, Dale placed a sticky note on this page and used it as an example to begin a lesson on long *e* featuring *ea*.

Chart: *The (meat) was   tasty.*

            met meat

Dale: Remember when we were reading this sentence, in this book? [Shows book.] This word [points to *meat*] was confusing. You thought it said *met*. You made a sound for each letter, like /me/ /at/.

           The word *met* is *m-e-t*, and it looks like this [points to the word *met* on chart].

But this word [points to word *meat* on chart] has two vowels together, an *e* and *a*, *m-e-a-t*. This word is *meat*. In this word you put the *e* and *a* together to make one sound, /ē/. We are going to start working on learning these words.

Long vowels are tricky. But after a month of focused, sequenced instruction, Dale noticed that Kayla had gained more confidence. Dale observed, "I think that I just helped organize the information." Most readers will need some organized instruction about how to tackle vowels in English, especially those beyond simple short vowels. The Beyond First Words unit helps teachers approach this complex content in a pragmatic and logical way.

Why Learning Vowel Digraphs Is Challenging

Children typically learn to read and spell words with vowel pairs (those spelled with two or more letters) after they have learned short vowels, blends, and consonant digraphs (Ehri 2005; Henderson and Beers 1980; Treiman 1993; Treiman, Stothard, and Snowling 2013). (Note: The terms *vowel digraph* and *vowel team* are used synonymously to name vowels with two or more letters that represent a sound other than the short sound.) For beginning readers, words with more than one vowel are difficult for four reasons:

1. *Groups of letters are more complex than a single letter*. One-to-one relationships are easier to understand than two-to-one relationships. So words like *got*, in which each visual symbol represents a sound, are more intuitive than words like *seat*, in which some visual symbols combine to represent a sound.

2. *There is more to learn*. In comparison to short vowels, there are more sounds. As described in Chapter 1, English has over twenty vowel sounds and only five are short sounds, most of which are pretty consistent in single-syllable words. That leaves over fifteen additional vowel sounds in English (e.g., /oo/, /oi/, /ā/, /ar/) that must be learned.

3. *There are different ways to spell the same sounds*. Many of the long and other vowel sounds have more than one spelling, and the only way to know which words take which patterns is to practice building the words.

   Long *o* sound: oa   o_e   ow   oe

   boat   hope   bow   toe

4. *There are different sounds for the same spellings*. In some situations, the same pattern will represent two or more different sounds (e.g., *book, tool, now, tow*).

   oo   book   tool

   ow   now   tow

   ea   head   meat

How Should I Teach Vowel Digraphs?

Children must use a sophisticated approach to decode sounds represented by vowel teams (Ehri 2005; Ehri and McCormick 1998; Juel 1983). In earlier stages, they simply decode letter-by-letter from left to right, in linear fashion. See Figure 6.1. Unfortunately, this does not work with vowel digraphs. You must focus on the entire pattern. Your eyes must skip ahead a bit to do some analysis. People have called this the "consolidated" phase of word recognition because children group or consolidate letters. They use a hierarchical approach to decoding in which they recognize grapheme units composed of multiple letters to represent a sound. This usually occurs in mid–first grade after students have become fluent with simpler patterns (Bowey and Hansen 1994; Ehri 1991; Juel 1983, 1991). Figure 6.1 shows the difference between linear and hierarchical decoding.

FIGURE 6.1   Linear Decoding Versus Hierarchical Decoding

Principles for Teaching Vowel Teams

As a teacher, you have to teach vowel teams differently. Following are some basic principles to guide you.

- **Recognize that long vowels take a long time.** As Thelma, a first-grade teacher, said to a student teacher with a very ambitious plan, "Yep. The long part of long vowels is that they take a long time! You're not just going to pull that off in a few weeks." Children do not learn to decode long vowel patterns in the same amount of time that they acquire consonants, short vowels, and digraphs and blends. Within the Common Core Reading: Foundational Skills standards, for example, these vowel spellings are introduced over the course of first and second grade (NGA and CCSSO 2012).

- **Target groups of letters.** Vowel patterns in this phase are based on *two* vowels together, so instruction will almost always talk about how vowels work together. Usually two letters are adjacent. For example, usually when you see a vowel + *r*, you will have an *r*-controlled sound. In some cases, the vowel sound pronounced is the long sound of the first vowel (e.g., *ay, ee, ea* as in *beat, ai*) or even a short sound (e.g., *ea* as in *head*). Many people grew up hearing the controversial mnemonic "When two vowels go walking, the first one does the talking." Figure 6.2 addresses this.

FIGURE 6.2

What *really* happens when two vowels go walking?

The rule "When two vowels go walking, the first one does the talking" doesn't always work. The idea is to remember that in digraphs like *ea* the long sound of the *e* is heard. However, Clymer (1963) claimed that the rule only worked 45 percent of the time. The real problem with this rule is that it is not well stated (Johnston 2001). In many situations where two vowels go walking, the sound created is *pretty consistent*, but *neither* letter does the "talking" (e.g., *toil, paw, bow, boot, hook, shout*). Other times, a consonant influences the sound (e.g., *toy, claw, bear, torn, fir*). Teach the vowel pairs with an eye for predictability (see the table following). For example, *oi, oy,* and *aw* are very predictable. Pairs like *-ay, -oa, -ee, -ai, -au,* and *-ey* are more predictable than they are not. Other vowel pairs, like *ea*, can make up to three sounds, but even so, often have one dominant sound (e.g., *seat* [49.6%], *head* [16.7%], *fear* [14.3%], or *toes* [44.4%], *shoes* [33.3%], *does* [22.2%]). Still others might seem like "exceptions," but if you consider patterns, you will find collections that can be grouped together (e.g., *bread, head, read, dread, tread*).

continues

Vowel Teams That *Are* More Consistent			
Makes One Sound Nearly 100% of Time	Makes One Sound 95%–75% of Time	Makes One of Two Alternative Sounds	
-aw: law, raw	**-ay:** play, day [96.4%]	**-ow:** bow, tow [68%]	**-ow:** how, now [31.9%]
-oi: foil, toil	**-oa:** coat, boat [95%] **Exception:** roar	**-oo:** boot, hoot [50%]	**-oo:** book, took [40.4%]
-oy: toy, boy	**-ee:** feet, see [95.5%] **Exception:** deer	**-ew:** blew [88%]	**-ew:** view [11%]
	-ai: wait, paint [75%] **Exceptions:** hair, said		
	-au: cause [78.9%] **Exception:** laugh		
	-ey: key [77%] **Exception:** prey		

Source: Johnston 2001

Note: Pattern words and exception words are examples *only*. Lists are not exhaustive.

- **Remember that distributed practice and repetition are key.** Because vowel patterns cannot be differentiated by sound, it is important to explicitly describe each pattern and then provide lots of opportunities for children to read and spell words. Distributed practice across weeks is crucial. Think about it. The word *date* is spelled with *a_e*, but there is no hint in the pronunciation of *date* to indicate that you would use *a_e* and not *ai*. The only way to learn that it's *date* and not *dait* is to see it read and to *spell* it over and over. When students can spell words themselves, we know that they really "own" the patterns. This is why so many of the activities in this stage are games or word-building activities, in which students just practice spelling.

- **Organize "outsiders," "exception" words, or "rule breakers" into groups.** As described in Chapter 1, English is not as consistent as other languages, but this does not mean that it is *not consistent.* This is particularly true with words that seem like exceptions. When grouped together, these words often create a category that suggests that they do not operate in complete isolation. For example, with the *o_e* pattern there are some words that do not have a long *o* sound (e.g., *some, come, dove, love, above, done, one, none, gone*). If you look carefully at these, you will see that they actually form a group, with all but *gone* having the /ŭ/ sound. Teaching these together as a group helps students organize the information cognitively.

Beyond First Words: Scope and Sequence

The scope and sequence for Beyond First Words covers the basic vowel sounds learned after short vowel sounds. See Figure 6.3. The whole unit takes about twenty-three weeks and is divided into four subunits: (1) Sneaky Silent *e*, (2) Teamwork (vowel teams), (3) *R* the Robber (*r*-controlled vowels); and (4) Diphthongs. This list is *not* comprehensive. It is a first pass for students who are just starting to learn vowel patterns. There are several patterns that are not covered (e.g., *-old, -eigh, -ey, -al, -ie*). The exclusion of these does not indicate that they should not be taught; it just indicates that there are others that are more useful.

When are readers ready to learn all these vowel patterns? Students who are ready for learning vowel digraphs are readers. They have a solid collection of about 500 words that they can decode or read by sight automatically. They can read single-syllable short vowel words with blends and digraphs. Generally, teaching long vowel patterns will not start until first grade for most students. The Common Core places the easier patterns (e.g., silent *e*, very common vowel digraphs) in first grade and those that are more complicated (e.g., *r*-controlled vowels) in second grade.

FIGURE 6.3

Week	Letter–Sound Pattern	Example Words

1. Sneaky Silent *e*

1	**a_e** [77.7%)1]	**a e** **-ake*** bake, rake, take, cake, shake, brake, lake, make, stake, wake, fake **-ale*** male, pale, sale, kale, stale, tale **-ame*** blame, came, dame, fame, name, game, came, shame **-ate*** plate, gate, state, Nate, rate, date, late, ate, grate
2	**i_e** [74.2%]	**i_e** fine, dine, lime, pine, time, nine, bike, like, hike, hive, mile, time, wife, line **-ide*** ride, hide, side, bride, slide, tide, pride, glide
3	**u_e** [76%]	**u_e** cute, mute, cube, rude, tube, use (Note: As described in Chapter 1, some of these have the /yoo/ sound.)
4	**o_e** [58%]	**o_e** hope, cope, rope, slope, mope, note, vote, tone, hole, role **-oke*** joke, poke, stoke, broke, stroke, woke
5	**Sneaky *e* exceptions**	**o_e** some, come, one, done, none, once, love, glove, shove, above, dove **a_e** have, dance (Note: Words with -*ore* are taught below with *r*-controlled vowels.)

2. Teamwork (Vowel Teams)

| 6–7 | **Long *a* (ai & ay)** | **ai** [75%]
-ain* rain, plain, chain, gain, plain, stain, train, grain, drain, brain
-ail trail, sail, hail, fail, jail, mail, nail, rail, bail
exceptions: said, again
-ay* [96%] hay, may, ray, tray, say, lay, day, gray, play, pay, clay, stay, slay |

1. These percentages reflect *estimates* of the percentage of time the target pattern represents the sound in K–3 reading materials. They are based on Johnston (2001) and Gates and Yale (2011). Patterns without percentages did not have information.

Week	Letter–Sound Pattern	Example Words
8	**Long _e_** (ee & ea)	**ee** [95%] deep, sleep, sheep, keep, see, bee, tree, weed, seed, sheet, meet **ea** [50%] meal, speak, leap, heal, team, east, feast, peach **-eat*** heat, meat, beat, neat, seat, wheat, feat, cheat, treat
9	_ea_ **exceptions**	**ea** = /ĕ/ dead, head, ahead, instead, dread, tread, bread (The word _read_ can be pronounced with either a long _e_ or a short _e_.) **ea** = /ā/ steak, great, break (Note: There are very few instances of _ea_ = long _a_.) (Contrast short _e_ words [e.g., _dead_] with long _e_ words [e.g., _treat_, _heat_].)
10	**Long _o_** (oa & ow)	**oa** [95%] boat, goat, moat, soap, oak, coat, roam, foam **ow** = /ō/ [68%] bow, tow, row, stow, know, low, mow, show, grow, slow (_Ow_ as in _how_ is found in diphthongs.)
11	**Long _u_** (ue & ew)	**-ue** blue, glue, true, clue, due **-ew** [88%] dew, crew, few, grew, chew, mew, new, stew, blew, threw
12	**Long and short _oo_**	**oo** as in _boot_ (50%) boot, hoot, root, hoop, food, too, zoo, roof, pool, tool, cool, fool **oo** as in _book_ (40%) took, book, hook, look, brook, shook, good, cook, wood
13	**Long _i_** (-y & igh)	**-y** by, cry, try, dry, shy, sly, my, why, fly, sky **-ight*** sight, bright, fight, light, might, night, right, flight **-igh** sigh, high (Note: The letter _y_ also represents the long _e_ sound in multisyllabic words [e.g., _pretty_, _happy_, _naughty_, _many_]. But the focus in this chapter is single-syllable words.)

3. _R_ the Robber (_R_-Controlled Vowels)

Week	Letter–Sound Pattern	Example Words
14	**ar**	**ar** bar, car, far, jar, cart, harm, part, dark, bark, chart, smart, sharp, yarn, shark
15	**or**	**or** born, fort, corn, form, fork, horn, north, port, for, pork, torn

continues

Week	Letter–Sound Pattern	Example Words
3. *R* the Robber (*R*-Controlled Vowels) *continues*		
16	***or* sound (continued)** **ore** **our**	**ore*** bore, more, sore, wore, shore, chore, tore, snore, store, score, before **our** your, tour, pour, court, course, fourth
17–18 (2 weeks)	***er* sound** **ir** **er** **ur** **ear**	**ir** firm, girl, bird, dirt, squirt, first, chirp, firm, stir, twirl, third, birth **er** fern, germ, term, herd, perm, verb, serve, nerd, jerk, her, verse, herd **ur** turn, hurt, curl, curb, surf, nurse, purse, curse, urge, burst, burn, blur **ear** pearl, earn, heard, learn, search, earth, learn
(*R*-Controlled + Vowel Digraph)		
19	***air* sound** **are** **air** **ear**	**are** care, bare, hare, dare, rare, pare, stare, scare, share, square, fare **air** hair, fair, pair, chair **ear** tear, bear, wear, pear
20	***ear* sound** **ear** **eer**	**ear** ear, hear, rear, fear, dear, gear, near, year, beard **eer** deer, steer, jeer, peer, sneer, cheer
4. Diphthongs		
21	**oi & oy**	**oi** coin, boil, soil, foil, point, choice, voice, noise **oy** boy, toy, soy, joy, cowboy, annoy
22	**aw & au**	**aw*** paw, claw, yawn, hawk, saw, draw, straw, raw, thaw, awe, crawl, straw **au** sauce, launch, pause, caught, haunt, fault
23	**ou & ow**	**ou** out, shout, proud, loud, found, ouch, cloud, couch, pouch, doubt, about **ow** how, now, wow, cow, town, crowd, down, brown, frown, growl, owl

Notes: Example words have been specifically chosen as optimal "teaching words." Use these words during the Decode-It and Spell-It parts of the lessons.

Rimes / word parts marked by the * are in the 37 most frequently used rimes (Wylie and Durrell 1970). These will generate many words and are essential to teach; 12 are taught in Beyond First Words.

Beyond First Words Lesson Template

The lesson template in Figure 6.4 can be used to plan lessons for all the subunits in Beyond First Words.

FIGURE 6.4

Beyond First Words Weekly Lesson Template

Subunit: _____   Lesson #: _____   Letter/Sound Focus: _____

	Decode-It (Analyze) 5–7 min.	Spell-It (Synthesize) 5 min.	Read-It (Apply) 5–7 min.
Monday	Activity:[1] / Words/Notes:	Activity:[2] / Words/Notes:	Title:[3] / Decodable Words: / Content Words:
Tuesday	Activity: / Words/Notes:	Activity: / Words/Notes:	Title: / Decodable Words: / Content Words:
Wednesday	Activity: / Words/Notes:	Activity: / Words/Notes:	Title: / Decodable Words: / Content Words:

© 2019 by Heidi Anne Mesmer from *Letter Lessons and First Words*. Portsmouth, NH: Heinemann.

	Decode-It (Analyze) 5–7 min.	Spell-It (Synthesize) 5 min.	Read-It (Apply) 5–7 min.
Thursday	Activity: / Words/Notes:	Activity: / Words/Notes:	Title: / Decodable Words: / Content Words:
Friday	Activity: / Words/Notes:	Activity: / Words/Notes:	Title: / Decodable Words: / Content Words:

1 Decode-It Activities: Word Equations, Word Sort Fill-In, Word Sort, Word Changer (Silent e), Vowel Flexing, Highlighting Vowels, Unifix Cubes, Side-by-Side, Word Wheels, Charting Words Found in Literature

2 Spell-It Activities: Dictation, Word Building, This or That? Making Words, Dictation with Dry-Erase Boards

3 Read-It Steps: Bookwalk, First Read, Second Read, Praise and Practice, Reread

© 2019 by Heidi Anne Mesmer from *Letter Lessons and First Words*. Portsmouth, NH: Heinemann.

For a downloadable PDF of this template, go to http://hein.pub/letterlessons-login.

Subunit 1: Sneaky Silent *e*

The first subunit introduces the silent *e* pattern in a five-week period. Silent *e* is the vowel marker found at the end of a word that usually signals the long vowel sound in the middle. The silent *e* pattern is one of the more reliable patterns in English; as discussed in Chapter 1, it is not foolproof, but it is fairly consistent. As analyzed by Johnston (2001), the long vowel sound, as marked by the silent *e*, is very consistent with *a, u,* and *i*. It is used with *e_e* but there are very few words. With *o_e* there are exceptions. Teaching exception words together is useful because it shows that there are actually groups of words that follow the same pattern and that "break" the silent *e* pattern. The silent *e* pattern is a good place to start because children usually pick up on this pattern quickly.

Subunit 2: Team (Vowel Teams)

The next subunit, called Teamwork, dedicates eight weeks to learning the most common vowel digraphs or teams. Each week provides one to three different spellings for the same long vowel sound. The patterns in these subunits were chosen because they appear frequently in English and because several of them have rimes or word families that are found in the 37 most frequently occurring rimes (Wylie and Durrell 1970). These are marked by the * in the scope and sequence (see Figure 6.3).

Because there are a number of *ay* and *ai* patterns, an additional week is suggested at this point. There are also a number of *ea* words, and additional time could be dedicated to those as well. The scope also addresses an *ea* exception group (e.g., *great, dead*). In addition, it addresses two sounds for *oo,* the sound in *book* and the sound in *hoot.*

Subunit 3: *R* the Robber (*R*-Controlled Vowels)

The *r*-controlled vowels are some of the most complex graphemes in English. This is why they are taught near the end of the unit. There are multiple ways to spell each sound (e.g., /er/: *ir, ur, er*), and in some cases the same grapheme will represent two different phonemes (e.g., *ear* as in *hear, tear,* and *earth*). (See the box "Vowel Flexing in Single Syllable Words," p. 187.) Thus, the *r*-controlled vowels take a while to teach and a while to learn. The *r*-controlled subunit takes seven weeks and has two sections. The first section introduces three basic *r*-controlled sounds: /ar/, /or/, and /er/. The *ar* sound, when there is no *e* at the end of the word, is pretty consistent (e.g., *car*). The *or* sound can be represented with just *or* as in *corn* but also can be represented by *ore* and *our* (e.g., *bore, chore, your, pour*). The straight *or* is taught in one week, and then the two additional spellings, *ore* and *our,* are addressed in the following week. The last two weeks of the first section address the multiple ways to spell the *er* sound (e.g., *firm, herd, hurt*).

"Watch out for the letter *r*! It will steal that vowel sound." So goes the clever mnemonic. For the vowel pairs listed below when the letter *r* appears, the sound is usually changed from a typical long sound to an *r*-controlled or *r*-influenced sound. Reminding readers to be on the lookout for *r* gives them a handy generalization to use to pronounce a word.

Vowel Flexing in Single-Syllable Words

When a student sees a single vowel in a single-syllable word, the sound will usually be short (e.g., *tack*, *tip*), and if it is not, it will usually be long (e.g., *cold*, *go*). But vowel teams can be tricky. The sound is sometimes long, sometimes short, and sometimes something different. Vowel flexing, also called vowel alert or TOTO (try one, try the other), is a strategy to help students approach the pronunciation of vowels (not short vowels) with flexibility (Lovett, Lacerenza, and Borden 2000; Meese 2016; Steacy et al. 2017. This is important because in one study as many as 50 percent of words read contained a variant vowel (Steacy et al. 2017). Teachers and researchers approach vowel flexing with different steps. The following three-step process is a compilation of the general principles. My approach is to guide students to stop and think about different sounds in words with vowel patterns.

Step 1: STOP

When students see two vowels in a word, the first step is to STOP. This helps them be aware. They know they should proceed with caution.

Step 2: TRY ONE SOUND

In this second step, students try one sound that could possibly fit in the word. This is the one sound they know or the one that is most common. Then they try that one pronunciation and test it against the meaning in the sentence. If the word does not make sense, they go to Step 3: TRY ANOTHER SOUND.

Step 3: TRY ANOTHER SOUND

In the third step, they try another sound that could work. This could be the short sound of the first letter, the long sound of the first letter, or some other sound they know. Then they try that one pronunciation and test it against the meaning in the sentence.

Two Examples for Vowel Flexing

Example 1: *dread*

> **STOP**
>
> **TRY ONE SOUND.**
>
> The student sees *ea* and attempts the first sound that he knows that goes with *ea*: long *e*. *Dreed*?
>
> The student evaluates the word in the sentence: "He saw the car and was filled with dreed." No.

continues

TRY ANOTHER SOUND.

The student tries the short sound of the first letter, /e/. *Dread*?

The student evaluates the word in the sentence: "He saw the car and was filled with dread." Yes. That's it!

Example 2: *vow*

STOP

TRY ONE SOUND.

The student sees *ow* and attempts the first sound that she knows: long *o*, as in *know*. *Voe*?

The student evaluates the word in the sentence: "The knight knelt, ready to take a *voe*." No.

TRY ANOTHER SOUND.

The student tries the *ow* sound as in *how*. *Vow*?

The student evaluates the word in the sentence: "The knight knelt, ready to take a *vow*." Yes. That's it!

Note: This is only one strategy to support students in decoding vowel patterns. It is not foolproof. Sometimes a student might not know the two different sounds for a pattern. Sometimes the long vowel and short vowel attempts don't work (e.g., *head* works for the long/short vowel in Example 1, but *row* does not work in Example 2, nor does *tear/earth* in Example 1). The goal of this strategy is to get students to stop and think when they encounter a vowel pattern.

In the second section of the *r*-controlled subunit are vowel pairs + *r*. See Figure 6.5. These are organized by sound. The first is *air* (e.g., *bare, hair, tear*) and the second is the sound *ear* (e.g., *fear, deer*). As with the other *r*-controlled vowels, there are multiple ways to spell each of those sounds. Several *r*-controlled representations are not directly taught in this unit because they are not as common (e.g., *oar, ure, ire*).

FIGURE 6.5

R the Robber How the Letter *R* Influences Vowel Pairs	
Vowel Pair	**+ *r***
ee	-eer deer, steer, cheer
ai	-air pair, stair, hair
ea	-ear rear, hear, fear tear, wear, bear

Subunit 4: Diphthongs

The last three-week subunit is Diphthongs. Although linguists use a different definition for diphthongs, in this unit the term refers to the three sounds typically represented by the following letter pairs: (1) *oi/oy*, (2) *aw/au*, and (3) *ou/ow*. In these situations, the vowel combinations do not take the long or short sound of either of the letters in the team. Rather, they make a glided sound. Both *oy* and *oi* were nearly 100 percent consistent in a sample of words found in elementary grades (Johnston 2001). However, as mentioned in Chapter 1, these sounds can be tricky for kids due to the change that the mouth makes as that sound is made. The *aw* sound, which is also very consistent, is taught next (e.g., *claw*, *caught*). The last sound in the unit is *ou* (e.g., *shout*, *how*). Note that *ow* also represents the long *o* sound, as in *now*. There are almost equal numbers of words that have *ow* as in *how* and words that have *ow* is *glow*.

Lesson Framework and Activities

Lessons for Beyond First Words are shorter than those in the previous subunits and typically take place about three times per week. They all use the same lesson framework with three parts: (1) Decode-It, (2) Spell-It, and (3) Read-It. There is no phonemic awareness (Hear-It) or Review-It section. The lessons can be fifteen to twenty minutes and might be included at the beginning or end of small-group reading instruction or in a separate phonics small group. Decodables can be used at this stage, although students at this stage are more fluent and will be reading a range of other materials during their language arts block. During the days that students are not meeting with the teacher for instruction, they practice patterns independently. See Figure 6.6.

The lesson has three goals:

- **Decode words with vowel patterns automatically (Decode-It).** Readers build their abilities to pay attention to multi-letter units and decode hierarchically. They look for units that represent sounds that are not the short sounds.

- **Spell words with the target patterns (Spell-It).** The ultimate gauge of students' understanding of the patterns that are being taught is their ability to spell those patterns. This task requires synthesis. When students can spell the various patterns, they are able to match each pattern with the proper word even when the sounds are similar (e.g., *ate* vs. *ait*).

- **Read words in books (Read-It).** Several times a week, during their small-group phonics work, students can read texts that possess some of the vowel patterns that they are learning. At this point in development, these words can be read in texts with some level of decodability, poems, and even children's literature. (See Figure 6.10 for popular titles and the words in them that contain vowel patterns.)

FIGURE 6.6

	Time	Lesson Part	Content	Sample Language	Activity Choices
1	5–7 minutes	**Decode-It** (Analyze)	Decode words with vowel teams.	Teacher: Let's use the cubes to make the word *teen*. That word has the /ee/ sound. To make that sound which letters do I need? Student: *ea*? Teacher: Yes, that makes the long sound but it doesn't go in this word. Is there another set of letters? Think about the word *see*. Student: *ee*	Unifx cubes Word Equations Word Sort Fill-in Word Wheels or Flip Books This or That? Side-by-Side Word Finds in Literature Vowel Flexing Word Sorts
2	5 minutes	**Spell-It** (Synthesize)	Spell words letter-by-letter.	Teacher: We are going to do a Word Building starting with the word *bat*. We are going to review patterns that we learned a while ago and also use the ones we know. *bat* *boot* *boat* *coat*	Dictation Dry Erase Boards Making Words Word Building
3	5–7 minutes	**Read-It** (Apply)	Read connected texts and poems with vowel teams.	Teacher: We are going to read this book, *A Store for Norm* but first let's do a Book Walk. We are looking for words that have the /or/ sound like Norm. Look at the first page. Do you see an *or* word? Student: *For*.	Read-it routine with decodables or poems Word Finds in Literature

Decode-It (Analyze)

During Decode-It, the activities provide opportunities to remember different patterns for the same sounds or compare words. See Figure 6.7. Earlier in the week, when the patterns are newer, use word wheels, word changers, or word sorts. Toward the end of the week, as students gain more practice, use Word Sort Fill-In, where students must supply the correct vowel pair for each word. Word Changer is a great activity for the Sneaky Silent *e* because students must pronounce a word *with* a silent *e* and a word *without* a silent *e*. Sometimes students use highlighters to identify the patterns or Unifix cubes with preprinted patterns to read or build words. During this part of the lesson, students could also be taught vowel flexing. (See the box "Vowel Flexing in Single-Syllable Words.") Word finds in literature are also useful. There is a list of children's literature in Figure 6.10 with specific words that follow the many different vowel patterns taught in the unit. These are all delightful, entertaining stories that children can and should read first for their own pleasure.

FIGURE 6.7

Activities for Decode-It: Reading words with multiletter vowel teams

Unifix Cubes with Letter Units

Use unifix cubes to build words with vowel teams.

VIDEO 6.1

Unifix Cubes

For an example of a lesson using letter cubes to teach vowel patterns, watch this video.

Word Equations

Call out a word and ask the students to use a dry erase board or word cards to create word equations with the different parts of the word.

goat = g + oa + t

hope = h + ope

snow = s + n + ow

continues

Word Sort Fill-In

In a Word-Sort Fill-In, students are given word cards with the vowel team omitted and then must sort words and fill in the correct vowel pattern.

ea meat	ee feet
n_ _t	tr_ _

This activity gets students to think about the pattern that appears in the word instead of simply visually sorting.

Caveat: This activity works best toward the end of the unit, when students have had some practice trying to remember the patterns. If you choose to do it at the beginning, give students access to a set of word cards with the correct spellings to help them.

Word Wheels

As described in Chapter 4, word wheels are a useful way to draw attention to a particular part of a word. In a word wheel, for example, a Sneaky Silent *e* might change the pronunciation of a base word.

Word Changer with Sticky Notes

This is essentially like a word wheel, but instead of using a wheel, students use a stack of sticky notes to change letters.

This or That?

Present two words with vowel patterns, one that is correct and one that is incorrect. The students have to decide if the proper way to spell the word is "this" or "that."

This?	That?
sope	soap
hirt	hurt
burp	berp
hed	head

Extensions: Students can make up their own This or That? and bring it to group meeting. Check each This or That? before it is shared.

Caveat: Play this game when students know a lot of patterns and have a repertoire from which to pull. If played too early, it falls flat.

Charting Words Found During Word Finds with Literature

After reading children's literature, have students find words with the target pattern. They can keep their own lists in a notebook.

Example: *Where Is the Green Sheep?* by Mem Fox

ee	ear	ai	a_e
sheep	near	train	brave
green	hear	rain	wave
peep			page
asleep			take

See Figure 6.10 for a list of children's books with target patterns.

Spell-It (Synthesize)

For vowel digraphs, the Spell-It section of the lesson is particularly important because spelling the words letter-by-letter helps students remember which patterns go with which words. Simple dictation is a great way to practice. Make sure to take away word cards or other cues so that the students really have to think about how to spell. At this stage, Word Building is optimal because students usually have a larger repertoire of letter–sounds. It is easier to plan Word Building or Making Words when you can include short vowel words, words with digraphs, words with blends, and words with target vowel digraphs. The activities listed below are the same ones that are in Chapter 5.

FIGURE 6.8

Activities for Spell-It: Spelling words

Dictation

Identify two to three words from the lesson to dictate. Children should correctly spell each word.

continues

Making Words and Word Building

Making Words and Word Building are two activities for spelling. (See p. 171 for more information.) In a Making Words lesson, children use five to seven magnetic letters or letter cards to spell words.

Word Building with vowel teams will have letters that change at the beginning, middle, and ending of words.

t	a	l	e
b	a	l	e
r	a	i	l

Don't wing it. Plan the words that your students will spell. (See "Making Words or Word Building Lesson" on p. 171.)

Read-It (Apply)

During Read-It in Beyond First Words, students practice reading vowel patterns in text. Certainly, texts with some level of decodability are useful at this point, but students can read poems with vowel patterns and may even find vowel patterns literature like *Sheep in a Jeep* by Nancy Shaw. In Beyond First Words, students can read more words, so texts with less control that still have target vowel patterns can be read. Figure 6.9 shows the "Read-It Routine" with procedures for reading a decodable text at this stage. It is very similar to the procedure shown in Chapter 5, but there are some differences. In addition, during Read-it, children can read poems or stories and find words with vowel teams.

WATCH

VIDEO 6.2

Finding Words in a Poem

Children finding *ee* words in the poem "The Sweet Jeep" (and then creating a tune for the poem!), see this video.

FIGURE 6.9

Read-It Routine

Before the Lesson: Preview the Book

Never use a book in a lesson without first previewing it.

Before using a book or poem in Beyond First Words, preview it and check to see that *there are a number of words* that contain taught vowel patterns. Students at this stage are more advanced. Typically they can read about 500 different words, including 100–200 high-frequency words and about 300 additional words with short vowels (Snow, Burns, and Griffin 1998). For this reason, the very close match between text words and taught patterns is easier to establish—students know more. However, in order to practice reading words with vowel teams in connected text, ask yourself, "Does the book have words with vowel teams? Will it provide opportunities to practice patterns?"

Step 1: Book Walk

The purpose of the book walk is to quickly review decodable words with taught vowel team patterns or complex content words *before* reading. (Note: At this stage, it is usually not necessary to review high-frequency words during the Book Walk.) The book walk usually takes about three minutes. During the book walk, call students' attention to words with target patterns: "Oh look, here's a word that has *-ee*. What is that? Let's practice reading that word. Here's another one on the next page."

Define decodable words with unknown meanings. For example, "Look at this word [point to *greed*]. How would we read that? *Greed*? Do you know what that means? It's when people want everything for themselves."

Note: A book walk is not a picture walk. Don't feel the need to go through every page and every picture in a book, especially if it's a long book.

Step 2: First Reading

By Beyond First Words, students can usually read the book the first time on their own, especially if some type of book walk has been conducted. If the book is particularly hard, a choral read with the teacher filling in at tough parts could help.

Choral read: Read and point the book all together. The teacher's voice stays in the mix and scaffolds through harder words but then "backs off" if students are more secure.

Independent read: This method is for books with words that students can decode very easily. The students read on their own without the teacher's voice.

continues

Step 3: Second Reading

Each child reads independently.

Decoding words is the idea in these decodables, so make sure it happens.

The child reads and decodes the story alone. Watch and listen for accurate decoding and help when a student is struggling to decode.

Use vowel flexing with single-syllable words, as described in the box on p. 187.

Remember, don't turn the reading into a phonics lesson. If the child cannot decode the word fairly quickly, provide three quick prompts and move on. (See "Word Prompting: What to Say When They Struggle with a Word" on p. 64.) The first prompt is to pause; the second prompt is to say, "Something tricked you"; the third prompt is based on the child's letter–sound knowledge. If these prompts do not work, model the word.

Step 4: Praise and Practice

At the end of the book, praise something the students have done well.

"When you came to the word *beam*, you stopped and were not sure. Then you said the /bea/ and then put that word together. Good job! What is that word [*beam*, point to word]?"

Then practice something that was difficult.

"When you came to *hat*, you said '*ham*.' Then you stopped and you reread the sentence and you said '_____' [let the child fill in the correct word]. You used your letter–sounds to read that word."

Step 5: Reread

After the children have read the book once by themselves, have them reread it to other teachers, cafeteria staff, counselors, family members, and friends. I like to say, "If you read it once, you should read it again !"

Independent Work

At the end of the lessons, the teacher can ask students to do independent work that's to be completed before the next lesson. One great activity for students is to make their own version of This or That? The practice of developing the wrong answers for This or That? and identifying the right answers can be very powerful. Another good independent activity is to have students word find, or identify words with target patterns in the books they are reading. It sometimes helps to have a specific book selected that students can use, so that you know they will find words. A list of children's literature with long vowel words appears in Figure 6.10. I suggest you read these aloud for enjoyment during small-group time and then let students reread a copy on their own and find words. Another approach might be to make several of these titles available to students and allow them to choose a book that interests them and read it. The word find activity usually works better if you ask students to find *single-syllable words*. Some activities, although very popular for homework, are not particularly useful. These are discussed in the box below.

Homework and Practice: What to Avoid

Rainbow Writing Words

It is very common for students to be asked to "rainbow write" words with each letter in a different color or to cut out letters from magazines to spell words. The supposed purpose of these activities may be to cement the word in memory. However, rainbow writing is time-consuming and the time costs do not match the benefit. Sometimes students do this activity without really thinking about the words. For example, I've seen a child write the first letter for a word five times and then write the second letter for the word five times and so on.

Search and Find Puzzles

Search and find puzzles require students to identify target words "hidden" within a sea of letters. Although the student does have to pay attention to the sequence of letters within the words, the main focus is sorting out the word among the letter "noise" in the puzzle. The main skills used are different from those used in spelling words. In addition, we don't write English words backwards, vertically, or diagonally, the way that they may be found in a word search.

Writing Sentences for Each Word

There is probably no one in the United States over the age of twenty who has not had to write sentences for each spelling word. This laborious activity has produced some of the dreariest and flattest sentences known to man. The main issues are that children do not need to write an entire sentence to practice the words and that this is not really an expressive or authentic application of writing.

Giving Everyone the Same List of Words

Another homework practice to avoid is giving everyone the same list of words to practice. Because students differ in their knowledge of words, they are usually working on different patterns. Thus, sending home one list of words for students to memorize and regurgitate on a weekly spelling test is pointless. In fact, the authors of *No More Phonics and Spelling Worksheets* remind us that children often will not know the words they memorize for a spelling test weeks later (Palmer and Invernizzi 2015).

FIGURE 6.10   **Books to Use for Word Finding: Children's Literature with Target Long Vowels**

Title, Author	Long A	Long E	Long I	Long O	Long U	Exceptions
Sheep in a Jeep, Nancy Shaw	**a_e:** sale	**ee:** beep sheep jeep steep deep weep sweep **ea:** leap heap cheap	**i_e:** driver	uh-oh go don't goes		shove comes
Should I Share My Ice Cream?, Mo Willems	**ai:** wait **ea:** great **ay:** maybe day	**ea:** cream please eat easy **ee:** sweet **ea:** easy	**i_e:** ice like **y:** my	**ow:** know **o:** no oh	**ew:** blew	love some give have
Kate and Nate Are Running Late!, Kate Egan	**a_e:** shakes wake takes make makes late Nate Kate hate plate date **ace:** races **ai:** straight wait **ea:** great **ay:** day okay today Saturday	**ee:** creeps asleep coffee feeds teeth seems feeling streets need speedy speed see **ea:** leap please eats squeal **e:** he she be	**i_e:** time ice slices **ie:** tries **igh:** sigh eyes	**oa:** toasts **ow:** flow	**u_e:** use **ui:** juice **ue:** clue	have some been one

Title, Author	Long A	Long E	Long I	Long O	Long U	Exceptions
Rain, Manya Stojic	**ai:** rain plain **a_e:** taste shade	**ee:** see deep feel tree trees green **ea:** leaves eat **e_e:** these	**i_e:** time like **y:** dry	**o_e:** hole shone **ow:** know	**ew:** grew	have
Where Is the Green Sheep?, Mem Fox	**ai:** rain train **a_e:** wave brave page take	**ee:** sheep green peep asleep	**i_e:** wide slide		**ue:** blue	
Ten Sleepy Sheep, Phyllis Root	**a_e:** race gate **ay:** gray	**ee:** sleep sheep knee-deep green bees tree three asleep **ea:** leap bleats	**i_e:** time vine nine beehive hive five **igh:** sighs **ie:** cries fireflies tried	**o_e:** rose close doze lope **oa:** roam	**ue:** blue	
The Rain Came Down, David Shannon	**ai:** rain paint rainbow **a_e:** came made plane baker cakes snake make shave gave **ay:** day **air:** hair	**y:** baby **e:** me **ea:** cream stream each **ee:** see three need sweet **ere:** here	**i_e:** wife driver ice inside time nice **y:** cry **ie:** dries	**o_e:** woke poked nose whole drove home cones **ow:** owner **oa:** boat		have done

continues

Title, Author	Long A	Long E	Long I	Long O	Long U	Exceptions
Rainy Day!, Patricia Lakin	**ai:** rainy paint rain hail **ay:** day play way **a_e:** make bake came whale face place	**ea:** each	**i_e:** outside line sliding **ight:** right sight	**o:** go no **oa:** road soaking **ow:** know **o_e:** home		
Mice on Ice, Rebecca Emberley and Ed Emberley	**a_e:** skate skates skating **ai:** waiting		**i_e:** mice ice nice	**ow:** snow		
Green Eggs and Ham, Dr. Seuss	**ai:** train rain **ay:** say may	**ee:** green see tree **ea:** eat **e:** be	**i:** I **i_e:** like **y:** try	**oa:** goat boat		
Which Witch Is Which?, Judi Barrett	**ay:** playing saying	**ea:** lean mean clean reading sneaky eating **ee:** green feeling	**y:** trying lying tying **i:** wild **i_e:** riding	**o:** holding	**oo:** broom balloon moon **u_e:** prune	

Title, Author	Long A	Long E	Long I	Long O	Long U	Exceptions
Fun Dog, Sun Dog, Deborah Heilingman	**ay:** stay away sprayed way **a_e:** take	**ee:** sweet greet need **ea:** treat beach reach teach	**i_e:** ride slide side **igh:** right **y:** by my	**o_e:** home		
Snow Dog, Go Dog, Deborah Heilingman	**ay:** play yay day stray away **a_e:** chase race place	**ee:** feeling sweet greet **ea:** treat	**i_e:** hiding ride slide	**ow:** snow **o:** go fro **o_e:** home		loves have

Note: Some very common multisyllabic words are included here.

Closing

"I wasn't really completing the job with phonics," explained Darla, a first-grade teacher in New Jersey. "I kind of got the kids to a place where they could blend short vowel words and then just taught other vowels as they came up. Mostly, I just didn't know how to approach anything beyond short vowels. With all these exceptions and rule breakers, it didn't feel like it made sense. Since it didn't make sense to me, I couldn't really teach it in a way that made sense to kids. I was not organized. It was like these long vowels were a tangled ball of yarn and I would go to the ball of yarn when I needed a piece of string and just grab a piece from anywhere and cut it off. It had all these loose, cut-off pieces in it. I never really knew where the ball of yarn started. Now, I have this nicely wound ball of yarn and I know where the yarn starts. I can unravel the content for the kids in a way that helps them."

Darla's experience is very common. So many very strong readers and teachers don't really have an organized plan for teaching the vowel sounds outside of the short vowels. What this unit does is organize the content and present it in a more logical way. The vowel digraph patterns are not easy and they will take a longer time to learn and more practice, but with an organized approach readers will understand how these patterns work and will move forward empowered with their knowledge.

References

Adams, M. J. 1990. *Beginning to Read: Thinking and Learning About Print*. Urbana-Champaign, IL: University of Illinois.

Allington, R. L. 1980. "Teacher Interruption Behaviors During Primary-Grade Oral Reading." *Journal of Educational Psychology* 72 (3): 371–77.

Anthony, J. L., and D. J. Francis. 2005. "Development of Phonological Awareness." *Current Directions in Psychological Science* 14 (5): 255–59.

Anthony, J. L., C. J. Lonigan, K. Driscoll, B. M. Phillips, and S. R. Burgess. 2003. "Phonological Sensitivity: A Quasi-parallel Progression of Word Structure Units and Cognitive Operations." *Reading Research Quarterly* 38 (4): 470–87.

Armbruster, B. B., F. Lehr, J. Osborn, and C. R. Adler. 2003. *Putting Reading First: The Research Building Blocks for Teaching Children to Read: Kindergarten Through Grade 3*. Washington, DC. National Institute for Literacy, National Institute of Child Health and Human Development, U.S. Department of Education.

Bailey, M. H. 1967. "The Utility of Phonic Generalizations in Grades One Through Six." *Reading Teacher* 20 (5): 413–18.

Bear, D. R., M. Invernizzi, and F. Johnston. 2006. *Words Their Way: Letter and Picture Sorts for Emergent Readers*. New York: Pearson.

Bear, D. R., M. Invernizzi, S. Templeton, and F. Johnston. 2000. *Words Their Way: Word Study for Phonics, Vocabulary, and Spelling Instruction*. New York: Pearson.

Bizzochi, A. L. 2017. "How Many Phonemes Does English Have?" *International Journal on Studies in English Language and Literature* 5 (10): 36–46. doi:10.20431/2347-3134.0510006.

Bond, G. L., and R. Dykstra. 1967. "The Cooperative Research Program in First-Grade Reading Instruction." *Reading Research Quarterly* 2 (4): 5–142. doi:10.2307/746948.

Bowers, P. N., and J. R. Kirby. 2010. "Effects of Morphological Instruction on Vocabulary Acquisition." *Reading and Writing* 23 (5): 515–37.

Bowey, J. A., and J. Hansen. 1994. "The Development of Orthographic Rimes as Units of Word Recognition." *Journal of Experimental Child Psychology* 58 (3): 465–88.

Brown, K. J. 2003. "What Do I Say When They Get Stuck on a Word? Aligning Teachers' Prompts with Students' Development." *Reading Teacher* 56 (8): 720–33.

Burmeister, L. E. 1968. "Usefulness of Phonic Generalizations." *Reading Teacher* 21 (4): 349–60.

Bus, A. G., and M. H. Van Ijzendoorn. 1999. "Phonological Awareness and Early Reading: A Meta-Analysis of Experimental Training Studies." *Journal of Educational Psychology* 91 (3): 403–14.

Calfee, R. 1998. "Phonics and Phonemes: Learning to Decode and Spell in a Literature-Based Program." In *Word Recognition in Beginning Literacy*, edited by J. L. Metsala and L. C. Ehri, 315–40. Mahwah, NJ: Lawrence Erlbaum.

Carroll, J. M., M. J. Snowling, J. Stevenson, and C. Hulme. 2003. "The Development of Phonological Awareness in Preschool Children." *Developmental Psychology* 39 (5): 913.

Chall, J. S. 1967. *Learning to Read.* New York: McGraw-Hill.

Cheatham, J. P., and J. H. Allor. 2012. "The Influence of Decodability in Early Reading Text on Reading Achievement: A Review of the Evidence." *Reading and Writing* 25 (9): 2223–46.

Chomsky, N. 1986. *Knowledge of Language: Its Nature, Origin, and Use.* New York: Praeger.

Clay, M. M. 1991. *Becoming Literate: The Construction of Inner Control.* 2nd ed. Portsmouth, NH: Heinemann.

Clymer, T. 1963. "The Utility of Phonic Generalizations in the Primary Grades." *Reading Teacher* 16 (4): 252–58.

Compton, D. L., A. C. Appleton, and M. K. Hosp. 2004. "Exploring the Relationship Between Text-Leveling Systems and Reading Accuracy and Fluency in Second-Grade Students Who Are Average and Poor Decoders." *Learning Disabilities Research and Practice* 19 (3): 176–84.

Connor, C. M., F. J. Morrison, B. J. Fishman, C. Schatschneider, and P. Underwood. 2007. "The Early Years: Algorithm-Guided Individualized Reading Instruction." *Science* 315 (5811): 464–65. doi:10.1126/science.1134513.

Cunningham, P. 1988. "Names—a Natural for Early Reading and Writing." *Reading Horizons* 28 (2). http://scholarworks.wmich.edu/reading_horizons/vol28/iss2/5.

Cunningham, P. M., and J. W. Cunningham. 1992. "Making Words: Enhancing the Invented Spelling-Decoding Connection." *Reading Teacher* 46 (2): 106–15.

Davis, M. 2018. "Responding to Jumbled Letters." http://www.mrc-cbu.cam.ac.uk/people/matt-davis/cmabridge/.

Dolch, E. W. 1936. "A Basic Sight Word Vocabulary." *Elementary School Journal* 36 (6): 456–60.

Drouin, M., S. L. Horner, and T. A. Sondergeld. 2012. "Alphabet Knowledge in Preschool: A Rasch Model Analysis." *Early Childhood Research Quarterly* 27 (3): 543–54.

Duke, N. K. 2016. *Notes on Choosing Good Alphabet Key Words.* Ann Arbor, MI: Self-published.

Ehri, L. C. 1991. "Learning to Read and Spell Words." In *Learning to Read: Basic Research and Its Implications*, edited by L. Rieben and C. A. Perfetti, 57–73. Hillsdale, NJ: Lawrence Erlbaum.

———. 2005. "Learning to Read Words: Theory, Findings, and Issues." *Scientific Studies of Reading* 9: 167–88. doi:10.1207/s1532799xssr0902_4.

———. 2015. "How Children Learn to Read Words." In *The Oxford Handbook of Reading*, edited by A. Pollatsek and R. Treiman, 293–310. New York: Oxford University Press.

Ehri, L. C., and S. McCormick. 1998. "Phases of Word Learning: Implications for Instruction with Delayed and Disabled Readers." *Reading and Writing Quarterly* 14 (2): 135–63. doi:10.1080/1057356980140202.

Ehri, L. C., E. Satlow, and I. Gaskins. 2009. "Grapho-phonemic Enrichment Strengthens Keyword Analogy Instruction for Struggling Young Readers." *Reading and Writing Quarterly* 25 (2–3): 162–91.

Ehri, L. C., and J. Sweet. 1991. "Fingerpoint-Reading of Memorized Text: What Enables Beginners to Process the Print?" *Reading Research Quarterly* 26 (4): 442–62.

Elkonin, D. B. 1963. "The Psychology of Mastering the Elements of Reading." In *Educational Psychology in the USSR*, edited by B. Simon and J. Simon, 165–79. London: Routledge and Kegan Paul.

Ellefson, M. R., R. Treiman, and B. Kessler. 2009. "Learning to Label Letters by Sounds or Names: A Comparison of England and the United States." *Journal of Experimental Child Psychology* 102 (3): 323–41. doi:10.1016/j.jecp.2008.05.008.

Evans, M. A., M. Bell, D. Shaw, S. Moretti, and J. Page. 2006. "Letter Names, Letter Sounds and Phonological Awareness: An Examination of Kindergarten Children Across Letters and of Letters Across Children." *Reading and Writing* 19 (9): 959–89.

Foorman, B. R., D. J. Francis, K. C. Davidson, M. W. Harm, and J. Griffin. 2004. "Variability in Text Features in Six Grade 1 Basal Reading Programs." *Scientific Studies of Reading* 8 (2): 167–97.

Fry, E. B. 2004. *The Vocabulary Teacher's Book of Lists*. New York: Jossey-Bass.

Gates, L., and I. Yale. 2011. "A Logical Letter-Sound System in Five Phonic Generalizations." *Reading Teacher* 64: 330–39. doi:10.1598/RT.64.5.3.

Griffith, P. L., and Olson, M. W. 1992. "Phonemic Awareness Helps Beginning Readers Break the Code." *Reading Teacher* 45: 516–52.

Groff, P. 1971. "Sequences for Teaching Consonant Clusters." *Journal of Reading Behavior* 4 (1): 59–65.

Henderson, E. H., and J. W. Beers, eds. 1980. *Developmental and Cognitive Aspects of Learning to Spell: A Reflection of Word Knowledge*. Newark, DE: International Reading Association.

Hiebert, E. H. 2002. "Standards, Assessment, and Text Difficulty." In *What Research Has to Say About Reading Instruction*, edited by S. S. Jay and A. E. Farstrup, 337–69. Newark, DE: International Reading Association.

———. 2005. "The Effects of Text Difficulty on Second Graders' Fluency Development." *Reading Psychology* 26 (2): 183–209.

Hines, S. J., D. L. Speece, C. Y. Walker, and L. M. DaDeppo. 2007. "Assessing More Than You Teach: The Difficult Case of Transfer." *Reading and Writing* 20 (6): 539–52.

Hoffman, J. V., and R. Clements. 1984. "Reading Miscues and Teacher Verbal Feedback." *Elementary School Journal* 84 (4): 423–39.

Huang, F. L., L. S. Tortorelli, and M. A. Invernizzi. 2014. "An Investigation of Factors Associated with Letter–Sound Knowledge at Kindergarten Entry." *Early Childhood Research Quarterly* 29 (2): 182–192.

Hulme, C., P. J. Hatcher, K. Nation, A. Brown, J. Adams, and G. Stuart. 2002. "Phoneme Awareness Is a Better Predictor of Early Reading Skill Than Onset-Rime Awareness." *Journal of Experimental Child Psychology* 82 (1): 2–28.

Hulme, C., V. Muter, and M. Snowling. 1998. "Segmentation Does Predict Early Progress in Learning to Read Better Than Rhyme: A Reply to Bryant." *Journal of Experimental Child Psychology* 71 (1): 39–44.

International Dyslexia Association. 2018. *Dyslexia Basics*. December 12. https://dyslexiaida.org/dyslexia-basics/.

Invernizzi, M., and J. Buckrop. 2018. "Reconceptualizing Alphabet Learning and Instruction." In *Pivotal Research in Early Literacy: Foundational Studies and Current Practices*, edited by C. M. Cassano and S. M. Dougherty. New York: Guilford Press.

Invernizzi, M., and L. Hayes. 2004. "Developmental-Spelling Research: A Systematic Imperative." *Reading Research Quarterly* 39: 216–28.

Invernizzi, M., L. Justice, T. J. Landrum, and K. Booker. 2004. "Early Literacy Screening in Kindergarten: Widespread Implementation in Virginia." *Journal of Literacy Research* 36 (4): 479–500. doi:10.1207/s15548430jlr3604_3.

Johnston, F. P. 2001. "The Utility of Phonic Generalizations: Let's Take Another Look at Clymer's Conclusions." *Reading Teacher* 55 (2): 132–43.

Johnston, F. R. 2000. "Word Learning in Predictable Text." *Journal of Educational Psychology* 92 (2): 248.

Johnston, F. R., M. Invernizzi, D. R. Bear, and S. R. Templeton. 2005. *Words Their Way: Word Sorts for Syllables and Affixes Spellers*. 3rd ed. Boston: Pearson.

Jones, C. D., S. K. Clark, and D. R. Reutzel. 2013. "Enhancing Alphabet Knowledge Instruction: Research Implications and Practical Strategies for Early Childhood Educators." *Early Childhood Education Journal* 41 (2): 81–89.

Jones, C. D., and D. R. Reutzel. 2012. "Enhanced Alphabet Knowledge Instruction: Exploring a Change of Frequency, Focus, and Distributed Cycles of Review." *Reading Psychology* 33 (5): 448–64.

Juel, C. 1983. "The Development and Use of Mediated Word Identification." *Reading Research Quarterly* 18 (3) 306–27.

———. 1988. "Learning to Read and Write: A Longitudinal Study of 54 Children from First Through Fourth Grades." *Journal of Educational Psychology* 80: 243–55.

———. 1991. "Beginning Reading." In *Handbook of Reading Research*, edited by R. Barr, M. Kamil, P. Mosenthal, and P. D. Pearson, 2: 759–88. New York: Longman.

Juel, C., and D. Roper. 1985. "The Influence of Basal Readers on First Grade Reading." *Reading Research Quarterly* 20 (2): 134–52.

Justice, L. M., K. Pence, R. B. Bowles, and A. Wiggins. 2006. "An Investigation of Four Hypotheses Concerning the Order by Which 4-Year-Old Children Learn the Alphabet Letters." *Early Childhood Research Quarterly* 21: 374–89.

Justice, L. M., P. C. Pullen, and K. Pence. 2008. "Influence of Verbal and Nonverbal References to Print on Preschoolers' Visual Attention to Print During Storybook Reading." *Developmental Psychology* 44 (3): 855.

Kirby, J. R., S. H. Deacon, P. N. Bowers, L. Izenberg, L. Wade-Woolley, and R. Parrila. 2012. "Children's Morphological Awareness and Reading Ability." *Reading and Writing* 25 (2): 389–410.

LaBerge, D., and S. J. Samuels. 1974. "Toward a Theory of Automatic Information Process in Reading." *Cognitive Psychology* 6: 293–323.

Landerl, K., H. H. Freudenthaler, M. Heene, P. F. De Jong, A. Desrochers, G. Manolitsis, R. Parrila, and G. K. Georgiou. 2018. "Phonological Awareness and Rapid Automatized Naming as Longitudinal Predictors of Reading in Five Alphabetic Orthographies with Varying Degrees of Consistency." *Scientific Studies of Reading*. doi:10.1080/10888438.2018.1510936.

Liberman, I. Y., D. Shankweiler, F. W. Fischer, and B. Carter. 1974. "Explicit Syllable and Phoneme Segmentation in the Young Child." *Journal of Experimental Child Psychology* 18 (2): 201–12.

Lonigan, C. J., and T. Shanahan. 2009. "Developing Early Literacy: Report of the National Early Literacy Panel. Executive Summary. A Scientific Synthesis of Early Literacy Development and Implications for Intervention." Washington, DC. National Institute for Literacy.

Lovett, M. W., L. Lacerenza, and S. L. Borden. 2000. "Putting Struggling Readers on the PHAST Track: A Program to Integrate Phonological and Strategy-Based Remedial Reading Instruction and Maximize Outcomes." *Journal of Learning Disabilities* 33 (5): 458–76.

Lundberg, I., J. Frost, and O. P. Petersen. 1988. "Effects of an Extensive Program for Stimulating Phonological Awareness in Preschool Children." *Reading Research Quarterly* 23 (3): 263–84.

McBride-Chang, C. 1999. "The ABCs of the ABCs: The Development of Letter-Name and Letter-Sound Knowledge." *Merrill-Palmer Quarterly* 45 (2): 285–308.

McCandliss, B., I. L. Beck, R. Sandak, and C. Perfetti. 2003. "Focusing Attention on Decoding for Children with Poor Reading Skills: Design and Preliminary Tests of the Word Building Intervention." *Scientific Studies of Reading* 7 (1): 75–104.

McKay, R., and W. H. Teale. 2015. *No More Teaching a Letter a Week*. Portsmouth, NH: Heinemann.

Meese, R. L. 2016. "We're Not in Kansas Anymore: The TOTO Strategy for Decoding Vowel Pairs." *Reading Teacher* 69 (5): 549–52. doi:10.1002/trtr.1393.

Menon, S., and E. H. Hiebert. 2005. "A Comparison of First Graders' Reading with Little Books or Literature-Based Basal Anthologies." *Reading Research Quarterly* 40 (1): 12–38.

Mesmer, H. A. E. 1999. "Scaffolding a Crucial Transition Using Text with Some Decodability." *Reading Teacher* 53 (2): 130–42.

———. 2001. "Examining the Theoretical Claims About Decodable Text: Does Text Decodability Lead to Greater Application of Letter/Sound Knowledge in First-Grade Readers?" *Yearbook: National Reading Conference* 50: 444–59.

———. 2003. "The Art of Balancing Instructional Materials for Beginning Readers: Becoming a Wise Consumer." *Balanced Reading Instruction* 10: 1–11.

Mesmer, H. A. E., and P. L. Griffith. 2005. "Everybody's Selling It—but Just What Is Explicit, Systematic Phonics Instruction?" *Reading Teacher* 59: 366–76. doi:10.1598/RT.59.4.6.

Mesmer, H. A. E., and K. Lake. 2010. "The Role of Syllable Awareness and Syllable-Controlled Text in the Development of Finger-Point Reading." *Reading Psychology* 31 (2): 176–201.

Moats, L. C. 1995. *Spelling: Development, Disability, and Instruction*. Baltimore: York Press.

———. 1998. "Teaching Decoding." *American Educator* 22 (1): 42–49.

Morris, D. 1983. "Concept of Word and Phoneme Awareness in the Beginning Reader." *Research in the Teaching of English* 17: 359–73.

Morris, D., J. W. Bloodgood, R. G. Lomax, and J. Perney. 2003. "Developmental Steps in Learning to Read: A Longitudinal Study in Kindergarten and First Grade." *Reading Research Quarterly* 38 (3): 302–28.

Murray, B. A., and T. Lesniak. 1999. "The Letterbox Lesson: A Hands-On Approach for Teaching Decoding." *The Reading Teacher* 52 (6): 644–50.

Muter, V., C. Hulme, M. Snowling, and S. Taylor. 1997. "Segmentation, Not Rhyming, Predicts Early Progress in Learning to Read." *Journal of Experimental Child Psychology* 65 (3): 370–96.

Nation, K., R. Allen, and C. Hulme. 2001. "The Limitations of Orthographic Analogy in Early Reading Development: Performance on the Clue-Word Task Depends on Phonological Priming and Elementary Decoding Skill, Not the Use of Orthographic Analogy." *Journal of Experimental Child Psychology* 80 (1): 75–94.

Nation, K., and C. Hulme. 1997. "Phonemic Segmentation, Not Onset-Rime Segmentation, Predicts Early Reading and Spelling Skills." *Reading Research Quarterly* 32 (2): 154–67.

National Reading Panel and National Institute of Child Health and Human Development. 2000. *Report of the National Reading Panel: Teaching Children to Read: An Evidence-Based Assessment of the Scientific Research Literature on Reading and Its Implications for Reading Instruction: Reports of the Subgroups*. Washington, DC. National Institute of Child Health and Human Development, National Institutes of Health.

NGA and CCSSO (National Governors Association Center for Best Practices and Council of Chief State School Officers). 2012. *Common Core State Standards for English Language Arts and Literacy in History / Social Studies, Science, and Technical Subjects*. Washington, DC: NGA and CCSSO. www.corestandards.org/ assets/Appendix_A.pdf.

Odden, D. 2011. "The Representation of Vowel Length." In *The Blackwell Companion to Phonology*, edited by M. van Oostendorp, C. J. Ewen, E. Hume, and K. Rice, 465–90. Malden, MA: Wiley-Blackwell.

Palmer, J. L., and M. Invernizzi. 2015. *No More Phonics and Spelling Worksheets*. Portsmouth, NH: Heinemann.

Pence, K. T., A. B. Anthony, L. Justice, and R. Bowels. 2009. "Preschoolers' Exposure to Language Stimulation in Classrooms Serving At-Risk Children: The Contribution of Group Size and Activity Context." *Early Education and Development* 20 (1): 53–79.

Piasta, S. B. 2014. "Moving to Assessment-Guided Differentiated Instruction to Support Young Children's Alphabet Knowledge." *Reading Teacher* 68 (3): 202–11.

Piasta, S. B., Y. Petscher, and L. M. Justice. 2012. "How Many Letters Should Preschoolers in Public Programs Know? The Diagnostic Efficiency of Various Preschool Letter-Naming Benchmarks for Predicting First-Grade Literacy Achievement." *Journal of Educational Psychology* 104 (4): 945.

Piasta, S. B., D. J. Purpura, and R. K. Wagner. 2010. "Fostering Alphabet Knowledge Development: A Comparison of Two Instructional Approaches." *Reading and Writing* 23 (6): 607–62.

Piasta, S. B., and R. K. Wagner. 2010. "Developing Early Literacy Skills: A Meta-Analysis of Alphabet Learning and Instruction." *Reading Research Quarterly* 45 (1): 8–38.

Rayner, K., S. J. White, R. L. Johnson, and S. P. Liversedge. 2006. "Raeding Wrods with Jubmled Lettres: There Is a Cost." *Psychological Science* 17 (3): 192–193.

Rose, J. 2006. *Independent Review of the Teaching of Early Reading*. Nottingham, UK: Crown. http://dera.ioe.ac.uk/5551/2/report.pdf.

Seidenberg, M. 2017. *Reading at the Speed of Sight*. New York: Basic Books.

Share, D. L. 1995. "Phonological Recoding and Self-Teaching: Sine Qua Non of Reading Acquisition." *Cognition* 55 (2): 151–218.

———. 2004. "Knowing Letter Names and Learning Letter Sounds: A Causal Connection." *Journal of Experimental Child Psychology* 88 (3): 213–33.

———. 2004. "Orthographic Learning at a Glance: On the Time Course and Developmental Onset of Self-Teaching." *Journal of Experimental Child Psychology* 87 (4): 267–98.

———. 2008. "On the Anglocentricities of Current Reading Research and Practice: The Perils of Overreliance on an 'Outlier" Orthography.' *Psychological Bulletin* 134 (4): 584–615.

Shaywitz, S. E. 2003. *Overcoming Dyslexia: A New and Complete Science-Based Program for Reading Problems at Any Level*. New York: Knopf.

Snow, C. E., M. S. Burns, and P. Griffin. 1998. *Preventing Reading Difficulties in Young Children*. Report from Committee on the Prevention of Reading Difficulties in Young Children, National Research Council. Washington, DC: National Academy Press.

Stahl, K. A. D. 2004. "Proof, Practice, and Promise: Comprehension Strategy Instruction in the Primary Grades." *Reading Teacher* 57 (7): 598–609.

Stahl, S. A., A. M. Duffy-Hester, and K. A. D. Stahl. 1998. "Everything You Wanted to Know About Phonics (but Were Afraid to Ask)." *Reading Research Quarterly* 33: 338–55. doi:10.1598/RRQ.33.3.5.

Steacy, L. M., D. M. Kearns, J. K. Gilbert, D. L. Compton, E. Cho, E. R. Lindstrom, and A. A. Collins. 2017. "Exploring Individual Differences in Irregular Word Recognition Among Children with Early-Emerging and Late-Emerging Word Reading Difficulty." *Journal of Educational Psychology* 109 (1): 51.

Suggate, S. P. 2016. "A Meta-Analysis of the Long-Term Effects of Phonemic Awareness, Phonics, Fluency, and Reading Comprehension Interventions." *Journal of Learning Disabilities* 49 (1): 77–96.

Taylor, B. M., P. D. Pearson, K. Clark, and S. Walpole. 2000. "Effective Schools and Accomplished Teachers: Lessons About Primary-Grade Reading Instruction in Low-Income Schools." *Elementary School Journal* 101 (2): 121–65.

Treiman, R. 1993. *Beginning to Spell: A Study of First-Grade Children*. New York: Oxford University Press.

Treiman, R., and B. Kessler. 2003. "The Role of Letter Names in the Acquisition of Literacy." *Advances in Child Development and Behavior* 31: 105–38.

———. 2004. "The Case of Case: Children's Knowledge and Use of Upper- and Lowercase Letters." *Applied Psycholinguistics* 25: 413–28. doi:10.1017/S0142716404001195.

———. 2005. "Writing Systems and Spelling Development." In *The Science of Reading: A Handbook*, edited by M. J. Snowling and C. Hulme, 120–34. Malden, MA: Blackwell.

Treiman, R., S. E. Stothard, and M. J. Snowling. 2013. "Instruction Matters: Spelling of Vowels by Children in England and the US." *Reading and Writing* 26: 473–87.

Treiman, R., R. Tincoff, K. Rodriguez, A. Mouzaki, and D. J. Francis. 1998. "The Foundations of Literacy: Learning the Sounds of Letters." *Child Development* 69 (6): 1524–40.

Treiman, R., S. Weatherston, and D. Berch. 1994. "The Role of Letter Names in Children's Learning of Phoneme–Grapheme Relations." *Applied Psycholinguistics* 15 (1): 97–122.

Tivnan, T., and L. Hemphill. 2005. "Comparing Four Literacy Reform Models in High-Poverty Schools: Patterns of First-Grade Achievement." *Elementary School Journal* 105 (5): 419–41.

Torgeson, C., G. Brooks, and J. Hall. 2006. *A Systematic Review of the Research Literature on the Use of Phonics in the Teaching of Reading and Spelling.* Nottingham, UK: DfES Publications.

Turner, V. S. 2017. "The Power of Overlearning." *Scientific American* 317 (2). www.scientificamerican.com/article/the-power-of-overlearning/.

United States Department of Health and Human Services. 2016. *Head Start Early Learning Outcomes Framework.* Washington, DC: United States Department of Health and Human Services Author.

Vadasy, P. F., E. A. Sanders, and J. A. Peyton. 2005. "Relative Effectiveness of Reading Practice or Word-Level Instruction in Supplemental Tutoring: How Text Matters." *Journal of Learning Disabilities* 38 (4): 364–80.

Vygotsky, L. 1986. *Thought and Language.* Cambridge, MA: MIT Press.

Wang, H. C., L. Nickels, K. Nation, and A. Castles. 2013. "Predictors of Orthographic Learning of Regular and Irregular Words." *Scientific Studies of Reading* 17 (5): 369–84.

Willingham, D. T. 2015. *Raising Kids Who Read: What Parents and Teachers Can Do.* San Francisco: Jossey-Bass.

Wylie, R. E., and D. D. Durrell. 1970. "Teaching Vowels Through Phonograms." *Elementary English* 47 (6): 787–91.

Yopp, H. K., and R. H. Yopp. 2000. "Supporting Phonemic Awareness Development in the Classroom." *The Reading Teacher* 54 (2): 130–43.

Ziegler, J. C., and U. Goswami. 2005. "Reading Acquisition, Developmental Dyslexia, and Skilled Reading Across Languages: A Psycholinguistic Grain Size Theory." *Psychological Bulletin* 131 (1): 3–29.

Zucker, T. A., A. E. Ward, and L. M. Justice. 2009. "Print Referencing During Read-Alouds: A Technique for Increasing Emergent Readers' Print Knowledge." *Reading Teacher* 63 (1): 62–72.

Index